ALL THE **2**S OF THE BIBLE

ALL THE 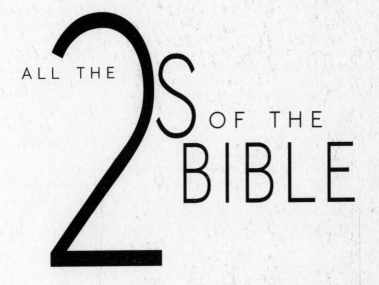 2S OF THE BIBLE

HERBERT LOCKYER

WHITAKER
HOUSE

ALL THE 2S OF THE BIBLE
Previously published by Baker Book House as *Twin Truths of Scripture,* 2 volumes.

ISBN: 978-1-62911-011-0
eBook ISBN: 978-1-62911-035-6
Printed in the United States of America
© 1973, 2014 by Ardis A. Lockyer

Whitaker House
1030 Hunt Valley Circle
New Kensington, PA 15068
www.whitakerhouse.com

Library of Congress Cataloging-in-Publication Data (Pending)

1 2 3 4 5 6 7 8 9 10 **LU** 20 19 18 17 16 15 14

CONTENTS

FOREWORD

Because of its marvel and magnificence, Scripture can be approached in many different ways, and this variety of method of study provides both pleasure and profit in the endeavor to "rightly divide the word of truth." (See 2 Timothy 2:15.) We consider here the way in which the sacred writers combined contradictory and complementary truths in a single verse or paragraph. Too often, one of these double truths is dealt with to the exclusion of the other, or one is so magnified as to minimize the other. Thus the pair becomes "a cake not turned," overdone on one side, underdone on the other, and so spiritually indigestible. But both sides deserve equal attention, as this book illustrates.

The Bible speaks of itself as a two-edged sword (see Hebrews 4:12), and many truths it reveals have a double aspect. Two passages in the Apocrypha emphasize this interesting feature. First of all, we are told to *"look upon all the works of the Most High; they likewise are in pairs, one the opposite of the other"* (Sirach 33:15 RSV). We also read that *"all things are twofold, one opposite the other, and he has made nothing incomplete*" (Sirach 42:24 RSV). Solomon expresses a similar idea: "*In the day of prosperity be joyful, but in the day of adversity consider: God also hath set the* **one over against the other**" (Ecclesiastes 7:14).

In the human body, we have one against another—one eye against another, one ear against another, one arm against another, one leg against another, and so on. Browning has the phrase "What hand and brain went ever paired?"[1] So in the Word, there are two and two, and if we ignore one of the two or unduly exalt one at the expense of the other, then we are guilty of not "*rightly handling the word of truth*" (2 Timothy 2:15 RSV). Are we not warned against the error of keeping back what is profitable and admonished to declare all the counsel of God? (See Acts 20:20, 27; see also Jeremiah 26:2.)

In many instances, we find pairs well matched; in other cases, there seems to be conflict between the twin truths presented. There is a proverb to the effect of "every couple is not a pair," meaning that the one is adverse in many ways to the other, and, in a verse where double terms are used, it may appear that one is contradictory to the other. But in God's infallible Word, there are no contradictions. What seems to be contradictory is really complementary. The numeral *one* excludes all others and denotes that which is sovereign, but *two* affirms there is another, and possibly a difference, whether for good or evil. The two may be different in character, yet one in testimony and friendship. Too often, the stamp of difference is that of enmity. Light can never agree with darkness. There can never be any agreement between holiness and sin.

It is not difficult to make a spiritual application of the doubles Solomon reminds us of:

---

1. Robert Browning, "The Last Ride Together," line 56.

Two are better than one....For if they fall, the one will lift up his fellow....If two lie together, then they have heat: but how can one be warm alone? And if one prevail against him, two shall withstand him. (Ecclesiastes 4:9–12)

As we are to prove in the examples of twin truths we have chosen, often when found lying together in the bed of one verse, the one truth warms and supports the other. If the one seems to fall in our understanding, the other is there to lift it up and help it. It is to be hoped that the following illustrations of this unique pairing of scriptural themes and qualities will serve as an incentive to a more extensive coverage.

"They likewise are in pairs, one the opposite of the other."
—Sirach 33:15 (RSV)

CHAPTER 1

GOODNESS AND SEVERITY

*"Behold therefore the goodness and severity of God: on them which
fell, severity; but toward thee, goodness, if thou continue in his
goodness: otherwise thou also shalt be cut off."*
—Romans 11:22

In the verse cited above, we have one of the conspicuous passages in the Bible where two important truths are set forth in one sentence and where there is an apparent paradox, or contradiction. But contradiction is only apparent, seeing that these twin but opposite qualities set forth different aspects of the divine nature. W. C. Procter has shown that "the goodness and severity of God" are visible in many realms. Take nature: The same hand that formed the beautiful flowers for no other reason than to delight us also forges the thunderbolts that are so destructive. Take providence: Here again the same double aspect can be traced in the fact that joys and sorrows, blessings and bereavements, all come from God. Take biblical history: The chief manifestation of the pair of actions Paul describes is before us throughout Scripture. Although God caused the godless inhabitants of the earth to be drowned, He saved Noah and his family. While He destroyed the ungodly Sodomites, He preserved Lot and his two daughters. All the firstborn of Egypt were suddenly slain, but God spared His chosen people.

It is at Calvary, however, that we have the most appealing evidence of the harmony between God's *goodness* and *severity*, between His boundless love, fathomless mercy, and infinite grace and His inflexible justice, immaculate holiness, and unalterable truth. (See Psalm 85:10; Isaiah 45:21; Romans 3:24–26.) We have *"the riches of his goodness"* (Romans 2:4) in *"spar*[ing] *not his own Son, but deliver*[ing] *him up for us all"* (Romans 8:32) and His severity in *"condemn*[ing] *sin in the flesh"* by that *"offering for sin"* (Romans 8:3). The same principles can be found in God's revelation of Himself to Moses: *"The Lord God* [is] *abundant in goodness…by no means clear*[ing] *the guilty"* (Exodus 34:6–7).

In Romans 11, where Paul dwells upon the opposite attributes of God, the contrast is between Jew and Gentile. The apostle stresses the present privilege of Gentiles and affirms that they have no room for boasting, because all their advantages were of grace. Further, their privileged position depended upon them remaining in the *goodness* that was its source. The exclamation "Behold!" usually precedes some great truth. It is as a bell calling for one's attention: *"Behold therefore the goodness and severity of God"* (Romans 11:22). The two extremes are not contradictory but complementary, not perverse but parallel, just as the parallel lines of a railway are necessary for transportation.

A danger we have to guard against is the undue emphasis of one side of the divine nature at the expense of the other side. It is essential to preserve balance between the two. To dwell upon the goodness of God to the exclusion of His severity—thinking only of His love, kindness, and provision, and as One too good to allow any to suffer for sin—makes Him a false deity.

Do you think He ne'er reproves me,
What a false friend He would be?[2]

Then we must not go to the other extreme and present Him as one too stern, austere, and severe to forgive; one who only ministers terror. True, He is the God of Sinai, but He is also the God of Calvary. The One who is *just* is also the *justifier* of all who seek the shelter of the blood.

With mercy and with judgment,
My web of time He wove,
And aye, the dews of sorrow
Were lustered by His love.[3]

We disapprove of those who affirm that the God of the Old Testament is distinct in character from the God of the New Testament. Modernists apologize for the Deity as depicted in ancient revelation; but we make no such apology, for as much space, if not more so, is devoted to the *goodness* of God in Old Testament Scriptures as to His *severity*. The loving and merciful side of the divine nature is exhibited, as well as the sterner side. Nothing can so affect the character of a person, or of a nation, as a deep conviction of sin combined with a clear understanding of a loving Father who is also a God of severity and intensely intolerant of sin and rebellion in any form.

The contention of the Modernist is that the more severe side of the divine character is associated with the Jewish Jehovah, a tribal deity who was jealous and wrathful and must, therefore, be rejected. Men must be directed to Jesus Christ, who, instead of presenting the wrathful autocrat as God appeared in the past, taught man to believe in a loving Father, ever kind and

---

2. Ellen L. Goreh, "In the Secret of His Presence," 1883.
3. Anne R. Cousin, "The Sands of Time Are Sinking," 1857.

good. But what must not be forgotten is the fact that nowhere in the Gospels did Jesus give any hint that He regarded God as a tyrannical deity, nor did He ever speak of Him disparagingly as the "Jewish Jehovah." Why, when His disciples wanted to call fire down from heaven to consume His enemies, He rebuked them, saying, *"Ye know not what manner of spirit ye are of"* (Luke 9:55).

While Jesus taught us to look to God as our loving, heavenly Father, and did not actually ascribe to God terms of severity and righteous anger, He did use two parables to symbolize this side of the divine character. He said, *"The master of the house being* **angry** *said to his servants..."* (Luke 14:21). *"His lord was wroth, and delivered him to the tormentors"* (Matthew 18:34). Even when Jesus spoke of God's forgiveness, He was careful to state that this was granted only on certain conditions. (See Matthew 6:14–15.) The apostles likewise believed that the God of the Old Testament and of the New were one. Paul could write, *"The wrath of God is revealed from heaven against all ungodliness and unrighteousness of men"* (Romans 1:18). As for John, the apostle of love, he declared that *"the wrath of God abideth on him"* (John 3:36) who rejects Christ.

We greatly err, then, when we speak of goodness and severity, or love and anger, as if they were two forces inconsistent with each other. Human relationships, as well as the Bible, show us that often they are inseparably associated, and that only those who truly love know what it is to be angry. The Old Testament teaches this truth. The God of unbending justice was ever ready to forgive and receive back into His arms of love the sinner willing to return home.

To the Lord our God belong mercies and forgivenesses, though we have rebelled against him.   (Daniel 9:9)

*I will heal their backsliding, I will love them freely: for mine
anger is turned away from him. I will be as the dew unto
Israel: he shall grow as the lily.* (Hosea 14:4–5)

*The Lord is merciful and gracious, slow to anger, and plen-
teous in mercy. He will not always chide: neither will he
keep his anger for ever. He hath not dealt with us after our
sins; nor rewarded us according to our iniquities.*

(Psalm 103:8–10)

If space permitted, many more similar passages from the
Old Testament might be added.

As one looks at the whole Bible as it reveals the character of
our God, it cannot be denied that one finds a certain intermix-
ture of severity and love in both the early and the later revela-
tions. The same loving Father is depicted in both; but also in
human life, parental love has to be sometimes combined with
severity when the child defies all restraints and law. Our God is
one of severity because He is a God of love. The sacred poet has
well expressed God's love to us:

> On fruitful boughs My care I spend,
> And sharpness with My love I blend:
> When most severe, then most their Friend.[4]

The weak father often spoils his son, because he is not far-
seeing enough to perceive how much injury the boy is doing to
himself by sowing seeds that will bear a frightful crop of selfishness and other forms of sin. The weak commanding officer of a
regiment, by overlooking crime, often causes the evil spirit of
insubordination to spread to such an extent that nothing but
very severe measures will restore discipline. A little firmness

---

4. Richard Wilton, "The Pruning of the Vine," *Lyra Pastoralis* (1902), 107.

at the beginning might have repressed the evil, but when once the disease has spread, nothing but very severe penalties will succeed.

As the three Persons of the Godhead are coequal, it is profitable to consider how this twofold representation of the divine character can be applied to each Person of the blessed Trinity.

1. THE GOODNESS AND SEVERITY OF GOD THE FATHER

Goodness comes first, which is as it should be, seeing that His "goodness faileth never."[5] There are some fifty references to this quality so abundant in God, which leads men to repentance. Romans 11:22 is the only place where the term *"severity"* occurs. The continued goodness of God is seen in His very name, for *God* is but a contraction of *good.* Both in name and nature, God is good. Twice over we have the simple yet sublime declaration *"God is love"* (1 John 4:8, 16), which was manifested in the surrender of His Son for our salvation. Such sacrificial love suffers long and is kind, and severity comes only after such goodness is spurned and outraged. God's predominating desire toward us is one of love. Severity is His last resort.

But because He is our loving heavenly Father, His is not the lax indulgence of an easygoing parent with love as a weak sentiment and severity as a necessary part of His character as the righteous Judge of the universe. He would be unworthy of our worship and surrender if He were "a God all mercy is a God unjust."[6]

He is a jealous God, a consuming fire. We have the repetition of the phrase *"The wrath of God"* not only in the Old

---

5. Henry W. Baker, "The King of Love My Shepherd Is," 1868.
6. Edward Young, *Night IV,* line 233.

Testament but thirty-five times in the New. It is blessedly true that He is a God of love, and that Christ came to reveal such a fact in all its fullness; but it is also true that because He is love incarnate, He must be a God of severity. In both Testaments, He is revealed as being intensely severe and particular as to the transgression of His laws, for He alone knows how much disaster sin has brought to His fair creation.

2. THE GOODNESS AND SEVERITY OF GOD THE SON

In the days of His flesh, Jesus affirmed, *"I and my Father are one"* (John 10:30). And they were one in all divine qualities and attributes. His goodness is clearly evident in His ways, words, and works. He did not come to be ministered unto but to minister and give His life as a ransom for sinners. He was rich, but for our sakes became poor. (See 2 Corinthians 8:9.) He loved us and gave Himself for us. His goodness, then, is revealed in His self-sacrificing life and atoning death. A previous Countess of Pembroke wrote:

> Christ placed all rest, yet had no resting place;
> He healed each pain, yet lived in sore distress;
> Deserved all good, yet lived in great disgrace;
> Gave all hearts joy, himself in heaviness;
> Suffered them live, by whom himself was slain;
> Lord, who can live to see such love again?[7]

Because of His love, God surrendered His beloved Son to the death of the cross, and there the sword of justice awoke against Him who came as the Good Shepherd. Death and the

---

7. Mary Sidney Herbert (Countess of Pembroke), "Wondrous Love."

curse were in His cup. At Calvary, goodness and severity kissed each other, revealing that the great act of divine love sprang from the same loving heart that previously punished a godless world by means of catastrophes. And Calvary will ever remain as the

> Trysting place where Heaven's love
> And Heaven's justice meet.[8]

The severity of Jesus can be found in His stern denunciations of those who finally reject His goodness. Some of the most terrible statements of the final doom of the impenitent fell from the lips of the loving Savior. It was He who spoke of *"eternal fire"* (Jude 1:7), *"weeping and gnashing of teeth"* (Matthew 8:12), and the abode where *"their worm dieth not, and the fire is not quenched"* (Mark 9:46). John used the expression, *"The wrath of the Lamb"* (Revelation 6:16). At the great white throne, He will be the Judge, ratifying the condemnation of the lost. *"Depart from me, ye cursed"* (Matthew 25:41). How imperative it is for those of us who have been saved by His grace to urge sinners to *"kiss the Son, lest he be angry"* (Psalm 2:12)!

3. THE GOODNESS AND SEVERITY OF GOD THE SPIRIT

Being one in essence with the Father and the Son, the Holy Spirit shares the virtue of divine goodness. For that reason, He is called *"thy good Spirit"* (Nehemiah 9:20), and *goodness* is stated as being part of the fruit of the Spirit. (See Galatians 5:22.) As He is the direct agent between Christ and us in this dispensation of grace, His goodness operates within the hearts

---

8. Elizabeth C. Clephane, "Beneath the Cross of Jesus," 1868.

of the unregenerate and the regenerate alike. Because He is the good Spirit, He never ceases to convict the ungodly of their sin.

How He strives to woo the sinner! He can say with the Savior He ever magnifies, *"How often would I have gathered* [you] *together"* (Luke 13:34). For those born anew by His power, there is the assurance of His gracious indwelling and likewise the endeavor never to grieve Him who loves us equally as the Father and the Son.

But recognizing *"the love of the Spirit"* (Romans 15:30), we must not overlook His severity. Do we not read of those who were the recipients of divine love and pity who rebelled against the tender Holy Spirit and vexed Him so much that He turned to be their enemy and fought against them? (See Isaiah 63:10.) Then there is our Lord's solemn warning about blaspheming the Spirit and the dire results of such an unforgivable sin. (See Mark 3:28–29.) We have a striking evidence of the goodness of the Spirit on the day of Pentecost as He brought salvation to thousands, yet His severity is seen in His act of smiting Ananias and Sapphira with sudden death for the way they lied against Him. (See Acts 5:5, 10.) Was it not the same with Joshua of old? There was victory at Jericho, but terrible punishment for Achan, who disobeyed the divine commandment. May grace be ours never to despise the riches of divine goodness!

CHAPTER 2

WHEN GAIN IS LOSS

"What things were gain to me, those I counted loss for Christ."
—Philippians 3:7

For one to turn losses into gains is a notable achievement, but how many businessmen would agree that gains should be counted as losses? In the spiritual realm, however, Paul knew how to lose in order to win and to look upon personal gains as losses for Christ's sake. (See Philippians 3:7–8.) This epistle to the Philippians as a whole is a kind of balance sheet of gains and losses. Paul must have been in a mercantile frame of mind when he wrote, for it is made up of adding, subtracting, and balancing. Some things the apostle reckoned as losses he carried over to the profit side, while the riches he had gained he wrote down as loss. What a precious paradox Paul gives us!

THE NATURE OF PAUL'S GAINS

Circumcised the eighth day, of the stock of Israel, of the tribe of Benjamin, an Hebrew of the Hebrews; as touching the law, a Pharisee; concerning zeal, persecuting the church; touching the righteousness which is in the law, blameless.

(Philippians 3:5–6)

The apostle had belonged to the very kind of aristocracy that excited dreams and kindled aspirations in the hearts of men like himself. In two verses, he enumerates the boastings of the flesh, and with minute distinctness, he describes the superiority of the majority of his age.

1. "*CIRCUMCISED THE EIGHTH DAY*"

This meant that Paul was born a Jew, not a proselyte to the Jewish faith who might or might not submit to the rite of circumcision. To be circumcised the eighth day after birth was the exclusive privilege of the Jewish male.

2. "*OF THE STOCK OF ISRAEL*"

What a gain this was—to be a descendant of the covenanted royal race! As Saul of Tarsus, he gloried in being a blue blood of a distinguished religion. This pedigree gave him entrance into the most exclusive and exalted circles of his nation's life.

3. "*OF THE TRIBE OF BENJAMIN*"

It was from this particular tribe, named after the son Rachel died giving birth to, that Saul, Israel's first king, came. It was reckoned as a royal tribe, and now another Saul boasts of the same tribal genealogy. This was the tribe that was faithful to the house of Judah after the division of the kingdom.

4. "*AN HEBREW OF THE HEBREWS*"

Such a phrase implies that his was a Hebrew ancestry on both sides of the family. Moffatt's translation of this phrase is,

"[Paul was] *the Hebrew son of Hebrew parents*" (Philippians 3:5 MOFFATT). Abraham is named as the first Hebrew, and all Jews were embraced in the covenant God had made with the patriarch. As a true Jew, Paul, when Saul of Tarsus, never mixed with the thoughts and habits of the Gentiles. He retained the customs and language of his fathers.

5. "*TOUCHING THE LAW, A PHARISEE*"

These words suggest a rigid profession and punctilious orthodoxy. He belonged not only to the strictest sect who had inherited Judaistic principles, but he also observed an intense Judaism in his own personal life. There were those who nationally were Jews but who were not Jews in nature. But to Paul, before his conversion, Judaism was not a profession—it was his very life.

6. "*CONCERNING ZEAL, PERSECUTING THE CHURCH*"

The tragedy was that this flaming religious zealot thought he was doing God's will in threatening to slaughter those who became Christ's followers. To him, the new teaching they had embraced was diametrically opposed to Judaistic theology. His callous, pugnacious antagonism of the saints is seen in the act of holding the garments of those who murdered Stephen, the first martyr of the church whom he would also eventually die for.

7. "*TOUCHING THE RIGHTEOUSNESS WHICH IS IN THE LAW, BLAMELESS*"

This seventh gain made him an apparently perfect Hebrew. He was "*immaculate by the standard of legal righteousness*" (Philippians 3:6–7 MOFFATT). He had blameless conduct and righteousness according to the rule of the scribes and Pharisees, which our Lord described as *their* righteousness. (See

Matthew 5:20.) There is righteousness created and imparted by God that reveals itself in true love to God and man. Then there is an apparent righteousness that is practiced to impress others. It is made up of outward observance of rites and public duties. When Paul came to testify of his changed life, he explained how he had tried to establish *his own* righteousness. He excelled in an exterior, manufactured righteousness, but was destitute of the divinely provided righteousness, *"the righteousness which is through the faith of Christ"* (Philippians 3:9).

THE RENUNCIATION OF GAINS AS LOSSES

> *Yea doubtless, and I count all things but loss for the excel-*
> *lency of the knowledge of Christ Jesus my Lord: for whom*
> *I have suffered the loss of all things, and do count them but*
> *dung, that I may win Christ.*   (Philippians 3:8)

Here we have what Jowett described as "revising the balance sheet." All the coveted treasures and gains Paul boasted about and counted as precious assets worthy of being placed on the credit side of life's account, he now deliberately transfers to the debit side and crosses them out as *loss*. Paul uses two phrases to describe the transfer.

1. "COUNTED AS LOSS"

The word for *"loss"* in this Scripture means "damage" or "detriment." His boasted gains were not merely worthless; they were worse than worthless because they prevented a sense of spiritual need and the hopelessness and helplessness a sinner must feel. In gaining the whole world of Judaism, Paul had lost his soul. Now his intelligent renunciation is complete, and he has found salvation and satisfaction through what he had lost. Although his old life was fascinating in its way, he came to see it as a detriment to the highest life. Indeed, "the loss of a loss is a gain."

2. "COUNTED BUT DUNG"

The term *"dung"* refers to refuse, scraps from the master's table for the dogs. When Saul of Tarsus had a vision of Jesus on that Damascus road, all his fancied greatness vanished and did not cost him a tear, for in the place of inferior gains, he had found eternal wealth. Renouncing all joy in past glory, he treated it as dirt, just as a beggar discards his rags and poverty if he discovers treasure. He surrendered his own self-righteousness, which had made him a hated, much feared persecutor, and by grace, he became the greatest character next to Christ in the New Testament account.

Is there not an application of Paul's balancing of accounts we can make?

THE WORLD'S ESTIMATION OF GAIN AND LOSS

Health, money, comfort, ease, prosperity, outward moral conduct, and exterior religiosity are counted clear gains and carried on the profit side of the ledger. Sickness, disappointment, death, loss of trade, and curtailment of selfish desires and pleasures are entered on the debit side as unmixed losses. But Paul came to reverse the order. Now the loss of life and all it held would be gain to him. *"To die is gain"* (Philippians 1:21). To every believer who has lost his life for Christ's sake, the grave is a gain.

THE DIVINE RECKONING

Paul became skilled in spiritual arithmetic and careful in his reckoning. Twice over he uses the words *count* and *loss*. Before he met Christ, his fancied gains were losses, but after his transformation by Christ, his losses were gains. For Christ's sake, he accounted all that was deemed worthy in the past as waste. He had believed that God was satisfied with outward religious rites and that life consisted only of all his aristocratic privileges and gains. Isn't this the folly of many people today who are self-satisfied with their pride of race, their exterior religious profession, strict orthodoxy, and boasted morality? They try to be as good as other people, to live as best as they can, but all they have and seek to do is insecure as a ground of confidence and can never bring them peace of heart and favor with God. F. W. Charrington had all he could wish for as a son of the famous Charrington brewing family, but, for Christ's sake, he surrendered a fortune from selling beer and gave his life to service among the slaves of strong drink.

HOW GAINS BECAME LOSSES

When Paul penned the words about past gains being losses, he was not in the flush of the early dawn of his faith. He had been serving the Lord for some twenty-five years, and, having suffered every worldly loss for Christ, he now revises his balance sheet. This autobiographical touch exemplifies a characteristic feature of Paul, namely, his constant habit of quoting his own experience as an illustration of truth. When he had counted his privileges and possessions as gains, he did not know the Lord as his personal Savior. It was only after God's dazzling glory had burst upon his vision that he saw what he had estimated as gold as but tinsel or dross. Once he saw the Lord, the old fancied greatness vanished, and he was revealed as a mean and miserable sinner. "He who loses anything and gets wisdom by it is a gainer by the loss."[9] In receiving Christ, Paul got wisdom and found himself a tremendous gainer.

There is nothing on the debit side of the balance sheet to account for the change of gains into losses—except for one item. The adverse change came not by creed, conduct, culture, or church, but only by Christ. Appropriating Him as Savior and Lord outweighed all past advantages and acquirements. Impelled by the example of Jesus, whom Paul saw and heard on that Damascus road, he emptied himself. Quickly he pulled down his old barns and built greater ones, so that he could offer roomier and more glorious hospitality to his Lord. That transforming vision was the motive in the revolution that swept out the past. When he gained Christ, all the boasted glory of the old days faded away. Paul had found Him and needed nothing more. It would seem that there were three steps in this change of gains into losses:

1. ABANDONING

Paul said, to put his confession in modern dress,

> I count all things to be loss for the excellency of the knowledge of Christ Jesus my Lord: for whom I suffered the loss of all things, and do count them but refuse, that I may gain Christ.   (Philippians 3:8 ASV)

Paul did not believe in unearned income. As a miser lives only to pile up his gold, so it was the passion of the apostle to amass Christ as his fortune, not to hoard Him up but to share such a treasure with the world. For a long time, he had lived on

9. Roger L'Estrange.

the outside, on the circumference; now he had discovered the true wealth, and it became his passion to have his own veins filled with the blood-currents of his Redeemer's heart. As he had labored passionately to amass the old wealth, now that such had been shown to be loss, he diverts all his energy to possessing the secret of the risen Lord. Home, reputation, and material prospects were all sacrificed after he fell in love with the lowly Nazarene and became His love-slave. It is still so when a Jew transfers allegiance from a dead faith to the Lord Jesus. He is stripped bare, severed from all tender relationships, and counted as dead by Orthodox Jews. Yes, and such a price is what many Gentiles have to pay as well.

2. ABIDING

Another phrase worthy of consideration is the one where the apostle speaks of the goal before him, *"That I may win* [or gain] *Christ, and be found in him"* (Philippians 3:8–9). The phrases *"in him," "in Christ,"* and *"in whom"* are particularly Pauline, and they imply that Christ is the element in which the believer lives, moves, and has his being. Paul desired to win or gain Christ and to be found in Him as the bird is in the air, the fish in the sea, the branch on the vine, the fugitive in a hiding place. He sought to be lost to all else and all others and to find in Christ his all in all. He realized that he could only hide from God *in* God.

The old rags of legal righteousness and his own hard-earned reputation were cast away for the magnificent offer of Christ's perfect robe of righteousness, which outdazzles an angel for whiteness and makes a contrite sinner whiter than snow. Paul was willing to abandon the thin, fading robe of his own righteousness and reputation for the glorious garment of sanctification of character, which is not the product of works or fashioned by human hands, but the workmanship of God. Clad thus, it was the consuming passion of Paul to be found in Christ, who had become his refuge. *"That I may...be found in him"* (Philippians 3:8–9) and *"that I may know him"* (verse 9) became his constant incentives.

3. APPREHENDING

There is a further stage in Paul's spiritual quest indicated in the words *"I follow after...that I may apprehend"* (Philippians 3:12). Although he could not cash all the checks of faith into current coin, he was not disheartened. Daily he appropriated more of the vast possessions in Christ for the exercise of his high and holy calling. The apostle compares himself to a charioteer stretching eagerly forward in a flying car to reach the prize. What a glorious race he found it to be! The very running of it seemed to transform all his mortal powers.

When the eternal Light of heaven physically blinded Paul but opened the eyes of his soul, it was like an earthquake, shattering altogether his past life. It revolutionized his estimation of values, for he came to see his past gains as worthless because he had built on them and had come to count them as solid wealth, whereas they were actually as dung. Arthur Way's translation of the phrase *"For whom I have suffered the loss of all things"* (Philippians 3:8) is most expressive: *"For His sake have I let all that wealth of mine be confiscated"* (verse 8 WAY). Often in a storm at sea things that are greatly prized have to be thrown overboard in order that life may be saved and may outride the storm. The apostle, in order to win Christ, flung the whole cargo of his much-loved confidences overboard.

The word *apprehend* means "to capture, to seize, to believe, to comprehend." As soon as Paul saw Christ, he knew he had seized hold of such a treasure, for he believed He would compensate him for all he had lost. Having gained Christ by an act of faith, he daily appropriated Him and increased in the knowledge of Him as his all-sufficiency. It was Chrysostom who said, "When the sun hath appeared, it is loss to sit by a candle." Having captured the Sun of Righteousness, Paul never went back to sit by the candle of his own righteousness. Losing his worldly reputation, he shone with God's honor. Losing his friends, he found that the Lord was near to strengthen him when brooks dried up. With the chaff blown away, Paul found the wheat. Had he known Lavater's expressive hymn, he would have sung the lines so true of his unceasing desire:

> Make this poor self grow less and less,
> Be Thou my life and aim;
> Oh, make me daily through Thy grace
> More meet to bear Thy name.[10]

---

10. Johann C. Lavater, "O Jesus Christ, Grow Thou in Me," 1780.

CHAPTER 3

WHEN LOSS IS GAIN

"My brothers, I want you to be under no misapprehension—the truth is, that what has here befallen me has, so far from justifying your fears, resulted in giving a fresh impetus to the Glad-tidings."
—Philippians 1:21 (WAY)

This meditation is logically an extension of the preceding one, for what Paul said in his reassuring message to the saints in Philippi was that his bondage was a blessing in disguise, that prison was a part of the divine plan. We are to understand the words *"the things which happened unto me"* (Philippians 1:12) as a reference to the apostle's imprisonment and suffering in a Roman jail, chained to a soldier of the guard. This terrible experience greatly troubled his friends, but he consoled their anxious hearts by writing that what they feared as a calamity was actually a channel of spiritual prosperity; that his disadvantage was being turned into an advantage for the cause of Christ; that his loss of liberty was the gain of spiritual liberty for those around him.

This weak and fettered Christian Jew was fond of speaking of his bonds as disguised blessings—that in poverty, there is wealth; that there is advancement in limitation; that hindrances often become helps; that a fortune is hidden in misfortune. Paul found his prison cell in Rome the appointed place of a richer and more glorious vision and the avenue of evangelism. Let us try to enumerate those things the apostle experienced in his confinement and discover how his loss of liberty was a real gain.

GAIN OF A GREATER INFLUENCE

Read what the prisoner of the Lord says:

My imprisonment has become the general topic of talk (as being in Messiah's cause...) through all the vast barracks of the Household Troops, and, indeed, among the population of Rome generally. (Philippians 1:13 WAY)

His limitation meant expansion. His imprisonment was an introduction or ticket of admission to the select guards of Caesar's palace. But for his fetters he would not have had the opportunity of furthering the cause of Christ as widely as he did. Think of the remarkable influence he had on the changing guards who had to listen to him because they were chained to him. Those soldiers soon found out that Paul was no ordinary prisoner; but, different from all others who were bound, he was serene, calm, tranquil, unperturbed by disturbing circumstances.

Paul made his prison a pulpit and shared the good news of Christ's redeeming love and grace with sovereigns and soldiers alike. Chains limited his physical movements, but they could not fetter his tongue. His bonds gave him the privilege of preaching the threefold message of righteousness, temperance, and judgment before Felix in such a way as to make him tremble. Brought from his cell to stand before King Agrippa, Paul gave his testimony of a transformed life with such power that the king was forced to say, *"Almost thou persuadest me to be a Christian"* (Acts 26:28). The apostle had longed for the privilege of preaching the gospel in Rome, the metropolis of the ancient world, but he had to preach it as a fettered prisoner.

Christian history is full of classic illustrations of the fact that "stone walls do not a prison make"[11]; that when godly men and women have been thrown into prisons, the gospel was spread thereby. Had it not been for his forced sojourn in Bedford prison, John Bunyan would not have had the liberation of mind that enabled him to give the world his three masterpieces: *The Pilgrim's Progress*, *The Holy War*, and *Grace Abounding*. Samuel Rutherford, that seraphic soul, would never have given to the church his rich heritage of *Letters*, extolling as they do the worth and beauty of Christ, had he not been imprisoned for Christ's sake. To this lover of the Lord, the bare stones of his cell shone like rubies. Iron bars were never to him a cage. Had it not been for saint and mystic Madam Guyon's sufferings in the dreaded French prison, the Bastille, we would not have had her appealing poem:

> A little bird I am,
> Shut from the fields of air;
> And in my cage I sit and sing
> To Him who placed me there;
> Well pleased a prisoner to be,
> Because, my God, it pleases Thee.
>
> ...
>
> My cage confines me round,
> Abroad I cannot fly;

---

11. Richard Lovelace.

> But though my wing is closely bound,
> My heart's at liberty;
> My prison walls cannot control
> The flight, the freedom of my soul.[12]

There are some birds that sing best in a cage; others beat their little lives out against the bars. They fight against the limitation and, struggling to overcome it, they lose their song. If God in His providence puts us in a cage, then let us learn to sing, that others may be blessed by the way we are able to turn loss into gain. Singing in the cage is better than beating our wings against its bars. Singing opens doors more readily than struggling, as Paul and Silas proved when, in spite of bleeding backs and feet in stocks, they could cause their songs of praise to shake the dark, damp dungeon in which they had found themselves. If you find yourself in bonds and surrounded by restrictions you cannot break through and feel that your fetters prevent you from witnessing for the Master, then look up and ask for grace to adjust your life to your bonds so that they further the gospel and become greater opportunities for service.

GAIN OF ENCOURAGEMENT FOR OTHERS

Paul goes on to tell us of another evident gain through his loss. It came in the encouragement it gave to those saints who were somewhat fearful, timid, and diffident. Not only did the gospel spread among *"the vast barracks of the Household Troops, and, indeed, among the population of Rome generally,"* but we read that *"most of the brethren, having, through my imprisonment, learned to put their trust in the Lord, are growing bolder than ever*

---

12. Madam Guyon, "A Prisoner's Song."

to speak the Word fearlessly" (Philippians 1:14 WAY). The effect upon the believer at Philippi was like a spiritual tonic, and they said, "Well, if Paul is brave enough to be true and go to jail and be happy and content there, inspired by his faithfulness, we, too, will stand for Christ and proclaim His truth."

It was not merely the apostle's imprisonment that nerved those saints; it was the way he bore it. His undying attachment to Jesus made others bold. Those who were fainthearted put on courage as they witnessed his fortitude. The way he scorned his fetters drove cowardice away in others and enabled them to stand up and be counted for Christ. Let us never forget that others are watching us in our hours of grief, in our days of loss, anxiety, trial, and disappointment, and if ours are songs in the night, then trembling hearts around us will determine to make their wilderness blossom as the rose. Often, we come across invalid saints whose physical disabilities confine them to home, who feel they are useless in the furtherance of the gospel; yet by their unshaken faith in God and serene surrender to His will, they proclaim His grace as effectively as any healthy evangelist. Their limitations are of great value, for they have much time for traffic with heaven. Paul's frequent and lengthy prison experiences enabled him to pray for a wide circle of saints, bringing them great blessing.

Those we call "shut-ins" are interceding priests and priestesses of the Lord, exercising a most beneficial spiritual influence in the world. Although bound by the fetters of physical infirmity, they are yet free to intercede, and the church and her ministers owe much to their ceaseless prayers. They reflect the ministry of the Lord they love, who intercedes for His own continually. Many a preacher gains inspiration as he leaves the presence of an afflicted saint whose sickbed is a sanctuary and who

believes that the affliction happening to him is for the furthering of the gospel. Eternity alone will reveal what the world owes
to those forced to live in their prison of pain and privation.

GAIN OF A LARGER CHRIST

That there was a sense in which Paul felt his bonds made him
safer and brought him sweeter security is seen in his wonderful
confession *"Now also Christ shall be magnified in my body, whether
it be by life, or by death"* (Philippians 1:20). Conscious as he was
that his imprisonment might end with his head being severed
from his body, he knew that martyrdom would but bring him
into the immediate presence of the Lord he dearly loved. While
manacled, he would magnify his Master, presenting Him in a
greater and grander way. Of course, in one sense, the apostle
could not make Christ greater or more prominent than He is in
His own adorable person. But by his willing acceptance of what
He had permitted, He became more magnificent in Paul's eyes
and in the estimation of the saints he wrote to.

In the hour of his initial surrender to Christ, Paul received
an unmistakable sight of Him in all the glory of His risen form;
but as he journeyed on, Christ became increasingly precious to
his heart until now, almost at the end of the course, whether
he lived or died, he wanted more than ever to exalt his Master.
Imprisonment could not shut Christ out; it only resulted in a
clearer vision of His glory and majesty. In bringing his body
into subjection to the will of Christ, Paul daily magnified Him
in it by his life of utter devotion. When, if tradition be true,
Paul was taken out to the Appian Way and beheaded, we know
that having written *"O death, where is thy sting?"* (1 Corinthians
15:55), he died in triumph.

GAIN OF A COMPLETE SURRENDER

The most conspicuous gain that came to Paul as the result of his loss of liberty was a complete surrender to Christ, for whose sake he had counted gain but loss. *"For to me to live is Christ, and to die is gain"* (Philippians 1:21). Arthur Way's translation is most arresting: *"For (if I could think of myself alone) for me life is absorption in Messiah: death—ah, that is gain!"* (Philippians 1:21 WAY). Paul had no thought of life apart from Christ. Did he not write of *"Christ, who is our life"* (Colossians 3:4)? This was not simply living like Christ, whether in or out of prison, but *living Christ,* that is, having Christ express His life through his life.

To the apostle, living was not preaching or doing what he pleased or satisfying his own selfish desires, but absorption in the Messiah. No Roman emperor could exile Paul from any part of his life. Although in a dungeon below the ground—windowless so that no ray of light could lighten the darkness and without ventilation to give him necessary fresh air—Paul lived, for while he lived, even in bonds, he was lost in Him who had promised never to leave His own. Paul had come to the place of absolute committal to Christ and, accepting his sufferings as the divine will, had a soul flooded with light and life.

Accepting his fetters as God's plan, he thereby magnified Christ, not as Nero's prisoner, but as the prisoner of the Lord.

Surroundings were hostile, and Paul's plans to plant the gospel flag in the regions beyond were sadly checked by his imprisonment, but he learned that although it seemed as if present circumstances were marching against him, yet a friendly hand was overruling in the purposes of hostile forces. What hindered his outward activity for Christ furthered His cause among men. Jacob cried, *"All these things are against me"* (Genesis 42:36), when in reality all things were for him and working together for his good, for provision in Egypt in a time of universal starvation. If we are tempted to complain, grumble, and chafe over our seeming limitations, absorption in Christ will transform bonds into blessings and change our losses into gains.

What we place after the words *"For me to live is…"* shapes our lives and characters and determines our eternal destiny. Some say "For me to live is love"; for others, it is "business" or "wealth" or "success" or "prestige," and their lives are molded accordingly—too often with disastrous results. But when, with Paul, we have *Christ* as our ambition in life, then no matter what our sphere or occupation may be, as long as it is honorable, Christ will be magnified in it.

Further, death is never gain if we die without Christ as our personal Savior. Nothing but eternal loss overtakes those who live and die without Him who died that we might have life forevermore. Paul knew that it would be better for him to depart this life because Christ had been the center and circumference of his life, and death he knew would be but a door leading into His presence in heaven.

To live, to live, is life's great joy;
To feel the living God within;
To look abroad and in the beauty that all things reveal,
Still meet the living God.

CHAPTER 4

COME DOWN, COME UP

"Thou man of God...Come down."
—2 Kings 1:9

"For better it is that it be said unto thee, Come up hither...."
—Proverbs 25:7

While we fully realize that "a text taken out of the context is a pretext," here we are transgressing such a homiletical principle by taking two phrases out of their context and using them as pegs to hang a few thoughts on. *"Come down"* and *"Come up hither,"* apart from their interpretation in the light of the narrative, can be easily applied to antagonistic attractions confronting the believer who constantly finds himself between two forces. In science, there is the law of gravitation, which Isaac Newton discovered when an apple fell to the ground, but there is also the law of higher direction, found in the sun when it says to the water in a pool, "Come up higher," and draws it up into the atmosphere. Thus is it with us. There is the voice calling us heavenward but also the voice, equally insistent, urging us hellward.

The Trinity of heaven, the Father, the Son, and the Holy Spirit, unite in constraining us to "*Come up hither,*" for as Solomon says, "*Better it is that it be said unto thee, Come up hither; than that thou shouldest be put lower in the presence of the prince whom thine eyes have seen*" (Proverbs 25:7).

The trinity of hell—the world, the flesh, and the devil—are combined in their desire to drag us down. They continually join with the king of Samaria of old when he said to Elijah, "*Thou man of God…Come down*" (2 Kings 1:9)! But the prophet stayed on the mount, knowing that it would be a serious *comedown* had he descended.

Heaven inspires us to climb the pinnacle to a life seated in the heavenlies, fragrant with the aroma of heaven. "*Set your affection on things above, not on things on the earth*" (Colossians 3:2).Earth wants us on her plane, to be of "the earth, earthy," like the man with the muckrake John Bunyan depicts in *The Pilgrim's Progress*, raking among rubbish and blind to gold above his head.

The Savior ever seeks to draw us nearer to Himself. "*I am my beloved's, and his desire is toward me*" (Song of Solomon 7:10). He strives to bless us with "*all spiritual blessings in heavenly places in Christ*" (Ephesians 1:3). Satan, in subtle ways, tries to entice us to follow him. Jesus warned Peter, "*Satan hath desired to have you, that he may sift you as wheat*" (Luke 22:31).

These two great opposing forces or laws recur over and over throughout the Holy Writ. They appear already in the opening chapters of the Bible dealing with creation: day—night; light—darkness; heaven—earth; God—Satan; the Seed of the woman—the seed of the serpent. It is a most profitable exercise to trace references and illustrations of these dual powers confronting man, and how, in every case, the personal will is the deciding factor as to whether he is to be drawn up or dragged down.

PRIMEVAL HISTORY: ADAM TO THE FLOOD

The first eleven chapters of Genesis are the foundation of Scripture, and if a man wrongly interprets these, he wrongly interprets the rest of the Word of Truth. There are, at least, three striking evidences of the antagonistic forces at work in the world. Each of us forms a combination of Adam and Eve— the Adam of innocency and the Eve of covetousness and disobedience. We find ourselves forever losing and regaining the Paradise of God's conscious presence when the Eve tempts the Adam within us.

Then, take the history of Cain and Abel. *Cain* means "acquisition," and he gave himself to acquire things of the earth. *Abel* means "that which ascends," as his sacrificial offering did. Do not these two brothers represent the two principles of law and grace, works and faith, flesh and the spirit? Abel's offering ascended and foreshadowed redemption by blood; Cain, on the other hand, was content with the fruit of the earth; he was a rationalist. As Cain killed Abel, so the Cain of the flesh ever seeks to put to death the Abel of spirituality.

Further, there is the record of Noah and the antediluvians, and our own life mirrors both. Both Noah and Enoch walked with God, but those around them were corrupt and fallen. Although Noah communed with heaven, he became guilty of drunkenness. "When we would do good, evil is present with us." (See Romans 7:21.) Two birds were sent out of the ark, the raven and the dove. The raven can illustrate the old nature, which is satisfied with the garbage of earth; the dove can illustrate the new man, who finds satisfaction in the things of the new creation.

PATRIARCHAL HISTORY: ABRAHAM TO THE EXODUS

From Genesis 12 to 50, we can trace further impressive presentations of the twin truths we are considering. Take Abraham and Lot, whose New Testament counterparts are Paul and Demas. Often, we find these characters vying for supremacy in our own lives. Abraham was unselfish and content to live as a pilgrim; Lot was selfish and greedy, with his eye on luxurious Sodom. Many of us are lopsided: unselfish in some things, selfish in others. Israel was guilty of trying to serve the Lord and yet bowing to idols. As Lot left Abraham, and Demas left Paul, we are forever tempted to forsake the living Fountain and hew out cisterns that can hold no water.

Then what a wealth of suggestion can be found in the verse *"Thy name shall be called no more Jacob, but Israel"* (Genesis 32:28). What a mixture this grand character was. At times, we see him as "Jacob"—a cheat, supplanter, and deceiver; and at other times, as "Israel"—a prince having power or favor with God. He had his vision of a ladder to heaven, but he responded to earthly voices that said to him, *"Thou man of God...Come down"* (1 Kings 1:9). He was something like the dual person Robert Louis Stevenson portrayed in *Dr. Jekyll and Mr. Hyde.*

In the story of Joseph and Potiphar's wife, we have a further illustration of the adverse forces claiming our allegiance. Joseph is one of the more perfect characters of the Bible who put forth great effort to wear "the white flower of a blameless life."[13] But a lustful woman contrived to stain his record. Courageously he resisted and was grievously wronged, suffering for his determination not to come down. At the least evil suggestion of Satan, may we, as those who are the Lord's, confront him with the question, "How can we do this great wickedness and sin against God?"

ISRAELITE HISTORY

The history of the Jews in the Old Testament is one long conflict between twin decisions. At times, they were on the mount with God; then they descended to the valley of sin, disobedience, and idolatry. Theirs was an up-and-down experience and existence. This is particularly evident when the people were a theocracy. The book of Judges presents the constant repetition of sin, servitude, sorrow, and salvation. The Israelites were more often down than up, the reverse of the divine ideal. When the judges were good and godly, the people wholly followed the Lord. But when leaderless, they became lax and left the heights for the plain. How spasmodically they faced the contending forces! Samson summarizes this dual aspect of the nation he judged. He found himself pulled in two directions. Both the power of the Holy Spirit and the power of the flesh operated in his life, with the flesh, alas, more often the conqueror. Is this not so with ourselves? There are seasons when, endued with the Spirit, we are strong in Him, but, yielding to some Delilah of the world, we are shorn of our spiritual strength.

Under the monarchy, the people were guilty of worshiping the Lord *and* serving idols. Saul's life was a mixture of triumph and tragedy. He set out with high hopes and aspirations, but

13. Alfred Tennyson, *Idylls of the King.*

he was gradually overcome by evil and lost his crown—a type of those who have a saved soul but a lost life. David also was a combination of the angel and the beast. He loved to live on the mount of God. A man after God's own heart, he sought spiritual heights, yet he was capable of terrible sins. Falling into the mire, he cried, *"Create in me a clean heart, O God"* (Psalm 51:10). Too often, the world sees in us more of the bad side than the good and is perplexed.

Solomon was another whose life was torn in opposite directions. He carried in his heart a divided love, for he loved not only the Lord but also many strange women, and they won out in the end. Instead of having a heart that was fixed, his heart was mixed—and the Lord abhors mixtures. The same principle emerges in Solomon's Love Song. The Shulamite found herself between the royal sovereign and her shepherd lover, with her lover prevailing. Further, when Israel's kings were good, the nation climbed the mount, but when they were bad, as, for instance, in Jeroboam's reign, the people were dragged down to a very low level indeed.

After their release from captivity, into which the people were drawn because of their descent from the heights, the same dual forces were at work. This can be seen in the experience of Nehemiah, who was called to repair the damage the nation's sin had caused. Heavenly voices urged him on in such a noble task, but earthly voices expressed their scorn and ridicule of such an effort. Nehemiah's foes said, *"Come, let us meet together...in the plain"* (Nehemiah 6:2). But he, knowing that to come down would mean to stay down, replied, *"I am doing a great work, so that I cannot come down"* (Nehemiah 6:3). Had he descended, what a comedown it would have been for such a man of God!

What about ourselves? Are we conscious of mighty, spiritual forces urging us on to build the ruined walls of humanity, even at the cost of sacrifice? At the same time, are we aware of the opposite, crafty, subtle, wicked temptation of the devil to walk an easier road? (Peter, used of Satan, tried to dissuade Jesus from going to Calvary!) Seeing we savor the things that are of God rather than of men, do we command Satan to get behind us?

NEW TESTAMENT HISTORY

New Testament Scripture supplies us with an even fuller insight into the higher and lower forces operating in the lives of saints. As with the radio we have both the aerial and earthy wires, so all through the New Testament, we have forceful illustrations of the *aerial* and *earthy* wires in the lives of many who lived before us. First and foremost, there is the example of our blessed Lord Himself, who, while on the high pinnacle, heard the voice of the tempter say, *"Cast thyself down"* (Matthew 4:6). But He could not be tempted to leave the heights. At the cross, He met the same challenge. Delighting to do the will of God, He willingly offered Himself; but while hanging on the cross in agony and shame, He heard the shout, *"Come down from the cross, and we will believe [you]"* (Matthew 27:42). Had He yielded, there would not have been a Savior for a lost world. Does not the same temptation face all of us who take up our cross and follow Him? The flesh hates the sacrificial. It wants to serve God without cost. It is harder to stay *on* the cross than to *come down* from it.

There is the record of dear Peter, the big fisherman, who was also in the middle of powers contending for the control of his life. The effectual prayers of Christ rose on his behalf, but there was the sifting of Satan that brought him down for a while. At times, he reveals a character deeply spiritual, utterly unselfish, strong and loving. At other times, he appears impulsive, rash, hasty, and cowardly. After Pentecost, however, the apostle lived more consistently on the mount with God.

Paul's teaching is weighted with the two laws or twin forces believers are subject to. His epistles are full of classic illustrations of the struggle between the new and old natures within a saint. He constantly broaches the theme of the two laws—the law of God and the law of sin—the one law contrary to the other. In that heart-moving portion of his autobiography, the seventh chapter of Romans, he feels like a man in slavery and cries out, *"O wretched man that I am! who shall deliver me from the body of this death?"* (Romans 7:24). In his letter to the Ephesians, he sets forth the wrestlings against Satan on one hand and wrestlings against God in prayer on the other. When he would do good, evil was present with him. Although he was a child of God, he knew that there was no good thing in him. The new man was always in conflict with the old man. The flesh lusted against the Spirit, and vice versa. Endeavoring to be spiritual in thought, desire, and action, Paul felt the carnal dragging him down.

If only young believers, that is, those who are young in the faith, would remember the two natures within, it would save them from a good deal of error, confusion, and disappointment. When, by faith, Christ is received as our personal Savior, by the Holy Spirit we are made the recipients of a new nature, and we become new creations in Him. But He does not take away the old Adamic nature with which we were born. This remains and will remain until Christ returns. Then we will have one nature—a perfect, unsinning nature like His own. Presently, by the Spirit's power, the old nature can be kept in the state of dying daily.

It is said that one day a French poet read to Louis XIV these lines, which are so Pauline in thought:

> Within this surging breast of mine,
> Two men I seem to see:
> The one, devoted to Thy cause,
> Is set on pleasing Thee;
> The other, rebel to Thy laws,
> Revolts continually.

As Louis XIV listened, he remarked to the poet, "Ah, yes! I know those two men!"

If we would be more than conquerors, we must ever be conscious of these two men, one of whom calls, "Come up higher!" and the other, "Come down, thou man of God!"

PERSONAL HISTORY

He who is not saved by grace knows nothing of the constant struggle between opposite powers seeking mastery of his life, for the simple reason that he has only one nature, an unchallenged sinning nature. Born in sin, he lives in it. If a person, after a profession of conversion, goes on living the same loose, careless life, never fighting against sins of the past nor ever showing any concern about holiness of life, then we may well conclude that he never partook of the divine nature.

If a sheep and a pig are turned into a pasture where there is a vile bog and a clean grassy hill, where will each animal go and why? If the sheep should venture too near the edge of the bog, in which the pig is content, and fall in, it would immediately cry out for the shepherd, revealing its consciousness that it is in an environment foreign to its nature. A mark of the sheep of the Good Shepherd is hatred for the mud of sin, lest the new nature be defiled. True believers are not immune from falling into the pig's trough, for the soul is ever a battlefield in which they seek "[to escape] *the corruption that is in the world through lust*" (2 Peter 1:4). God's grace and power alone can prevent their return to sin as "*the sow that was washed* [returning] *to her wallowing in the mire*" (2 Peter 2:22).

The sweet, tender voices of heaven constantly entreat us to ascend the heights and breathe in the pure air. Over against them, rebellious, worldly, satanic voices urge us to come down to a lower level. Which of these voices conquer, dominate, control our daily lives depends on the place we give the Holy Spirit in our lives.

Let us return to Elijah, and discover how his experience tallies with our own. Several aspects require emphasis.

1. TEMPTED TO FORFEIT

We are tempted like the prophet to forfeit a God-given and God-placed position. "*Thou man of God...Come down*"! It is only such a man that can fall. Had Elijah not been a man of God, he would never have been asked to come down. If already down in the world, there is nowhere to fall. "He that is down need fear no fall." But the higher our life, the deeper our descent if we do fall. It is essential, of course, to distinguish between *position* and *practice*, or what we are in Christ and what we are in ourselves. If we are born of the Spirit, then we have been raised and made to sit with Christ in the heavenlies, and nothing can affect our standing in Him. Ours is an eternal salvation in Him.

The question is, Does our daily *practice* correspond to our judicial *position*, or our *standing* in Christ harmonize with our *state* on earth? While we cannot come down from our fixed position, we can indulge in habits and practices contradictory to a life with Christ hidden in God. It is the gracious, unceasing ministry of the Holy Spirit to transform and translate what we are in the heavenlies into what we should be here on earth. *In* Christ, we are to be *like* Christ.

2. TEMPTED TO YIELD

We are tempted as Elijah to yield to honor, position, wealth, and influence. Doubtless the diseased king would have bestowed honors upon Elijah had he come down from the top of the hill as commanded. But, obeying God rather than man, the prophet stayed on the heights, and because he did so, he received power to call fire down from heaven on those who had rejected God and spurned His faithful witness. Often the law of spiritual gravitation operates from the most unlikely and least expected sources. Satan is very subtle, and he knows that every man has his price. Time and again, preachers and churches become crippled, lacking power for God, because they become too dependent upon wealth and position. Rather than offend those who wield influence in a church, they yield to carnal wishes and plans.

3. ATTESTED OF GOD

We are attested of God when, like Elijah, we stay where God has placed us. What an impotent church needs is a band of Elijahs determined to stay on the mount and bring fire down upon antagonistic forces. We cannot keep ourselves on the top of the hill and overcome those forces that would drag us down by our own efforts. The flesh is too strong for us. There is no victory in resistance or suppression. Faced with such a struggle, Paul exclaimed, *"Thanks be unto God, which giveth us the victory"* (1 Corinthians 15:57). He is the counteracting power. My finger can defy the law of gravitation. Here clasped in them is a knife. The law is pulling it down, but it cannot succeed in doing so because the knife is held by living fingers. But if they are relaxed and release their grasp, immediately the knife falls to the ground. Our Lord referred to the Holy Spirit as the Finger of God (see, for example, Exodus 31:18; Deuteronomy 9:10), and it is He who holds the believer fast. Tersteegen expressed his experience in the following lines:

> The secret voice invites me still,
> The sweetness of Thy yoke to prove;
> And fain I would; but though my will
> Seems fixed, yet wide my passions rove;
> Yet hindrances strew all the way;
> I aim at Thee, yet from Thee stray.[14]

But if we want a life attested true by God—and man—then He must be the Lord of every notion of the heart, and we must stay on the mount in spite of demons and men. We must be aided by the Spirit to meet antagonistic forces in home, business, and Christian service. If we have been guilty of sacrificing heavenly principles on the altar of worldliness or convenience, and have become earthy, then we must repent and respond to the call of heaven, "Come up higher!" When satanic powers seek our descent and constantly urge us to come down, sustained by the Spirit, we must immediately respond, "By His grace, never! The heights for me!"

> Each moment draw from earth away
> My heart that lowly waits Thy call;

---

14. Gerhard Tersteegen, "Thou Hidden Love of God," 1729.

Speak to my inmost soul and say,
"I am thy love, thy God, thy all!"
To feel Thy power, to hear Thy voice,
To taste Thy love, be *all* my choice.[15]

---

15. Ibid.

CHAPTER 5

THE LION AND THE LAMB

"Behold, the Lion....I beheld, and, lo,
in the midst of the throne...stood a Lamb."
—Revelation 5:5–6

Within the particular part of that great Apocalypse from which our verses are taken, the inspired apostle John has given us his record of the strange spectacle of suspense in the heavenly courts. In the palm of the eternal One is a seven-sealed book; wonder abounds on every hand when no one is found worthy to open the scroll and read, and the failure caused grief and tears. An elder, however, bids John not to weep but to turn and see One who was able to unloose the sealed book and read. John looked to see the prevailing Lion, but he sees not a Lion in all its majesty but a Lamb—a "little lamb," as the term actually means.

It is said that at one time in the Roman coliseum, when the crowds sat watching a martyr standing in the arena waiting for a half-starved lion to leap forth from its cage and tear him to pieces, the keeper led forth a gentle lamb instead of the usual

lion as a play for the audience. The lamb came to the man awaiting death and licked his hand, and the audience responded with
surprise and thundering applause.

John expected to see a Lion, even Jesus the Lion of the tribe
of Judah, but instead, he saw a Lamb. One elder cried, "Behold
the Lion," and another nearby cried, "Behold the Lamb," and we
are to discover there is no contradiction here, for the one figure
is complementary to the other. We are taught by the two voices
a double truth we must be careful never to separate: The soul of
man needs not only the Lamb to expiate him from the *guilt* of
sin but also the conquering Lion to deliver him from the *power*
of sin. As the Lamb, Christ wins back a lost inheritance. As
the Lion, He unfolds it and makes it actual in our lives. As the
Lamb, He saves and redeems. As the Lion, He sways and rules.

The sealed book can be regarded as being the title deeds of
man's heavenly inheritance, which he lost by his fall in Eden, but
which was won back by the Lamb of God at Calvary. The title
deeds, however, were sealed and unavailable. One was found
who could break the seal. Christ is not only the Lamb of atoning sacrifice but also the Lion of majestic, royal conquest. Here,
then, are two sides of the one divine Person. He who, by His
priestly sacrifice, opened up the way to eternal life is He who,
with kingly power, makes His blood-washed ones victorious over
those sinful habits and desires hindering their spiritual progress
and the enjoyment of the full fruits of His finished work. As the
Lamb, then, He saves; as the Lion, He keeps us saved.

THE LION AND THE LAMB

What extremes these two creatures are in the animal
world! The one majestic, the other meek; the one strong,

the other weak; the one fearless, the other fearful. Yet there is no contradiction to the two beasts when applied to the Person and work of Christ who beautifully portrays both and combined both in His life and service here below. Isaiah, in describing the quality of the millennium, says that one distinguishing feature of it will be that *the wolf also shall dwell with the lamb*" (Isaiah 11:6). Some souls believe we are presently in the millennium. To prove that such is a fallacy, one has only to put a lamb alongside a wolf or lion. Will they dwell together? Yes! But the lamb will be *inside* the lion and not *alongside* it.

In Christ, however, the Lion and the Lamb dwell together in blissful harmony. One trait does not consume the other, as we hope to prove. What dignity and lowliness we discern in His bearing! At all times, He combined the brave, courageous attitude of a noble man and the gentle ministering touch of a loving mother. His was the royal bearing of a king, yet He could stoop to serve as a slave, as He did when He washed His disciples' feet. Mastery and suffering characterize His career. Authority and entreaty can be found in His teachings. The voice that quelled demons also pleaded with the demon-possessed to come to Him for rest. The eyes flashing wrath on hypocrites also melted with compassion over a doomed city.

All through the New Testament, we have this double strain, this mysterious blending of deity and humanity. The Lion and the Lamb are inseparable companions. His leonine passion of hatred for all those forces robbing humanity of peace and blessedness was coupled with a lamblike tenderness and compassion for poor, helpless sinners who were as lost sheep. Think of these twin aspects:

+ With leonine power, He rebuked the wind and waves and commanded them to be still. With lamblike meekness, He reviled not when He was reviled.

+ With leonine power, He brought Lazarus back from the grave. With lamblike patience, He opened not His mouth in Herod's presence.

+ With leonine boldness, He set His face steadfastly toward Jerusalem. With lamblike grace, He did not strive or cry.

+ With leonine sternness, He pronounced woes upon sinful Jerusalem. With lamblike tenderness, He weeps over her sins.

+ With leonine assertiveness, He utters His "I Ams." With lamblike self-denial, He died that men might have Him as the Bread of Life.

+ With leonine loftiness, He claimed the allegiance of men. With lamblike sacrifice, He made Himself of no reputation.

Although a King, He suffered as a helpless subject. Although the Lord of Life, He died.

THE LION AND THEREFORE THE LAMB

John has a pregnant phrase summarizing the book of Revelation. He penned, *"The Lamb shall overcome them: for he is Lord of lords, and King of kings"* (Revelation 17:14). The Lion and the Lamb are prominent in this concluding book of the Bible. The mystery of the incarnation is that of the eternal Lord becoming the Lamb. Although it may sound paradoxical, it is profoundly true. "The Captain of our salvation was made perfect through suffering." (See Hebrews 2:10.) Suffering perfects character and increases the sufferer's sympathy and power. Christ, because He was *the* Christ, the Anointed One, had to suffer. Because He was the Chief or King of men, He had to be foremost in self-sacrifice, as He was.

There is a legend to the effect that a chasm in the center of the Roman Forum was caused because the people had incurred the wrath of their gods, and that the chasm became wider and deeper day by day. The citizens poured all their richest possessions, gold, silver, jewels, into the gulf to appease the angry gods, but it yawned before them more terribly than ever. A message was received that the chasm would close only if one of the noblest of the citizens would cast himself in. Curtius, one of the finest youths in Rome, leaped into the abyss astride a white horse. Immediately, the chasm closed. The best man had to sacrifice himself for the rest. So Curtius still lives in the annals of Roman history as its lamb of expiation.

Christ, through His willingness to take upon Himself our frail flesh, became the noblest of all men and imposed upon Himself the work of atonement. It was expedient that a man die for the sins of the people, and He became that Man. The Lion became the Lamb, bearing away the sin of the world.

> There was no other good enough
> To pay the price of sin,
> He only could unlock the gate
> Of heaven and let us in.[16]

Bethlehem, where Christ was born a King, necessitated Calvary, where He died as the Lamb. Thus, He prevails in virtue of the cross, because first of all, He was the prevailing Lion. He was *God* manifest in *flesh*. As the strong, immortal Son of God, He alone had the right to die as the Son of man. Now, as the

---

16. Cecil F. Alexander, "There Is a Green Hill Far Away," 1847.

Lion of the tribe of Judah, He can break every fetter, crush every foe, and establish His kingdom on the ruins of opposition. His blood can make the vilest clean because it was the blood of God. (See Acts 20:28.)

THE LAMB AND THEREFORE THE LION

This is another facet of the dual truth before us. He became the Lion in His resurrection because He was willing to die as the Lamb. This is portrayed for us in the Lord's Table on the Lord's Day. Christ is lionized in heaven as the Lamb that was slain. *"Worthy is the Lamb...to receive...honour"* (Revelation 5:12).

> Crown Him with many crowns,
> The Lamb upon His throne.[17]

Isaiah, in his Calvary-resurrection prophecy, combines the Lion and the Lamb. *"He shall divide the spoil* [leonine] *with the strong; because* [lamblike] *he hath poured out his soul unto death"* (Isaiah 53:12). As the Lamb, He was led to slaughter; as the Lion, He leads to victory. As the Lamb, He was rejected; as the Lion, He reigns. Because of His cross, He has the crown. His scars earned Him His sovereignty. Honor is now His because of His humiliation. He reigns from the tree. Dying as the grain of wheat, He reaps a glorious harvest. We behold the Lion in Him who became the sacrificial Lamb.

A greater or more startling contrast could scarcely be conceived than that existing between a lion and a lamb. John looked for a Lion but saw a Lamb. The Christ of Jewish expectation was a lion, a conquering prince who would deliver an oppressed

---

17. Matthew Bridges, "Crown Him with Many Crowns," *The Passion of Jesus*, 1852.

people and restore the kingdom. The Jews rejected Christ because He looked more like a lamb than a lion. He did not come in royal robes and with a retinue of servants to take His place as king. Instead, He was despised and rejected, having nowhere to lay His head. He was born in a stable, not a palace; and when He grew up, He did not become the lion fighting His enemies, but He was willing to be led silently and submissively as a lamb to the slaughter.

Is not this still the world's concept? Men want power, force, and dominion. There is little room for tenderness, gentleness, sacrifice, and love. In national life, lions are desired, not lambs. Too often, the world's way to realize power is by war and the armored fist. The fittest are the only ones who should survive. But God's method of conquest is by the cross and through the nail-pierced hands of Him who died on it, and in virtue of His sacrifice, He will yet establish His kingdom on earth. Because He humbled Himself to the death of the cross, He has been highly exalted and will fulfill the fiat of having all His enemies under His feet. Universal worship will be His because of His wounds. His anguish will result in eternal adoration. There is a twofold application of this twin truth as far as we are concerned at the present time.

1. THE TWOFOLD NEED

Each of us needs to have the twofold office of Jesus as the Lamb and the Lion fulfilled in and through us. If we are to be delivered from the penalty and power of sin, it can only be accomplished through the Lamb slain for us. We must not only "behold the Lamb," but we must also accept Him as the sole ground of our acceptance before God. All those who attain heaven will have been washed in the blood of the Lamb.

If we are to be daily emancipated from the enticements and government of sin, then we must see in the Lamb the Lion who is able to rout all our foes and make us more than conquerors. We must have Him not only as our Savior but as the Sovereign Lord reigning over every part of life. We must constantly surrender to Him as the prevailing One. Saved by the blood of the Lamb, we have need of His protection; saved by the blood of the Lion, we have need of His protection from the evil machinations of the roaring lion, the devil.

2. THE TWOFOLD OFFICE

In the same narrative in which Christ is portrayed as the Lamb and the Lion, the saints are named as being "kings and priests unto God." (See Revelation 5:10.) What a well-matched pair of offices John gives us! Kings come first because, unless we first know what it is to reign in life by Christ Jesus, we cannot intercede effectively as priests. We require the leonine power, strength, and courage of noble kings, coupled with the lamb-like priestly qualities of meekness, gentleness, and submission. Balance must be preserved between the two.

As priests, we are to be meek under injury, patient amid suffering, as sheep among wolves, and ever active serving God and humanity. As kings, we must be bold as lions in fighting all that is alien to God's holy mind and will, ever manifesting those leonine characteristics so necessary in life's contest against the world, the flesh, and the devil.

CHAPTER 6

CRISIS AND PROCESS

"The Lord, whom ye seek, shall suddenly come to his temple."
—Malachi 3:1

"He shall sit as a refiner and purifier of silver."
—Malachi 3:3

The two verses we have cited from the book of Malachi have a direct application to the ministry of John the Baptist and also to the return of Christ when manifold blessings are to be poured out on Israel; but our purpose is to use the verses to illustrate a much-needed message concerning the ever-deepening spiritual experience of those who profess faith in Christ. The late Reverend Evan Hopkins, who was looked upon as the theologian of Keswick, loved to emphasize the twofold work of the Holy Spirit in the life of the believer.

THERE IS CRISIS

Such a crisis is reached and experienced when, by the act of faith, one is fully adjusted to the will of God and the pivot is changed from self and sin to God. This can be either in a person's regeneration or in his discovery of the ministry of the Spirit in his sanctification.

"The Lord, whom you seek, shall suddenly come to his temple" (Malachi 3:1). The *"temple"* is the biblical figure used by Christ for His own physical body. Paul applied this term to the church as a whole and to the individual believer. So the Lord comes in a new way to what is His already. In the temple of old, God's presence was localized. Coming suddenly to His temple, then, prefigures a crisis. We may ask why such a crisis is necessary in the experience of the majority of those who claim to be Christ's. One reason is that the person is ignorant of the truth of the Holy Spirit's presence at the time of conversion. Another is that the newly converted person is unaware that he possesses two natures, one carnal and one spiritual, and does not understand the difference between the two. Many live with only one half of the gospel, namely, salvation, and do not understand sanctification. Then there comes the moment when the truth of a fuller, richer, more victorious life bursts upon their vision, and the possibilities of a fuller submission to the Lord are realized.

Malachi speaks of the Lord sending a messenger before His face to prepare His way (see Malachi 3:1)—prophetic of the work of John the Baptist as he prepared the way for Jesus. This verse can also be applied to the preparatory influences resulting in the deeper sanctification of the child of God. Sorrow, disappointment, a sense of emptiness, spiritual impoverishment, fruitlessness, a consciousness of carnality and bondage can prepare the way for the Lord to come suddenly to His temple. Or a sense of need can result from private dealing with the Lord, reading works on holiness, listening to Spirit-inspired messages, and watching the fuller, more radiant lives of others.

As in regeneration, there is the instant communication of divine life to the soul hitherto dead in sin, for in so many cases, the Lord comes suddenly to unsaved hearts as He did when He instantaneously saved Saul of Tarsus. As the sinner realizes his insufficiency, the Lord comes suddenly and lifts the defeated, despairing one into a more blessed life altogether. An instant rectification and adjustment to the will and purpose of God often produces a thrill and change as marked as conversion. Some who have entered into this rest of faith refer to it as a second conversion.

Are you a born-again believer? If so, are you *being* saved? Are you fully surrendered? Does the Lord stand in the vestibule of your life? Or is He seated on the throne, reigning supreme over the empire of thought, the empire of love, and the empire of action? If He is not permeating the temple of your body, why not invite Him to come suddenly into it, as He did to the actual temple when He drove out all those who profaned His sanctuary? By a definite act, thoroughly adjust your regenerated life to the requirements of His holy will. He is the Messenger of the Covenant you will delight in. You have and love Him as Savior. Why not give Him His coronation as Lord of your life? This is the crisis saintly Bishop Handley Moule summarized for us in his Keswick hymn:

> Come, not to find, but make this troubled heart
> A dwelling worthy of Thee as Thou art;
> To chase the gloom, the terror, and the sin:
> Come, all Thyself, yea come, Lord Jesus, in![18]

Remember, if He is not Lord of all, He is not Lord at all. He stands at the door knocking for admission. The crisis comes when the door is opened from the inside, and the process begins

18. Handley C. G. Moule, "Come In, O Come!" 1890.

when the Lord enters and becomes the continual guest and host. *"I will come in to him, and will sup with him, and he with me"* (Revelation 3:20).

THERE IS PROCESS

As we receive the Lord Jesus (crisis), so we must walk in Him (process). There must be a daily sanctification, a constant growing to conform to His image, an unending advance in things divine. *"The path of the just is as the shining light, that shineth more and more unto the perfect day"* (Proverbs 4:18). Thus we have a crisis in an act of consecration or decision for holiness of life; then a process, gradual, continuous, and without finality. Before one can draw a line, he must start at a point—the crisis; then comes the line—the process. Two friends were discussing this matter. One was puzzled and could not understand it; the other had passed the crisis and had experienced full joy in the process. He used the following illustration to help his friend grasp the meaning:

"How did you come from London to Keswick to attend the Convention?" he asked.

His companion replied, "By train, of course."

"And did the train bring you on a sudden jump into Keswick?"

"Oh, no, I came along more and more."

"Yes, I see, but first you got into a standing carriage, and how did you do that? Was it more and more?"

"No, I just stepped in all at once."

"Exactly! That was the *crisis*; then you journeyed along more and more till you reached your destination, and that was *process*."

Do these two aspects not throw a flood of light on many of the Scripture passages that confuse some people? For instance, passages such as these: *"Let us cleanse ourselves from all filthiness of the flesh and spirit"* (2 Corinthians 7:1). *"Present your bodies a living sacrifice"* (Romans 12:1). These actions are deliberate and definite; they describe a crisis, an act. Then there are phrases that indicate a continuous attitude and a daily process. *"The very God of peace sanctify you wholly"* (1 Thessalonians 5:23). *"[Let us] perfect…holiness in the fear of God"* (2 Corinthians 7:1). And as these experiences are bound together in the Holy Scriptures, let no man put them asunder. (It is primarily the believer we have in mind in this present meditation.)

"And [the Lord] *shall sit as a refiner and purifier of silver"* (Malachi 3:3). Here we have what the poet describes as "the glory of going on, and still to be."[19] Once He not only *stands* but *sits* after He enters with His own bright presence and ordering hands, He begins to straighten up the dark confusion within His temple. Taking the throne, He sits as the refiner and purifier of silver—a metal referring to the believer, for it was redemption money in ancient Israel. It is here that we detect the difference between regeneration and sanctification. Regeneration is not capable of degrees. No one is more or less regenerated than another. Regeneration is a divine and immediate act. But the work of the Spirit in the sanctification of the born-again one is gradual and progressive and admits of degrees. All believers are saints, but some are more saintly than others; the degrees of spiritual progress depend on the fullness of trust and obedience.

What we are dealing with is our *practical* sanctification, not the *positional* sanctification Paul refers to when he says, *"Whom he justified, them he also glorified* [sanctified]" (Romans 8:30).

---

19. Alfred Tennyson, "Wages."

All regenerated ones are complete in Christ. But our *standing* in Him does not always correspond to the *state* of life here on earth. Thus it is the work of the Spirit to translate what we are in Christ into what we ought to be in our daily life and witness. Paul describes this progressive sanctification as a transformation: *"Beholding as in a glass the glory of the Lord, [we] are changed into the same image from glory to glory, even as by the Spirit of the Lord"* (2 Corinthians 3:18).

It should be clearly understood that this adjustment or process does not mean the complete extermination of the old nature from within. Accepting the Holy Spirit as Sanctifier does not imply eradication of the flesh. Nor does it signify absolute or sinless perfection or an experience in which there is no more temptation or a state from which we cannot fall or that we have reached a position in which we cannot sin again. What it does mean is the acceptance of a perfect Savior who is able to keep us from falling and redeem us from all iniquity, as well as give us the power to continually say no to the bent and gravitation of sin and self, thereby mortifying the deeds of the body. If you put your arm out of joint, the bonesetter adjusts or sets the bone—this is the *crisis*. But the arm is still sore, and there comes the gradual return of freedom to use it—this is the *process*. And so we sing—

> Work on, then, Lord, till on my soul
> Eternal light shall break,
> And, in Thy likeness perfected,
> I "satisfied" shall wake.[20]

Following the initial act of surrender, there comes the habit or attitude of surrender, and the thoroughness of dedication to God deepens and increases. Returning to the illustration of the

---

20. Handley C. G. Moule, "My Savior, Thou Hast Offered Rest."

refiner and purifier of silver, such refining is associated with the redeemed of the Lord, not with the unsaved whose first need is regeneration. Malachi speaks of the refining process in connection with the sons of Levi, meaning the Lord's separated ones.

"Refine" refers to the expulsion of the dross from the silver ore by the smelting of the fire. "Purify" signifies the separation or removal of the dross brought to the surface of the metal under intense heat.

How long does the refiner sit at his crucible? Until he sees the reflection of his face in the dross-free silver. How long will the divine Refiner sit at the crucible of your life and mine—until He comes to make up His jewels? Let us not be afraid of the purifying process, for what the Light reveals, the Blood can cleanse. *"I shall be satisfied, when I awake, with thy likeness"* (Psalm 17:15). The crisis, then, is when we sing, "Come in, O come"; the process when we further sing, "O Jesus Christ, grow Thou in me."

> Refining fire, go through my heart,
> Illuminate my soul;
> Scatter thy life through every part,
> And sanctify the whole.[21]

Between the crisis and the consummation, there are several characteristic traits of the progressive life of the believer. We can gather these from Malachi's prophecy:

1. THE PRESENCE AND PROVISION OF THE UNCHANGING LORD

What assurance and consolation for our hearts can be found in His declaration, *"I am the LORD, I change not"* (Malachi 3:6). We may change; so may our circumstances and times; but

---

21. Charles Wesley, "My God! I Know, I Feel Thee Mine."

He remains the same yesterday, today, and forever, and as the unchanged and unchanging One, He is able to perfect that which concerns us.

2. THE BRINGING AND THE BLESSING

The fullness of blessing God has for every one of His children is conditional. *If* we bring all our tithes into His storehouse, then He will open the windows of heaven and pour upon us an overwhelming blessing. But if we rob Him of all that should be His, we rob ourselves of all He has for us. (See Malachi 3:7–10.)

3. THE PROMISE OF VICTORY OVER SATAN

Through the death and resurrection of our Lord, ours is the authority to say to Satan, "*The* LORD *rebuke thee*" (Zechariah 3:2)! "*Get thee behind me*" (Matthew 16:23)! We have the Lord's promise, "*I will rebuke the devourer for your sakes*" (Malachi 3:11). Deliverance can be ours from the abortive fruit of the self-life, and conversely the preservation of the fruit of the Spirit. Through Calvary, Satan is a defeated foe, and so, by faith, we claim the victory.

4. THE ATTRACTIVENESS OF A CHRISTLIKE CHARACTER

C. H. Spurgeon once wrote of those who were "saved but sour." Sometimes, professionally good people are hard to live with and work for; they fail to be delightsome. But this should not be so. Those who know and follow the Lord ought to be the sweetest, easiest, and most reasonable people to get along with on the earth. Sanctification should add charm to character, making us "lovely and pleasant in our lives." (See 2 Samuel 1:23.) How apt is the child's prayer "O God, make the bad people good, and the good people easier to live with"! May we be found among the delightsome people. (See Malachi 3:12.)

> I ask this gift of Thee—
> A life all lily-fair;
> And fragrant as the place
> Where seraphs are.[22]

5. THE PRECIOUSNESS OF FELLOWSHIP WITH THE SANCTIFIED

We have the adage, A man is known by the company he keeps. In the spiritual realm, like draws to like. *"They that feared the Lord spake often one to another"* (Malachi 3:16). Then the prophet has a sweet touch, *"The Lord hearkened, and heard it, and a book of remembrance was written before him for them that feared the Lord, and that thought upon his name"* (Malachi 3:16). If ours is the ever-increasing thirst for holiness, we will not be found hankering after the company of the carnal and worldly but seeking the fellowship of kindred minds. Separation to God involves separation from fellowship with those who do not fear the Lord and constantly think upon His name.

In conclusion, then, we have the commencement and continuation of the abundant life Christ offers. There is the crisis, or, if you prefer, His sudden entrance to His temple. It is not for us to quibble over terms and isolate those who do not use our exact phraseology or pronounce our shibboleths. What is vastly important is not expression but experience. Entire sanctification, reception of the second blessing, baptism with the Spirit, infilling of the Spirit, readjustment of life and service to the will of God—these are all descriptive of what happens when we crown Christ the Lord of our lives.

---

22. Helen Bradley, "I Am Thine Own, O Christ."

One must be careful to add that it is possible to be so thoroughly yielded to God in the hour of conversion as not to require the spiritual crisis we have been dealing with. It was so with the apostle Paul, who, from the outset of his transformation on that Damascus road, knew what it was to be utterly yielded to the will of God. But with the majority of believers, it is otherwise. Those lacking a Christian parentage and upbringing know little about the Bible, the ministry of the Spirit, and the two natures in the hour of acceptance of Christ as a personal Savior. Consequently, there is an up-and-down experience, more often down than up, because of habits and desires carried over from their unsaved past.

Then, as we have already indicated, there comes the moment when they are fully conscious of their spiritual lack, and the Lord suddenly comes to His temple with the revelation of a glorious life of freedom and peace; and through a crisis of the will, a yielding up of the entire life is experienced, and mighty spiritual forces are released. Thereafter, the process begins, and the Lord patiently sits before the crucible of life, refining it day by day, tempering the fire until the dross is separated and removed and, with growing spiritual apprehension, the witness becomes more victorious and fruitful.

> Have you on the Lord believed?
> Still there's more to follow;
> Of His grace have you received?
> Still there's more to follow.[23]

The striking testimony of Frances Ridley Havergal, who came to traverse the lofty path of spirituality, will fittingly conclude our meditation of the twin truths of crisis and process—

---

23. Philip P. Bliss, "Have You on the Lord Believed?" 1873.

It was on Advent Sunday, December 2, 1873, I first saw clearly the blessedness of true consecration. I saw it as a flash of electric light, and what you *see* you can never *unsee*. There must be full surrender before there can be full blessedness. God admits you by the one into the other. He Himself showed this most clearly. You know how singularly I have been withheld from all conventions and conferences; man's teaching has, consequently, had but little to do with it. First, I was shown that "the blood of Jesus Christ His Son cleanseth us from all sin," and then it was made plain to me that He who had thus cleansed me had power to keep me clean; so I just utterly yielded myself to Him, and utterly trusted Him to keep me.[24]

> My spirit, soul, and body,
> Dear Lord, I give to Thee,
> A consecrated offering,
> Thine evermore to be.[25]

---

24. *The Primitive Methodist Magazine, for the Year of Our Lord*, vol. 63, 1882.
25. Mary D. James, "Consecration," 1869.

CHAPTER 7

LIFE AND DEATH

"I have set before you life and death, blessing and cursing: therefore choose life, that both thou and thy seed may live."
—Deuteronomy 30:19

"Behold, I set before you the way of life, and the way of death."
—Jeremiah 21:8

*"Broad is way, that leadeth to destruction...
And narrow is the way, which leadeth unto life."*
—Matthew 7:13–14

*"The wages of sin is death; but the gift of God is
eternal life through Jesus Christ our Lord."*
—Romans 6:23

The four passages cited indicate that the supreme, most momentous choice facing any man in his lifetime is between the alternatives of life or death, God or Satan, heaven or hell. No other decision confronting him compares to this solemn one with its eternal issues. A man may scorn, argue against, or neglect these stern alternatives of Scripture, but they remain inviolate and inviolable, reminding him that the choice is ever between life and death in eternal things. Everywhere this sharp division prevails. Distinct lines are drawn, and we cannot alter them. If we are not among the sheep, we must be with the goats. If we are not for Christ, we are against Him. If we are not children of God, then we are children of the devil. If we are not in the white, we must be in the black, for there is no mixture of gray in spiritual matters.

The endowment of free will is a most wonderful yet dangerous gift, for like a sword in the hand of a child, it can injure its possessor. When God created man, He did not make him a robot, a mere machine. Rather, He made him a free moral agent with power of choice and action. Sin exists in the universe because the first man used this precious gift against the Giver. Tennyson reminds us that

> Our wills are ours, we know not how;
> Our wills are ours, to make them thine.[26]

It is with the will that the battle is fought and the choice made between right and wrong, good or evil. George Matheson has taught us to sing—

> My will is not my own
>   Till thou hast made it thine;
> If it would reach a monarch's throne,
>   It must its crown resign.[27]

Both here and in eternity, we are what we *will* to be. Moses emphasized this fact in the charge he gave to the people of Israel

---

26. Alfred Tennyson, *In Memorium A. H. H.* (1849), prelude, stanza 4.
27. George Matheson, "Make Me a Captive, Lord," 1890.

as he was dying, facing a lonely, unmarked grave on Mount Nebo. What a majestic sight it must have been to see him stand forth calling heaven and earth to witness against the multitudes he had led for almost forty years. He had faithfully set before them life and death, blessing and cursing, warning them that "the life indeed" would only be theirs if they chose the living God! There is also in the call of Moses the suggestion of the abiding results of a right kind of choice: *"That both thou and thy seed may live"* (Deuteronomy 30:19). Choice shapes life and character and determines destiny.

Furthermore, the choice is ever personal. *"Choose you this day whom ye will serve"* (Joshua 24:15). No one other than you can choose Christ. Who is "the life" for you? Friends may pray for you, and try to influence and persuade you to accept Him as Savior; but the decision to do so is yours alone. *"If any man will to do his will, he shall know"* (John 7:17). When a soul is faced with the alternatives of life or death, only he can respond for himself. As Lowell puts it—

> Then it is the brave man chooses,
> while the coward stands aside,
> Doubting in his abject spirit, till his Lord is crucified.[28]

Not a few are troubled by the apparent contradiction between divine predestination and human choice. These cannot be fully harmonized by our finite comprehension. Although Israel was an elected nation, the realization of their privileges was conditional upon the obedience of the people. (See Exodus 14:5–6.) In connection with the church, the predestination the apostles speak of is related to present privileges, not to eternal blessedness. (See 2 Peter 1:10–11.) John Calvin declared that "some are preordained to eternal life, and others to eternal

28. James Russell Lowell, "The Present Crisis," lines 53–54.

damnation." But this assertion is contrary to the teaching of Holy Writ in that it nullifies the function of the human will and also does away with preaching the gospel to lost sinners. Arminius was also wrong in his assertion that "God, from all eternity, determined to bestow salvation on those whom he foresaw would persevere unto the end in their faith in Jesus Christ." But to make salvation dependent upon foreseen perseverance clearly contradicts the teaching of Paul that *"the election of grace"* (Romans 11:5) is all of grace. *"If by grace, then is it no more of works: otherwise grace is no more grace"* (Romans 11:6; see also Ephesians 2:8).

The scriptural position is that God's grace is the sole *source* of predestination, the work of Christ for us and the Holy Spirit in us as its sole *method,* and holiness here and happiness hereafter as its *object,* all of which is allied to the counterbalancing truth of human choice and decision. God always addresses us as responsible beings, endowed with free will and, therefore, able to determine whether or not our names will be written in the Book of Life. When C. H. Spurgeon was asked how he could reconcile divine election with personal choice, his wise answer was, "On this side of heaven I read, 'Whosoever will may come.' When I get to the other side of heaven I shall read, 'Whomsoever I have chosen.'" Let us now discover how these twin truths are expressed in Scripture.

TWO WAYS FROM WHICH TO CHOOSE

Our Lord was most explicit in His teaching regarding the options facing a sinner. He said, *"Broad is the way...narrow is the way"* (Matthew 7:13–14). There are only two roads, then, and as we cannot walk on two at the same time, a choice has to be made concerning the one we intend to travel. We speak about a person being a middle-of-the-roader. But in the spiritual realm, there is no middle road, although men may try to create one. *"There is a way which seemeth right unto a man, but the end thereof are the ways of death"* (Proverbs 14:12). It may help if we examine the nature of these opposite ways.

1. THE NARROW WAY

Why did Christ call it a narrow way? Because although it is wide enough for any sinner to walk on, there is no room for his sin. All that is alien to God's holy will is excluded from this way. We recognize that there are those who profess to have their feet on the narrow way but whose heart is on the broad way. These are the carnal Christians that Paul refers to. Traffic on the narrow way has never been heavy, for, as Christ put it, *"Few there be that find it"* (Matthew 7:14). Those who adhere to the fundamentals of the faith are often labeled as "narrow." Well, what else can they be if their feet are on the narrow way? Woe befalls the train that does not keep to the narrow rails all the way. In addition, our destination depends on the way we take. Awaiting all those on the narrow way is life forevermore in the presence of Him who never deviated from that way.

2. THE BROAD WAY

Some cities have a central road they call "Broadway," and usually, life on it is broad in every wrong sense. Christ called it "broad" because on it, there is plenty of room for sinners and their sin. Because it seems to be a very pleasant way, it is thronged with deluded travelers, for *"many there be which go in thereat"* (Matthew 7:13). The tragedy is that the majority of people much prefer the road leading to vanity fair, even although it ends in the City of Destruction. The psalmist said, "*The way of the ungodly shall perish*" (Psalm 1:6).

> Broad is the road that leads to death,
> And thousands walk together there;
> But wisdom shows a narrower path,
> With here and there a traveler.[29]

TWO COMPANIES FROM WHICH TO CHOOSE

To explain the purpose of His incarnation and crucifixion, our Lord said, "*The Son of man is come to seek and to save that which was lost*" (Luke 19:10). To Him, then, there are only two conditions or companies—the saved and the lost; and if we are not in the first group, we must be in the second. The difference is arbitrary. There are only two kinds of people in the world, the saints (the title the Bible gives Christians) and the "ain'ts." Many shirk the issue. If you ask them, "Are you saved?" they often reply, "Well, I don't know. I don't think I am." Then if you say, "If you are not saved, you must be lost," their immediate response is, "Oh, no, I am not a lost soul." It may clarify matters if we can determine the exact meaning of the terms *saved* and *lost*.

What does being saved imply? *Save* and *salvation* are among the terms most often used in the Bible. God is presented as our salvation. Christ died to save sinners, and there is no other name by which we can be saved from sin and hell. Because of our utter inability to save ourselves, deliverance must come from another. Apart from Christ, the sinner is both helpless and hopeless. To

---

29. Isaac Watts, "Broad Is the Road," 1709.

be saved, then, after the New Testament order, is to recognize our lost condition, repent of our past sin, receive by faith the Savior through whose death we have remission of sins, and then by the Holy Spirit's power, live the life, proving the reality of such a salvation. Being saved also includes deliverance from coming wrath and judgment; therefore, our past, present, and future are covered.

One can be morally good and upright, a church member and worker, a religious person, and yet not be saved. They may work *for* the faith but not be *in* it. Paul makes it clear that we are saved from sin's penalty and power by grace, not by works. *"By grace ye are saved"* (Ephesians 2:5). If we could work out our own salvation, then there would have been no need for Jesus to come and die. But He took upon Himself human flesh and died that we might be forgiven and saved, and that we might go "at last to heaven, saved by His precious blood."[30] Let us never be ashamed to confess that we have heard the joyful sound "Jesus saves!"

What does being lost mean? Words may have different shades of meaning. For instance, the term *lost* has a twofold implication: Something may be lost, and yet there may be every possibility of recovery, or something may be lost with no possibility of recovery. Years ago, while living in Glasgow, I came home one afternoon to find that our very small daughter had wandered away from home and was lost. I searched the neighborhood without avail; as a last resort, I went to the police station, and there I found her. Jesus spoke of a lost sheep, a lost silver coin, and a lost son—all lost in different ways. The blessedness of these parables is that the sheep, the coin, and the son were all found. Through disobedience, man has strayed from God and is lost in sin, but there is the prospect of recovery. "He

30. "There Is a Green Hill Far Away."

found the sheep that was lost." (See Luke 15:6.) Thank God there is a recovery office!

> I was lost, but Jesus found me,
> Found the sheep that went astray.[31]

But there is a more solemn side of the term *lost*—lost with no possibility of recovery. Suppose you are traveling on the ocean and, while standing at the rail of the ship, you accidentally drop a valuable ring or watch into the fathomless depths. Your treasure would be lost beyond recovery. We make no apology for stating that if a person dies lost, or out of Christ, he dies lost forevermore. As man is when he dies, so he is on the other side. The grave can work no miracle of transformation, and the Bible knows nothing of the purgatory Rome invented to fill her coffers. *"In the place where the tree falleth, there it shall be"* (Ecclesiastes 11:3). The rich man, hoping for some way out of the tormenting flame of hell, sought for mercy and a transfer to the blessed abode where Lazarus was. (See Luke 16:19–31.) But Abraham, in the parable told by Jesus, told him there was no relief from his torment and that any access to a more blissful sphere was impossible: *"Between us and you there is a great gulf fixed: so that they which would pass from hence to you cannot; neither can they pass to us, that would come from thence"* (Luke 16:26).

What a solemn declaration to come from the loving heart of Jesus! Yet He was only declaring the inevitable end of those who reject what He provided for them at Calvary, deliverance from eternal woe. He has no pleasure in the death of the wicked. Every sinner passing out into everlasting darkness gives the Savior a fresh pang. Heaven never sends a lost sinner to hell. All who depart to that place where the worm never dies and the fire

31. Francis H. Rowley, "I Will Sing the Wondrous Story," 1886.

is never quenched go to such a doom of their own volition. We have the priceless power of choice with which we will our salvation or our damnation.

How imperative it is for us to warn the lost to flee from the wrath to come. (See Ezekiel 3:17–21.)

TWO MASTERS FROM WHOM TO CHOOSE

How emphatic and unmistakable is our Lord's statement *"No man can serve two masters: for either he will hate the one, and love the other; or else he will hold to the one, and despise the other. Ye cannot serve God and mammon"* (Matthew 6:24). Joshua gave the people he commanded the choice between the living and true God and the gods of the heathen: *"Choose you this day whom ye will serve"* (Joshua 24:15). Boldly, he announced his own decision when he said, *"As for me and my house, we will serve the LORD"* (Joshua 24:15). Jesus was most emphatic about allegiance to only one master: *"Ye **cannot** serve God and mammon"* (Matthew 6:24; Luke 16:14). When He fashioned the heart of man, He made it a throne capable of holding only one master.

Who are the two masters bidding for the throne of your life and mine? The Savior and Satan—the two who are diametrically opposed in their designs for humans. If we are not the happy servants of the former, we must be the helpless slaves of the other. If we love the one, we hate the other. Some may try to serve both masters, taking the privileges of the Savior with one hand and the pleasures of Satan with the other, boasting that they can have the best of both worlds. But how contradictory it is to sing on Sunday, "Were the whole realm of nature mine, that were an offering far too small,"[32] and then go out and live the rest of the week as if there was no Savior demanding their soul, their life, their all.

Jesus, as a gracious Master, seeks to bless; Satan, as a gruesome master, is out to blast. The One provides us with goodness; the other, grief. The One died for our sins and sets us free; the other keeps us in our sins and makes us slaves. The One leads to heaven; the other, to hell. To be the friend of one master, then, is to be the enemy of the other. *"A friend of the world is the enemy of God"* (James 4:4). More than ever in these days of impotent Christian witness, it is imperative to preach the necessity of separation from worldly pleasures and pursuits on the part of those who profess to have chosen Christ as their Master. It can never be Christ *and* the world but always Christ *or* the world. If we hold to the one, we will despise the other. (See Matthew 6:24).

Jesus calls to separation,
And Himself hath led the way;
His own life the explanation,
His own life the illustration—
Who is ready to obey?[33]

TWO JUDGMENTS FROM WHICH TO CHOOSE

Among the various judgments mentioned in Scripture, the apostle Paul brings two together in one verse in the last letter he penned. In his farewell charge to Timothy, in which he urged the young evangelist to preach the Word and make full proof of his ministry, he reminded him of the judgment of the saved

32. Isaac Watts, "When I Survey the Wondrous Cross," 1707.
33. Lucy Ann Bennett, "Holy, Happy Separation."

and also the judgment of the lost. This, he said, was part of the Word he should preach: *"The Lord Jesus Christ, who shall judge the **quick** and the **dead** at **his appearing** and **his kingdom**"* (2 Timothy 4:1).

Here we have two different companies—the living and the dead—and two different judgments—one taking place at His appearing and the other at His kingdom. The living are those saved by grace, those who will never die the second death. The dead are those who were dead in their trespasses and sins, those who died in their sins and who consequently cannot be where Christ is—*"Whither I go, ye cannot come"* (John 8:21).

As to the respective times and particular nature of these two judgments, the first is before the judgment seat of Christ, which will take place after He appears the second time. Writing to saints, Paul declared that all must appear before this judgment and that it is a judgment specifically related to service and the rewards for this service. Every man's work will be tried by fire of what sort it is. (See Romans 14:10, 12; 1 Corinthians 3:12–15; 2 Corinthians 5:10; Revelation 22:12.) The tragedy is that some of us will stand before the Lord on this crowning day with a saved soul but a lost life. *"Saved; yet so as by fire"* (1 Corinthians 3:15). There will be nothing to our credit—no stars in our crown. God grant us a full reward!

The second judgment will be before the great white throne. John vividly describes this as taking place after the Lord has set up His kingdom. (See Revelation 20:12–15.) Before this august throne only the wicked dead will be brought, for the Lord who is the Judge can never say of any redeemed soul, "Depart from me you cursed, for I never knew you!" (See Matthew 7:23; 25:41.) Those whose names are not written in the Lamb's Book of Life are raised for the ratification of their condemnation, after which they will pass out into *"the second death"* (Revelation 20:14). If we are at the first judgment, we will not be at the second one. Our relationship to Jesus Christ determines the particular judgment we will face.

TWO DESTINIES FROM WHICH TO CHOOSE

It is remarkable to find how many gospel truths are foreshadowed in the Old Testament. Our Lord made it perfectly clear that, although we are all travelers to eternity, there are two different destinations—heaven and hell—and He died that we at last might go to heaven, saved by His precious blood. Think of the way Daniel expressed the alternate destination part of humanity is journeying to: *"Many of them that sleep in the dust of the earth shall awake, some to everlasting life, and some to shame and everlasting contempt"* (Daniel 12:2).

G. Campbell Morgan wrote, "I can choose heaven or hell. It is a tremendous issue, but it is a magnificent possibility." Have you ever paused to ask yourself the question "Where will I be a minute after death?" If it is not in paradise, then it will be in perdition. The moment we depart, we go to be with Christ, or else we enter the eternal abode of the lost without any hope of release. God would not be just if all men, irrespective of their life and character, entered heaven. Some people like to retain the idea of heaven but totally reject the necessity of hell. But God has never abrogated the scriptural revelation of hell; it is still in the Bible and must still be preached. It is to be regretted that there is a sinful silence in pulpits today concerning the eternal doom of those who die out of Christ. As we extol the glories of heaven, we must not neglect to warn sinners of the groans of hell. One wonders what would happen if a solemn, scriptural message from every pulpit next Sunday was preached on the verse *"The wicked shall be turned into hell, and all the nations that forget God"* (Psalm 9:17).

TWO ATTITUDES FROM WHICH TO CHOOSE

Pilate found himself in a dilemma when the Jews rejected Christ, an innocent prisoner, and chose Barabbas. He asked, *"What shall I do then with Jesus which is called Christ?"* (Matthew 27:22). Christ was on Pilate's hands, and he had to do something with Him. What should he do—release Him, as his conscience told him to do; or resign Christ to His fate, which he did against his better self and also against the entreaty of his wife? Pilate would have stood out in history as a courageous ruler had he acted nobly by defying the Jewish rulers who cried out for the blood of the Man he knew to be faultless and not worthy of death and releasing Christ. But instead, he released Barabbas, and then tried to rid himself of the responsibility of committing Christ to be crucified by washing his hands. But the damned spot remained.

The same Christ is on our hands, too. We must do something with Him. Two paths are before us; we must take one or the other. To put it simply, we can either receive Him or reject Him. As far as He is concerned, we cannot remain neutral. If we are not *for* Him, we are *against* Him, as He Himself declared. (See Matthew 12:30; Luke 11:23.) If we receive Him, He receives us and makes us the children of God. (See John 1:12.) He becomes our Savior, the savor of life unto life. If we reject Him, then we seal our doom and ultimately face Him as the righteous Judge, the savor of death unto death.

The breath from my mouth can both warm my cold hands and cool a bowl of hot soup. The sun shining in the heavens melts wax but hardens clay. Just so, the Christ who melts the heart and saves from sin also closes the door of hope on a sinner when he, having rejected the only remedy for his sin, dies. It is our solemn obligation to set before men life and death, blessing and cursing, and to lovingly challenge them to choose life with all its benefits both here and hereafter. Our appeal must be "The awful choice—life or death? Which will you choose? Which will you lose?"

> There is a time, we know not when,
> A point we know not where,
> That marks the destiny of men
> To glory or despair.
> There is a line by us unseen,
> That crosses every path;
> The hidden boundary between
> God's patience and his wrath.[34]

---

34. Joseph Addison Alexander, "The Hidden Line."

CHAPTER 8

HARPS AND SPEARS

"David played with his hand [upon his harp], *as at other times: and there was a javelin in Saul's hand."*
—1 Samuel 18:10

Many years ago, before we were obliged to leave our English home for extended service in America, there hung on the wall in my study a picture that never ceased to fascinate me. It minutely described a scene in King Saul's palace. Seated on a carpeted floor, with a lion's skin partly covering his perfectly formed body, was young David. His fingers, gliding over the strings of his much-loved harp, seemed to express the inspired music of his pure soul.

Reposing on a raised divan was Saul, gazing down into the innocent and ruddy countenance of the shepherd lad. For the time being, Saul's agitated mind was soothed by the melody of David's harp. Yet the jealous sovereign held in one hand a spear of death, ready to hurl at any moment.

I always found the contrast most marked. In the hand of youthful David was a lovely harp. In Saul's large, strong hand was a bejeweled spear. The lesson of the picture was obvious: While the gifted harpist played his instrument, producing music so soothing and sublime, Saul's anger was appeased and his deadly spear at rest. As David strummed his harp, and possibly sang one of his psalms, the evil spirit departed the unhappy king.

Are there not times when we all need the ministry of the minstrel? There are times when the harp conquers the spear, melody triumphs over murder, peace over war, good over evil, and Calvary over Satan. Then evil spirits descend upon us, and we are compelled to call for the minstrel to expel them from our lives. When fierce anger against another flames within the soul, we need to pray, "Calm me, my God…while these hot breezes blow"[35]; and as of old, when He bade the angry storm abate, there will be *a great calm* (Matthew 8:26; Mark 4:39).

SYMBOLIC OF TWO CHARACTERS

When we look at the instruments side by side, we see that the harp is the instrument of peace and the spear is the instrument of pain, portraying the opposite natures of David and Saul when Saul was the nation's first king. David is the melodious one; Saul, the murderous one. Think of King Saul. What an imposing appearance was his! Towering head and shoulders above others, he had height but not honor, brawn but not brains, personality but not deep piety. His was a feeble, changeable nature. He started out with high ideals, but these were never realized. Gradually, he degenerated until he became melancholy, jealous, and suspicious of those who fought for him and loved him; then, later, he was filled with remorse. Thus it was that, in a jealous

35. Horatius Bonar, "Calm Me, My God," 1857.

moment, he was ready to hurl his spear and murder the young man to whom he owed so much and whose character was so different from his own. Saul had great faith in his spear, which seldom missed the mark. It was always beside him, whether he was in repose, at meals, or in battle.

Such a destructive weapon was a symbol of his reign and descriptive of his character as a pampered hypochondria, as well as a madman when in the grip of an evil spirit. Saul was conspicuous as the man with a spear, especially when he was hunting David to kill him. *"Having his spear in his hand…"* (1 Samuel 22:6). *"Saul lay sleeping…his spear stuck in the ground at his bolster"* (1 Samuel 26:7). Saul and his spear were inseparable. He had failed to realize the Lord does not save with sword or spear (see 1 Samuel 17:47), and he had forgotten that when Goliath came out against Israel with sword and spear, it was a lad's feeble stone from a musical brook that had killed the giant.

Think of David, the shepherd lad. This sweet harpist was anointed king over Israel when he was only a youth, yet there is never any trace of impatience on his part to ascend the throne. He never lost his head and saw no incongruity in being both shepherd and sovereign. It was because of his gift and fame as a harp player that he was commanded to play for Saul, as to appease him in his evil moments and to soothe the temper of the very man who was bent on taking his life. Saul constantly eyed David with a close, keen scrutiny, but David, who had early mastered the lesson of self-government, acted wisely. James Beattie of the eighteenth century wrote in *The Minstrel:* "His harp, the sole companion of his way." In his exile, David's harp was his unfailing companion, its music expressing his nature. Later he wrote about praising the Lord with the harp. He certainly acted out his advice.

The harp depicts the harmony of David's discipline and buoyancy. He was ever calm and fearless in the consciousness of his divine calling. A cunning, or skillful, player, he rose to eminence because of his skill on the harp. The time came when he had to use a sword, but then the instrument of peace and harmony immortalizes the sweet psalmist of Israel. We know him not as a man of war but as the shepherd who loved to play and sing, and whose spiritual lyrics are still sung the world over. Saul may value his javelin, but David loved his lyre, and the contrast is startling and complete, as the artist has embodied in his canvas.

TYPICAL OF OPPOSITE QUALITIES

Is there not an irreconcilable difference between *harps* and *spears*? How adverse they are in construction and purpose! The one thrills; the other kills. The one soothes; the other slays. The one produces songs; the other produces sobs. The one draws out a benediction; the other draws blood. Further, a fool can throw a spear, but it takes gift and patience and practice to produce captivating music on a harp. Any coarse hand can throw a spear, and usually they are thrown by coarse hands prompted by coarse hearts. It takes soft, gentle, sympathetic hands to pluck the strings of a harp. The fine touch, producing heavenly music, is made possible by a still finer soul. One or two applications can be made of these different and contradictory instruments.

1. DAVID'S HARP REPLIED TO SAUL'S JAVELIN

The ancients attributed supernatural power to music. Apollo is represented as subduing everything with his lyre. There is also the legend of Orpheus and the power of his harp. As David played his harp, we read that *"Saul was refreshed, and was well, and the evil spirit departed from him*" (1 Samuel 16:23). Elisha also experienced the soothing influence of music. He was willing to exercise his prophetic gift on behalf of the armies of Jehoshaphat and those of his enemy, Moab. The prophet was angry with the wicked Jehoram, and he knew that in his angry mood, he was in no condition to prophesy aright, so he said, "*Bring me a minstrel*" (2 Kings 3:15). One who was with the army was brought, and as he touched the strings of his harp, and as the soft notes of his music floated over the desert and the tents of war, the anger in the heart of Elisha subsided. "*It came to pass, when the minstrel played, that the hand of the Lord came upon him*" (2 Kings 3:15), and once again, his spirit was calm and tranquil and he spoke to God. God, in turn, spoke to the prophet and gave the two kings directions, delivering them out of great danger. (See 2 Kings 3:11–27.)

So it was when David took up his harp and expressed the harmony of heaven. His flashing eye, glowing countenance, and fervor expressed his love for his instrument, and his fingers made the strings vibrate with divine music. Saul's spear held no fear for David, for the harp in his hand was attuned to heavenly inspired psalms. All the time his harp was in his hand, David was immortal. Saul's murderous weapon might leave a mark on the wall, but it could not pierce the psalmist's heart. Spears can never hurt the man who abides where God has placed him and who, when the darts of jealousy are hurled, takes up his harp and gives music for murder. Have we not the promises that "*no weapon that is formed against thee shall prosper*" (Isaiah 54:17) and "[the Lord] *cutteth the spear in sunder*" (Psalm 46:9)?

The triumph of the harp over the spear had a profound effect on the king, for we read that "*Saul was afraid of*

David" (1 Samuel 18:12). Sheltered by the presence of the Good Shepherd, we have no need to fear the pointed spears of demons and men or the fiery darts of the devil. Having the harp of faith in the Lord's protective care, *"darts are counted as stubble: he laugheth at the shaking of a spear"* (Job 41:29). If we are safe under the divine wings, then we have no reason to *"be afraid…for the arrow that flieth by day"* (Psalm 91:5). God will see to it that not a shaft will hit until He sees fit.

2. THE FUNDAMENTAL TRUTH AND WITNESS OF SCRIPTURE

David could have slain Saul, but he always used the harp against the spear, or returned good for evil, as the incident in the cave proves. (See 1 Samuel 24.) The psalmist was a fugitive because of Saul's determination to kill him. In the hunt, the king rested in the cave at Engedi, not knowing that the person he sought was nearby. While he slept, David crept near and cut off a part of Saul's garment to prove that he could have killed him. When the king awoke and saw how magnanimous David had been, he repented of his murderous intentions and said to him, *"Thou art more righteous than I: for thou hast rewarded me good, whereas I have rewarded thee evil"* (1 Samuel 24:17). The harp triumphed over the spear and honor over hatred, as it was with Jesus, David's greater Son. His foes came out against Him with swords and staves, but He went out to His bitter death with peace in His heart and a song on His lips. On the night He was betrayed, He gave thanks. (See 1 Corinthians 11:23–24). The murder that was planned and known to Him could not destroy the music of His soul. *"When they had sung an hymn, they went out"* (Mark 14:26)—to Calvary! Hatred was met with a hymn and swords with a song.

Those who had companied with Jesus came to see that harp playing was more pleasing and profitable than spear throwing. For instance, an angry mob might have hurled their stones at godly, defenseless Stephen, but as he died, the first martyr of the Christian Church, he played his harp for his murderers; and it was not long before Saul of Tarsus, after listening to such music, left his spear for a harp. After he became Paul the apostle, he preached by life and witness to do good to those who despitefully use you and to overcome evil with good. Isaiah visualized the time when even nations will beat their spears into pruning hooks. The consistent teaching of the Word is the transformation of piercing spears into musical harps.

The spear or javelin was a weapon of war in times past; in our present age, nations try to keep what they call "the balance of power" by the multiplication of spears. The nation having the greatest number of nuclear weapons, ships, and submarines is the one to be feared, because it is able to lord it over smaller nations whose bombs and battalions are not so numerous. Harps of peace are not popular these days, when all nations are arming to the teeth and are spending billions more to prepare for a holocaust of war than they are to spread peace throughout the earth. But nations as well as individuals who live by spears usually fall by them. The Holy Writ warns us, *"They that take the sword shall perish with the sword"* (Matthew 26:52). When the foes of Christ came out against Him with swords and staves, Peter, thinking that a spear should be used against a spear, drew his sword, and in defense of his Lord, he cut off the ear of a man. But Jesus said, *"Put up again thy sword into his place"* (Matthew 26:52). He did not require any protection the flesh could provide when He had myriads of angels at His disposal.

Saul's spear was often poised to fling at David, but the day came when he fell on it and killed himself. Judas was the means of Jesus hanging on a tree; shortly afterward, he chose from which to commit suicide because of his crime. Yes, we reap what we sow, whether it is in harps or spears. Wise Solomon wrote, *"Say not, I will do so to him as he hath done to me: I will render to the man according to his work"* (Proverbs 24:29). Peter's advice is, *"Not rendering evil for evil, or railing for railing, but contrariwise blessing"* (1 Peter 3:9). In other words, meet the spear with a harp. *"The LORD saveth not with sword and spear: for the battle is the LORD's"* (1 Samuel 17:47).

The ancient heathens had the custom of dipping their spears in poison to make death crueler. But spears poisoned with criticism, hatred, ill-will misinterpretation, and false accusations can cause us no harm if we are wearing the protective armor of God. Paul would have us remember that the shield of faith can ward off all the fiery darts of the wicked one. (See Ephesians 6:16.) How assuring is that beatitude of Jesus, *"Blessed are ye, when men shall revile you, and persecute you, and shall say all manner of evil against you falsely, for my sake. Rejoice, and be exceeding glad"* (Matthew 5:11–12). Take up your harp and meet reviling with rejoicing.

THE PERSONAL QUESTION

The question God presented to Moses is one we must honestly answer ourselves: *"What is that in thine hand?"* (Exodus 4:2). A harp or a spear? Are you keeping company with David and his beautiful lyre or with Saul and his deadly javelin? Are you handling a harp or hurling a spear? The ideal, of course, is to use the harp against the spear, for trouble always ensues when spear meets spear, whether among individuals or nations. Often our attitude toward anyone who is unjust in their sharp, pointed criticisms of us is, "Wait till I see them. I'll give them a piece of my mind!" If we do this, we give the wrong piece, for it is always further trouble when flesh meets flesh. *"Be not overcome of evil, but overcome evil with good"* (Romans 12:21).

Further, it we are on our way to heaven, we must become an expert in playing the harp, for there are no spears in heaven but only harpers on their harps, as John reminds us. (See Revelation 14:2.) If we have been more prone to use spears, we must bury them, not in the hearts of others, but in the grave of Him who died to make us good and triumphant. It certainly requires grace to manipulate the harp when spears are flying, proceeding on an even and harmonious way, allowing no discord without to ruffle our spirit. When attacked, we must leave the judgment of our foes to Him who is our defense. This was David's way and also that of David's greater Son *"who, when he was reviled, reviled not again; when he suffered, he threatened not; but committed himself to him that judgeth righteously"* (1 Peter 2:23). The Calvary way is to use the harp to overcome the spear.

Christ ever embodied the truth He taught. Although there were those bent on despitefully using Him, He went about doing good. When the spearlike nails were driven into His hands and feet, the music from His harp of forgiveness soothed the breasts of many. Just as He expired, a soldier thrust a spear into His side, but it only released the blood He was shedding to deliver men from the instruments of sin and death. Torturing nails and a piercing spear drew from His heart only the melody of grace and pardon. It is our obligation to follow that divine example. *"Bless them which persecute you: bless, and curse not"* (Romans 12:14). *"Avenge not yourselves"* (Romans 12:19). Never meet a spear with a spear.

Life seems to be full of misfits. Often in a home or a church, there are those who are difficult to get along with. They seem to be spear-y in nature, always having their dagger drawn. It is hard to play on the harp when we deal with such persons, yet this is the only way to triumph. When our enemy hungers, we are told to feed him, not make him bleed with a spear. The Holy Spirit enables us to be kind to the unkind, loving toward the unlovable, gracious to the ungracious. This is the truth we learn from David's pacification of Saul. There are times when we ourselves need a minstrel for the soul—the music of God's voice to chase away all doubt and fear when waves of adversity sweep over our lives.

The divine Minstrel comes to us in many ways: We are restrained from a wrong course by the intervention and advice of a friend, for instance. When David forsook his harp and took up the spear, determined to avenge churlish Nabal who had insulted him and his men, it was the beautiful and wise Abigail, Nabal's wife, who prevented him from shedding blood. When the wild passion of revenge had subsided, he blessed Abigail, saying, *"Blessed be thy advice, and blessed be thou, which hast kept me this day from come to shed blood, and from avenging myself with mine own hand"* (1 Samuel 25:33).

The royal harpist learned how to use the harp against the spear in a very practical way. Other minstrels for troubled hearts are the worship in the sanctuary, the gracious promises of the Bible, and the privileged refuge of prayer, whether personal and secret or communal. When the spears are flying thick and fast, or the waves and billows rage and fierce temptations assail, what a supreme resource we have in Him who is *"a very present help in trouble*" (Psalm 46:1). For every mood in life, we have on almost any page of the Bible a minstrel to charm and calm our fevered heart. No matter the spears that have been hurled, God has promised to deliver us from their destruction. So, if your harp has been hanging on a willow tree, take it down and sing the song of the Lord, even in a strange land.

CHAPTER 9

DYING TO LIVE

"If ye live after the flesh, ye shall die: but if ye through the Spirit do mortify [make to die] the deeds of the body, ye shall live."
—Romans 8:13

One of my earliest boyhood memories is that of daily passing a large shop owned by a man who dyed garments. Outside his dyeing establishment was displayed an arresting sign, with the words

We Dye to Live, We Live to Dye.

What a catchy way, I always thought, to draw attention to the dyer's dependence upon his particular craft. By changing one letter in this sign, we have a summary of what Paul teaches in Romans 8:13:

We Die to Live, We Live to Die.

Living after the flesh, we die; dying to the flesh, we live. Bishop Handley Moule's translation of Paul's spiritual paradox is helpful:

If you are living flesh-wise, you are on to the way to die. But if by the Spirit you are doing to death the practices, the stratagems, the machinations, of the body, you will live.

Sanctification, one of the prominent themes of the Bible, is explained and expounded upon in various ways by teachers of holiness; but the truest definition is the one Paul was fond of using, namely, that sanctification is a double process of dying and living, of mortification and vivification. The apostle points us to a life in which the old nature is daily subdued, done to death, and the new nature is daily strengthened and perfected, made to live—a life in which Christ increases and self decreases.

In teaching such a sacred theme, we have to guard ourselves from lopsidedness. It is essential to preserve balance and not to emphasize one phase at the expense of the other. There has been a tendency in some quarters to dwell on the death side. This leads to a practice of morbid mortification. Calvary, however, must lead to resurrection. The two sides, then, of dying and living must be held in unity and held fast both in knowledge and experience.

THE TWOFOLD PROCESS

> *For if ye live after the flesh, ye shall die: but if ye through the Spirit do mortify the deeds of the body, ye shall live.*
>
> (Romans 8:13)

All injunctions and incitements to holy living run along the lines of dying and living. Let us look at one or two passages where the double aspect of death and life, the cross and the resurrection, are clearly emphasized. What impresses one about Paul's use of the contrast in Romans 8:13 is that the *body* of the believer is the seat and vehicle of temptation and sin—"the doings of the body." Never are we exempt from the elements and conditions of evil residing within as well as surrounding us. But by the habitual recollection and appropriation of the Holy Spirit living within us, we are able to do to death the practices of the flesh and to die daily to sin so that we can live.

The word *"mortify,"* "doing to death," is in the present tense and denotes a continuing process that will continue until we die physically or are caught up to meet the Lord in the air. Then and only then will we be freed from the pressure of the lusts and affections of the flesh. Throughout our Christian pilgrimage, we will find that the ideal life is one in which there is a daily death to fresh discoveries of sin's enticements and a daily appropriation of a risen life in Christ, who waits to lead us in the train of His triumph over the world, the flesh, and the devil.

In a previous passage, Paul expresses the same truth in a somewhat different way when he says, *"Be not conformed to this world: but be ye transformed by the renewing of your mind"* (Romans 12:2). Do not be conformed to the course and state of this scene of sin and death. This is cross aspect. Christ died for us and saved us from our guilty past, not to reconcile us to the world, but to make us estranged, dissimilar, opposite to it in all ways. He could claim for His own, *"They are not of the world, even as I am not of the world"* (John 17:16).

"Be ye transformed by the renewing of your mind." This implies that our new life is distinct from our old life in the world, just as physical life is distinct from physical death. Here again, we have the idea of a continuous process, for the words *"conformed"* and

"*transformed*" are in the present tense, indicating a never-ceasing process; a life of constant, progressive death to the world and transformation to a life in Christ.

Then, in the third chapter of his letter to the Colossians, Paul rings the changes on the twin aspects of holiness in the phrases "*Mortify therefore your members which are upon the earth*" (Colossians 3:5); "*Ye are dead*" (verse 3); "*Risen with Christ, seek those things which are above*" (verse 1). Here the apostle stresses two practical conclusions: Our death in Christ must be made real in us, and our resurrection in Christ must be a reality in our lives. This twofold aspect perfectly agrees with what we find in nature as well as in the foundation and superstructure of our Christian life and faith.

1. THE HUMAN BODY

Scientists tell us that death is constantly going on in the human system so that it changes every seven years. Every day, a certain amount of living tissue dies and has to be borne out to burial, and every day, new tissue is formed. Does this not illustrate what takes place in the spiritual realm?

2. THE UNIVERSAL LAW OF NATURE

> The poet would have us remember that:
> Life evermore is fed by death,
> In earth and sea and sky;
> And that a rose may breathe its breath
> Something must die.[36]

Our Lord used the figure of a corn of wheat dying to bring life. When it dies, it produces much fruit. (See John 12:24.) Seeds die that fragrant flowers may appear. Winter merges into

---

36. Josiah Gilbert Holland, "Life from Death," *Bitter-sweet*, 1859.

spring, and spring into summer. All around us are reminders of death leading to resurrection.

3. THE TWO FUNDAMENTAL FACTS OF THE GOSPEL

Paul, in setting forth the nature of the gospel he was commissioned to preach, gives us two focal points: *"Christ died for our sins…he rose again the third day"* (1 Corinthians 15:3–4). These two historic facts must be accepted, for without faith in them, personal salvation is not possible. The spiritual reality of these two truths is experienced in baptism, which is a portrayal of death and resurrection. (See Romans 6:1–5.) It is true, in one sense, that Christ died for us, but it is truer to say that Christ died that we might die to the practices of the flesh and the appeal of sin. Christ died *for* sin that we might be dead *to* sin. He died *for* the world that we might be dead *to* the world. And let it be ever remembered that our old nature never dies; rather, we die to it.

> Dying with Jesus, by death reckoned mine;
> Living with Jesus, a new life divine.[37]

There is a sense in which crucifixion was not finished at Calvary but has continued through the ages and will continue until the church is saved to sin no more. Jesus said, *"He that taketh not his cross, and followeth after me, is not worthy of me"* (Matthew 10:38). Then, when Paul wrote about being *"crucified with Christ"* (Galatians 2:20), he implied a continuous experience of death to self and sin. In the same sense, resurrection is prolonged, for "the church keeps a perpetual Easter." Every soul quickened to newness of life by the Holy Spirit is a pulse beat of our risen Lord on His throne. The philosophy of this dual truth is written large over the Epistles. An Irishman passing

---

37. Daniel W. Whittle, "Moment by Moment," 1893.

a graveyard said, "Sure, that's the place where the dead live." Constant identification with Christ in His death and resurrection is the place where all who would die to sin must live.

THE FIVEFOLD SECRET

We are not left to the mere discipline of self, the exercise of willpower, or efforts of our own to bring to death the machinations of the body that are detrimental to spiritual progress. There can be no transition from death to life this way. The life of the believer is certainly a battlefield, but he does not struggle on to victory. Through the Spirit, his is a continuous march of triumph. God commands us to live a holy life, but what He commands, He supplies. His charges are His enablings. Paul exhorts us to the sanctification of our entire being; but he is careful to add, *"Faithful is he that calleth you, **who also will do it**"* (1 Thessalonians 5:24). There are at least five ways by which we can die as we live and live as we die.

1. APPROPRIATION OF CHRIST

John records a mystic truth in Christ's words, *"He that eateth me...shall live by me"* (John 6:57). The story is told of a sick soldier given up to die; his father traveled a long distance to be at his bedside in the hospital. There he lay half conscious, and nothing the father or attendants could do aroused him, until the father said, "Here, son, is a loaf of your mother's bread which I have brought to you."

"Bread from home," gasped the dying boy, "Give me some!" And from that hour he began to mend.

What Jesus meant when He said, "Eat of me," was the personal appropriation by faith of all that He had accomplished on our behalf and all that He is Himself as the Bread of heaven. We must feast on His death and resurrection and intercession on our behalf in heaven and upon all the revealed promises of God. Jesus spoke of Himself as the Life, and as we claim Him as such, everything in our lives unworthy of Him quickly dies.

Bread of Heaven,
Feed me till I want no more.[38]

2. MEDITATING ON CHRIST

While it is true that a glance is enough to save a soul, as it did the dying thief, it takes prolonged gazing at Christ to sanctify the saved soul. Paul would have us know that it is only as we keep beholding the glorified Lord as in a mirror that we can be changed into His likeness from glory to glory by the Spirit. (See 2 Corinthians 3:18.) The world, blinded by its god, cannot understand the most difficult of arts, namely, the constant contemplation of the cross and its meaning and message. Augustine, commenting on the divine fiat *"Thou canst not see my face: for there shall no man see me, and live"* (Exodus 33:20), wrote, "Then let me die if only I may see His face." As the glory of God is seen in the face of His beloved Son, we are able to see God and live, for *"he that hath seen [Christ] hath seen the Father"* (John 14:9). In a deeply spiritual sense, we must die in order to see the divine face, for the pure in heart alone can see Him. When John saw his glorified Lord, he fell at His feet as dead. It is in proportion to the degree we die to or mortify the deeds of the flesh that our eyes can behold the glory of our Savior's holy countenance. Often when one lives a very long time with another, they reproduce the likeness of that friend. Likewise, the longer we live in and with Christ, having no earthborn cloud

---

38. William Williams (1745), translated by Peter Williams (1771), "Guide Me, O Thou Great Jehovah."

to hide Him from our eyes, the more our lives will reflect Him for others to see and believe.

3. ABIDING IN CHRIST

In His parable of the vine and the branches, Jesus combined two features of our victorious life in Him. There is *union*—"**Abide in me**"—and *communion*—"*I in you*" (John 15:4). Both are necessary, not only positionally, but practically. His fullness can be imparted to us only if there is unhindered communion. The word "*abide*" has the idea of "being at home in." Paul, thinking of his martyrdom, could say, "*To depart, and to be with* [at home with] *Christ...is far better*" (Philippians 1:23). But throughout our Christian pilgrimage, He desires His own to dwell in Him, to have Him as our residence. How blessed it is to always be at home with the Lord.

One cannot emphasize too strongly that the mere imitation of Christ is utterly inadequate to make us dead to sin and alive to God. We must be incorporated into Him. There are many good, moral, religious people who seek to act as Christ did; but such an effort is simply a product of the natural man. One of the greatest enemies of holiness after the divine order is morality. A person may sit before the most perfect portrait of Jesus conceived by a gifted artist and say, "Let the beauty of Jesus be seen in me!" But the beauty of the Lord can never come upon them until it is wrought in them by the Holy Spirit and by unbroken union and communion with the beautiful Lord Himself. Morality and religion can be practiced by the unregenerated man, but holiness of heart and work within the renewed man is the work of the Spirit. One can be moral without being holy, but no person can be holy without being moral. Holiness is of the Lord, and unless we are grafted into Him, we can never reflect such a virtue. The branch of the vine does not produce the fruit; it only bears it. It is as life flows from the Vine that we, as branches, die to old habits, old natural instincts, old preferences, and bear fruit unto holiness.

4. THE ADVENT OF CHRIST

Another contributing factor to our practical sanctification is the glorious appearing of our blessed Lord. *"Every man that hath this hope in him purifieth himself, even as [Christ] is pure"* (1 John 3:3). A progressive holiness, or daily purity, depends on a daily expectancy of Christ's return. We cannot live just any kind of life if we believe that He may return at any moment. The second coming exercises a powerful influence in our present daily life; it is effective in putting to death worldly, sinful pursuits and practices, for—

> With such a blessed hope in view,
> We would more holy be.[39]

Emerson would have us "hitch [our] wagon to a star."[40] It is only as we fasten our hearts to Him who is the Bright and Morning Star that we can be lifted out of our low, selfish, unsanctified motives and ways, and into a serene, blessed, victorious life, bringing glory to Him who *"shall come...and will not tarry"* (Hebrews 10:37).

5. THE SPIRIT OF CHRIST

Death or life, mortification or vivification, these are not possible apart from the gracious aid of the Holy Spirit, who is the Lord of life and power. Paul strongly stresses the ministry of the Spirit in the work of sanctification. It is only through the Spirit that we can mortify the deeds of the body and then live in

---

39. Robert Boswell, "Behold, What Love!"
40. Ralph Waldo Emerson, "Society and Solitude: Civilization," 1870.

the newness of life. (See Romans 8:13.) We can only be transformed into the likeness of our holy Lord *"by the Spirit of the Lord"* (2 Corinthians 3:18). It is utterly impossible for a regenerated person to rescue himself from the practices and stratagems of "the old man." Paul tried it, but it did not work, and he was forced to cry, *"Who shall deliver me from the body of this death?"* (Romans 7:24). And he found a Deliverer—*"Jesus Christ our Lord"* (Romans 7:25)!

The indwelling Spirit, if He possesses the believer, is a divine and all-effectual counteragent to everything within and without that is alien to God's holy mind and will. It was by the Spirit that Christ accomplished His death at Calvary. *"Through the eternal Spirit* [Christ] *offered himself without spot to God"* (Hebrews 9:14). Christ also rose from the dead by the power of the Spirit: *"The Spirit of him that raised up Jesus from the dead"* (Romans 8:11; see verse 1:4). We can realize His death in ourselves and experience the risen life only through the self-same Spirit, the Spirit of life. As He fills our lives, habits of the flesh disappear, for death cannot resist life.

The practical conclusion of the whole matter, then, is, Are we dying to live? Are the two lines parallel, not only in knowledge, but experience? Is the old life flourishing less because we are doing to death the deeds of the flesh? Is the new life daily increasing through the constant appropriation of all we have as the result of Christ's death and resurrection? Is ours the consuming passion of Paul who said, *"That I may know him, and the power of his resurrection, and the fellowship of his sufferings"* (Philippians 3:10)? There is no comma, no break dividing this double truth; one flows from the other. Holiness, then, like salvation, is of grace by faith. "'I take'—'He undertakes.'"[41] An undertaker is one whose responsibility it is to care for us when

41. A. B. Simpson, "I Clasp the Hand of Love Divine."

we die. He does everything for us when we have no life to do anything for ourselves. The Lord is our wonderful Undertaker who will do everything for our growth in grace, if only we will reckon ourselves dead indeed unto sin.

> Take my poor heart, and let it be
> For ever closed to all but Thee!
> Seal Thou my breast, and let me wear
> That pledge of love for ever there.[42]

---

42. Nicolaus Zinzendorf and Johann Nitschmann (1735), translated by John Wesley (1740), "I Thirst, Thou Wounded Lamb of God."

CHAPTER 10

A CLEAN HEART AND A RIGHT SPIRIT

"Create in me a clean heart, O God;
and renew a right spirit within me."
—Psalm 51:10

Among the 150 psalms that make up the Psalter, none is as heart-moving as Psalm 51, one of the penitential psalms. It is blotted with the tears of anguish and penitence of David's guilty heart. There is no need to enlarge on the circumstances that preceded its writing; its heading tells the tragic story. Kingly power had been abused, and the worst passions yielded to. Darker guilt can scarcely be found in Scripture. This sorrowful psalm is a mirror of our own hearts, for it reveals that in each of us, there is something near hell and something near heaven, something diabolical and something divine. It also marks the steps of sinning saints returning to God. Although the psalm was written well over three thousand years ago, it might have been written yesterday, for its title proves that it is timeless.

The structure of the Psalm 51 is superb, significant yet simple, and constitutes a powerful message for any preacher to present. It can be organized into three marked sections:

1. The confession of guilt (See Psalm 51:1–6.)

2. The prayer for divine renewal (See verses 7–12.)

3. The reward of restored fellowship (See verses 13–19.)

All we are to do in this meditation is to concentrate upon David's double prayer expressing a twin need: *"Create in me, a **clean heart**, O God; and renew a **right spirit** within me"* (Psalm 51:10).

PRAYER FOR CLEANNESS OF HEART

The verse contains two requests, the one complementing the other. Clean hearts and right spirits go together, and *"what therefore God hath joined together, let not man put asunder"* (Matthew 19:6; Mark 10:9). If you have the clean heart, you will manifest a right spirit. You cannot have a right spirit toward God and others unless you have the clean heart God alone can create. Taking the twin desires together, we discover how one is complementary to the other.

The clean heart is the inward work of grace and is what God does in us. It represents the root of holiness. The right spirit is the outward work of God and is what He does through us, and suggests the fruit of holiness.

In one sense, this was a perplexing prayer from David's lips. Was he not God's already, and had he not already received a heavenly anointing? Did not God call him *"a man after mine own heart"* (Acts 13:22; see 1 Samuel 13:14)? How could he cry out for a clean heart if he already had a heart like God's? David had learned that there was something more than being born again. His soul's deepest need had to be met.

A regenerated heart is the possession of all believers, for it implies the removal of the past penalty and guilt of sin. A clean heart is one all saints pray and long for. This is the sanctification of spirit, soul, and body Paul describes in 1 Thessalonians 5:23: *"The very God of peace sanctify you wholly; and I pray God your whole spirit and soul and body be preserved blameless unto the coming of our Lord Jesus Christ."*

1. THE CLEAN HEART IS A NECESSARY CREATION

The psalm reveals the penitent's progress from outward sin to inward sin, from practice to principle. David came to discover hidden, evil springs within his being, although he had been a child of God for nearly fifty years. And is it not tragic that his life and royalty was marred by one sin? May God deliver us from the peril of indulgence in the sin that so easily troubles us. Many outstanding Bible saints stained their characters by a particular sin—one dead fly that caused the ointment to stink.

+ Noah marred his walk with God by intemperance.

+ Abraham lost his influence with Abimelech through deception.

+ Moses was shut out of Canaan because he lost his temper.

+ Miriam became a leper for criticizing the leadership of Moses.

+ Achan met his doom, as did his relatives, through covetousness.

+ The children of Israel were kept out of the Promised Land because of unbelief.

✦ David had his testimony marred through lust.

This renowned psalm is most valuable, then, because it digs down to the roots and arrives at the cause of a climax. Dr. Alexander Whyte says of David, "He lays on himself the blame of a tainted nature, instead of a single fault: not a murder only, but of a murderous nature." The creation of a clean heart was therefore a necessity. In a previous psalm, David wrote, "*Who shall ascend the hill of the* Lord....*He that hath clean hands, and a pure heart*" (Psalm 24:3–4). Clean hands are the result of a clean heart, and God is ever good to those who are of a clean heart. Have we not need to cry, personally, "Create in me a clean heart, O God"? Such a creation is necessary, for the pure in heart are the only ones who are able to see God. (See Matthew 5:8.)

2. THE CLEAN HEART IS A HOLY CREATION

Because the issues of life spring from the heart, it is essential for it to be purified and then be kept pure. Unless the fountain is clean, the water will not be wholesome. What exactly is implied by a clean heart? Perhaps we can best state what it is not. Having a pure heart does not mean one is in a state of absolute perfection, or sinlessness. The liability to sin is always present, even in the best of us. The tendency to sin, however, can be counteracted by the Holy Spirit, whose mission it is to produce divine holiness in our lives. There is a distinction between blamelessness and faultlessness. Often, we are blameless but never are we faultless. We make many mistakes, but are blameless in them, because of partial light—we did not know them to be mistakes. To be in a condition of faultlessness would mean we were incapable of making mistakes.

"Without fault" is a phrase always used to describe what we will be in glory. With increasing spiritual apprehension, there comes a fuller knowledge of sin, and the consciousness that in some past actions we had no compunction of conscience, though our thoughts or actions were actually blameworthy. The Old Testament Levitical sacrifices had a sacrifice for "the sins of ignorance." Our old nature is the seat of sin and ever subject to attractions of the flesh. Our Lord is the only One who lived on earth without blame and without fault. Being ever without fault, or sinless, He was never guilty of any blameworthy act. Our obligation is to live in harmony with the Holy Spirit who is able to make us sensitive to what is alien to the divine will.

> They who fain would serve Thee best
> Are conscious most of wrong within.[43]

Coming to the positive side of the cleanness of heart that David prayed for, may we never be guilty of watering down the full implication of such a request. Let us desire all that God means by it. We need all that David meant when he cried to God and all that God is able to accomplish. There is no sense in waiting for a definition of "clean heart." God waits to translate it into experience.

> Make me willing to receive
> All Thy fullness waits to give.

By a *clean* heart, we understand a heart in which there is no known, conscious, unjudged, or unforgiven sin. It is equivalent to *"a clear conscience toward God and toward men"* (Acts 24:16 rsv). When David spoke about *"secret faults"* (Psalm 19:12), he was not referring to those things he knew to be wrong and which he hid from others, but to depths of corruption within his being he did not know existed. They were not known to him, but they were known to God, and as he sought to walk

43. Henry Twells, "At Even Ere the Sun Was Set," 1868.

in the light, the unknown became known and the secret faults were revealed. Paul could say, *"I am not aware of anything against myself, but I am not thereby acquitted. It is the Lord who judges me"* (1 Corinthians 4:4 rsv). When we have a clean heart, then, we are conscious there is nothing between the Lord and ourselves to hinder communion. This inner condition is maintained, as the Holy Spirit brings what is unconscious to our consciences, and we immediately confess and repent of our sin.

Such a cleansing requires faith on our part—*"Purifying their hearts by faith"* (Acts 15:9). The word John uses for *"purifying"* implies a present and progressive tense. As we keep on confessing the uncleanness the Spirit reveals, the blood of Jesus keeps on cleansing us from it. (See 1 John 1:7.) Charles Wesley has taught us to sing—

> A humble, lowly, contrite heart,
> Believing, true, and clean,
> Which neither death nor life can part
> From Him who dwells within.[44]

3. THE CLEAN HEART IS A DIVINE CREATION

Solomon asked the question, *"Who can say, I have made my heart clean, I am pure from my sin?"* (Proverbs 20:9). No man can make his own heart clean, for sinful forces are beyond human control. He must rely on God to make him pure. The margin of the Revised Version has different wording: "Create *for* me a clean heart." God creates a clean heart not only *in* us but *for* us.

> Every virtue we possess,
> And every victory won,

---

44. Charles Wesley, "O for a Heart to Praise My God," 1742.

And every thought of holiness,
Are His alone.[45]

Because the cleansing of the heart is God's work alone, the creative name for God, *Elohim*, is used. In the Bible, the word *create* is always used strictly of the creative power of God. Self-effort and suppression are useless.

I watch to shun the miry way,
And staunch the springs of guilty thought;
But, watch and struggle as I may,
Pure I am, pure I am not.[46]

"To create" means to make something out of nothing, which is what God did at creation when "*he spake, and it was done*" (Psalm 33:9). When Paul wrote of the saints as being "*created in Christ Jesus*" (Ephesians 2:10), he employed the same term. What can we offer God to make a clean heart out of? All we can give Him is our sin, but out of the wreckage of our lives, He can create a new man in His likeness. The only God needs is a broken and contrite heart. (See Psalm 51:17.)

PRAYER FOR RIGHTNESS OF SPIRIT

"*Renew a right spirit within me*" (Psalm 51:10) is the other half of the prayer. Cleanness of heart and rightness of spirit are twin necessities. It is, unhappily, possible to seek after a clean heart and yet possess and maintain a wrong spirit in daily life. If David's heart was to be kept pure, then he had to have a steadfast spirit to resist temptation. The clean heart put David in right standing with God. His heart was created by God, but he

---

45. Harriet Auber, "Our Blest Redeemer, Ere He Breathed," 1829.
46. W. G. Smith, "One Thing I of the Lord Desire."

had to cultivate it by perfecting holiness in the fear of the Lord. God gives the seed, but the gardener cultivates it.

Being right with God involves being right with those around us. The right spirit adjusted David's relationship with Bathsheba and the others he had wronged.

The clean heart is the root, principle, fountain, of our life godward. The right spirit is the fruit, the spring, the practice, the conduct of holiness manward.

The two words *create* and *renew* offer a study of contrast: God creates something from what is not there; He brings all that is necessary into the heart requiring His attention. Grace feeds, not on what it finds, but on what it provides.

> Come, not to find, but make this troubled heart
> A dwelling worthy of Thee as Thou art.[47]

"Renew" implies a totally different aspect of divine action. One cannot renew what does not exist. David once had a right spirit, but because it had lost its rightness, he prayed for its renewal. The same thought can be found in his Shepherd Psalm, where he exclaimed, *"He restoreth my soul"* (Psalm 23:3), *"restore"* meaning to bring back to its original condition. *"Restore unto me the joy of thy salvation"* (Psalm 51:12). Sin had robbed David of such joy.

The prophet Ezekiel also reminds us of God's willingness to undertake for us the double blessing David prayed for: *"A new heart also will I give you, and a new spirit will I put within you"* (Ezekiel 36:26). What exactly are we to understand by the right spirit? What is its nature? Many a consecrated heart is marred by a wrong spirit. A clean heart is powerless if it lacks the right spirit, which is the medium of expression.

47. "Come In, O Come!"

Often we have a wrong spirit toward God for His providential dealings. We are also guilty of a jealous, unforgiving, critical, thoughtless, hard spirit toward those around us. Here the word *right* does not stand over against *wrong*; rather, it implies being upright, honest, transparent in every detail of our Christian lives. David, in committing adultery with Bathsheba, had been guilty of deception. To put it simply, then, the right spirit is the spirit of Jesus in everything to everybody. Within the psalm, other references to the spirit indicate what the renewal of a right spirit implies.

The margin of the Revised Version gives us the word *steadfast* for "*right*," while the margin of the Authorized Version has *constant*. Both of these terms describe a person standing tall with firmly planted feet and a braced-up frame, ready to meet a challenge. If soldiers have been standing at ease on a parade ground, and the officer cries, "Attention!" what a different posture is assumed! They stand at full height, eyes eager eyes, feet planted firm, and hands gripping their weapons. They stand erect as they wait for the next command.

There are no easy parade days for Christians. Satanic attack is always impending, and the adversary is alert, waiting to devour. David failed to remain steadfast in spirit when he was tempted. He found himself borne along by the rushing torrent of passion, and he discovered how unstable he was. He failed to remain firm and constant in faith and obedience. He was not rocklike in meeting the wiles of the devil. His heart was not "*set…aright, and* [his] *spirit was not stedfast with God*" (Psalm 78:8).

1. FREE SPIRIT

Other twin requests are found in this penitential prayer of David's. For instance, he prayed, "*Restore unto me the joy of thy salvation; uphold me with thy free spirit*" (Psalm 51:12).

The margin of the Revised Version gives us "willing" for "*free.*" Doubtless this is a reference to the Holy Spirit mentioned in the previous verse, who is not the Spirit of bondage but of liberty. "*Where the Spirit of the Lord is, there is liberty*" (2 Corinthians 3:17). A renewed spirit is a willing, noble, princely spirit. Christ requires noble, princely service, not a grudging, enforced obedience. When Christians have to be begged and pleaded with to serve God or to give of their substance to His cause, there is something wrong with their spirit. It lacks the glorious liberty of the children of God.

2. BROKEN SPIRIT

In his confession, David said to God, "*The sacrifices of God are a broken spirit: a broken and a contrite heart, O God, thou wilt not despise*" (Psalm 51:17). David's spirit had to be broken before God could renew it. In his treatment of Bathsheba and her husband, Uriah, the psalmist revealed a most evil, deceitful spirit, a spirit that had to be broken—and it was! Is our spirit one of humility? One that realizes its nothingness? Have we come to experience that we cannot bless unless we bleed? *Bleed* and *bless* are word-cousins. Through His bruising and bleeding, Jesus became the Savior of the world.

3. HOLY SPIRIT

David urgently prayed, "*Take not thy holy spirit from me*" (Psalm 51:11). Under grace, no believer with the promise of the abiding, or indwelling, Spirit should pray this prayer. (See John 14:16.) While Christian *position* is not found in David's cry, Christian *experience* is. The Holy Spirit is the only One who can renew a right spirit within us. The human spirit can only be renewed, sanctified, hallowed by the divine Spirit. As we yield to His control, He keeps our spirits right, steadfast, and pure, ready to serve wherever He appoints. Notice the pivotal wording in this psalm of contrition: *"**Then** will I teach transgressors thy ways; and sinners shall be converted unto thee"* (Psalm 51:13). *"Then."* When? After the heart has been cleansed, the spirit renewed, the soul made aware of the presence and power of the Holy Spirit and of the liberty He imparts, and the restored one is rejoicing again in God's salvation. Revival depends on spiritual renewal. The church will experience a mighty ingathering of the lost when her members seek clean hearts and right spirits from God.

> Stir me to give myself so back to Thee,
> That Thou canst give Thyself again through me.[48]

---

48. Bessie Porter Head, "Stir Me! Oh Stir Me, Lord."

CHAPTER 11

SOLITUDE AND SOCIETY

"And every man went unto his own house.
Jesus went unto the mount of Olives."
—John 7:53–8:1

"They broke up their meeting and went home,
while Jesus went off to the Mount of Olives."
—John 7:53–8:1 (PHILLIPS)

While the original Scriptures were certainly divinely inspired and, therefore, infallible, it is essential to realize that its division into chapters and verses, although most convenient, was man-conceived and consequently fallible. Occasionally, chapters and verses are wrongly split up. Take, for instance, the passage we have chosen as the basis of this meditation. Its first part is given in the King James Version as the last verse of John chapter 7, and the second part as the opening verse of John 8. But, as anyone can clearly see, the two verses are naturally one, and they are set as one verse in the Revised Standard Version. *"They went each to his own house, but Jesus went to the Mount of Olives"* (John 7:53–8:1 RSV).

If one had the ability to paint a moving masterpiece, it could well be a picture portraying the two extremes suggested by these two departures from the temple in Jerusalem. Surely there is material here for one of the greatest scenes ever depicted on canvas. On one hand, we have a glimpse of the chief scribes and Pharisees going home in small groups, wrangling and disputing about the claims of Christ. The Feast of Tabernacles had ended, and after farewells to friends, many of those who had attended returned to their homes in other parts of the country. Back they went to their comfortable dwellings; to domestic happiness, comfort, and ease; and to sleep soundly until another morning broke.

But for Jesus, it was totally different. He left the temple alone, and His solitary figure retired slowly, for He carried a heart crushed and broken by disappointment. At last He reached the mount and spent the night among the trees on the hillside with no human companion near, very commonplace to his daily routine. He went out, not to a home with its glowing fire and pleasant fellowship around an evening meal, but to the lonely, grassy slope, with the darkness of the night covering Him like a blanket. This impressive contrast suggests several themes we should look at closer.

SOCIETY AND SOLITUDE

The homes to which the Pharisees traveled indicate society—wives to love, children to play with, and friends to greet.

The Mount of Olives where Jesus retired to is eloquent of solitude. There was no room for Him in the cozy dwellings to which the others went. There was no one to show Him kindness, no one with the decency to offer Him a night's shelter. Pharisees and Jews had their homes just as foxes have their warm holes and the birds of the air their cozy nests; but Jesus had nowhere to lay His head. (See Matthew 8:20; Luke 9:58.) So, out He went to the cold mountain with its midnight air.

While others had the warm comfort of society, Jesus was forced out into the solitude of night. We read, *"Jesus was found alone"* (Luke 9:36). It had been the same at His birth. Other babes were born into homes where preparation had been made for their arrival and where they had every care and attention. But Jesus saw the light of day not in a loving home but in a stable where, on a bed of straw, Mary gave birth to Him. There was no room in the inn, suggestive of society. His birth outside a human dwelling place is symbolic of what He was to endure for our sakes. When He died, He experienced the same solitude. John and Mary went home together, but Jesus remained on dark Mount Calvary to die alone as the world's Sin-Bearer.

Can it be that you find yourself in fellowship with the lonely, lowly Nazarene—alone with the Great Alone? Other people seem to have plenty of company and all the pleasure and happiness their hearts desire, but somehow your lot is different. Your existence is somewhat apart from others. Relatives are either dead or have deserted you, and you live alone. Many around you seem to live in a whirl of society, but yours is a solitary existence. Take courage, for you are in the royal company of Him whose calmness of spirit on the Mount of Olives is so obvious.

> Why should you be lonely,
> Why for friendship sigh,
> When the heart of Jesus
> Has a fully supply?[49]

---

49. Alice Pugh, "In the Heart of Jesus," 1916.

SLUMBER AND SOBS

The Pharisees passed out into the night and finally reached their homes to sleep and rest through the silent hours of the night. But Jesus went not to a home to sleep but to the mount to sob and sorrow over those who slept. This was not the only time He spent the night sobbing over sinning souls. He beheld the city from the height of the mount *"and wept over it"* (Luke 19:41). His great task brought Him much solitude and sorrow. How He burned with zeal to vindicate God and save man! The Jews who rejected Him were ignorant of His glowing passion and His utter dedication to the work He was sent to do. When in the garden of Gethsemane, with the cross so near, His disciples went to sleep under the shade of the trees. But Jesus went a little farther and there sweated and sobbed. He gave His eyelids no rest during those final hours. In the night season, He cried and was not silent. He could not do otherwise, seeing He was about to bear the terrible load of human sin and taste death for every man.

Whose company do we share? Is it that of those who think only of sleep, ease, indolence, and their own selfish comforts? *"Let us not sleep, as do others; but let us watch and be sober"* (1 Thessalonians 5:6). Has the challenge come to us, *"Watchman, what of the night?"* (Isaiah 21:11). Do we have solitary times when, unknown to others, we yearn over lost ones in and out of our homes? Let our friends go to their homes and engage in things perfectly legitimate and lawful and enjoy the company they love to have. For those who follow the Lamb the obligation is clear: They must be willing to go outside the camp where He is, bearing His reproach. It is to be feared, however, that we do too much sleeping and resting. We love self-ease and pleasure, and do too little sobbing and wrestling. The Pharisees went home to sleep, but Jesus went to the mount to pray and agonize and weep. Dr. Alexander Smellie would have us remember,

> It is inexcusable that Christians should go to their own homes, and make no real sacrifice of leisure, or money, or comfort, or reputation, or affection. It is high time that on God's behalf and on man's, we should be found with Jesus on the mount of loneliness and prayer. The Father seeks servants who will glorify Him at any cost. The world is sick unto death. And how can we sit still?

DIVISION AND DEVOTION

There is a further application we can make of the twin truths we are considering. Those chief scribes and Pharisees who went to their own houses left the Sanhedrin a divided company, as the context shows. There were those who recognized Christ as a prophet. (See John 7:40.) Others saw in Him as the Messiah. (See verse 41.). Still others were impressed with His authority as a divine Teacher—*"Never man spake like this man"* (John 7:46). So we read that there was a division among them because of Jesus. Can you not picture in your mind's eye the heated discussion among those religious leaders, and how, when they left the temple, they would continue arguing stoutly and strongly about His claims? Some in the company would speak up and say, "He is our man, and the preacher we want to follow." A few would angrily dispute and deny His assertions, pick holes in His life and teachings, and thus prove Him unworthy and unsuitable as a Messiah. There were those against Him who went home to hatch fresh plots to destroy His influence and life. But others retired to discover fresh means of defending and enhancing the reputation of Him who they knew to be the Christ.

What about the One causing such divisions? Which side did He take? None! He went out to the mount to talk everything over with His heavenly Father. He steals away from those who are fighting over His claims to spend the night in prayer with Him who knew the truth about His Son. Men were willing to talk and argue about Jesus but not so willing to open up their hearts to Him, so He sought the solitude of the night to speak face-to-face with God. He left others to discuss their ideas about Him and knelt in the grass for their sakes. The morning star found Him where the evening star had left Him, praying over the spiritual blindness of those who claimed to be all that was righteous. He sacrificed rest for wrestling in prayer and slumber for sorrow.

What a wonderful example He has left us to follow! Often people leave churches and go to their homes criticizing and misjudging the preacher, singers, and other worshipers. But others retire commending and singing the praises of those who ministered the Word. When possible, it is best to leave a solemn service and find some quiet, lonely spot where we can pray for spiritual results to follow all we heard proclaimed. We must bear in mind that if we strive to live on the mount with God, then we will be beyond both the blame of some and the good intentions of those who defend us. It matters little what people think or say about us as long as we know we have God above who knows us like no other. Then the good things will not cause us to be unduly proud or elated, for we have the assurance that we live to please Him. Further, the bad things others may do and say will not cross or annoy us, seeing we keep company with Him *"who, when he was reviled, reviled not again"* (1 Peter 2:23). The pure air of the lonely mount is a perfect antidote for the effect of poisoned lips.

REJECTION AND REIGN

It is not difficult to make a further application somewhat prophetic of the society and solitude our basic text suggests. Those Jews went out to their homes only to gather more time to feed their fires of hatred, as can be seen when they later took up stones to kill Jesus. (See John 8:59.) So this going of every man to his own house spoke of rejection, of going out into life without Him. Leaving Jesus, every man took his own road, but not one of them had the courtesy to ask Jesus over for the night. There was no room for Him in their society. It is still true that men go out to live their sinful, selfish, indulgent, and independent lives, while Jesus continues to intercede for them.

The day is coming when, with His pierced feet planted on the Mount of Olives, Christ will reign over all homes and command the allegiance of all who dwell on earth. (See Isaiah 2:2; Zechariah 14:4.) The solitary Man will then be seen as the sovereign Lord ruling over all. No longer will He be alone, sobbing over the sins of men. Instead He will be attended by myriads of blissful and glorified saints. No longer will those of earth dispute His claims. All will own His right to rule, and every knee will bow and confess Him as Lord. (See Romans 14:11; Philippians 2:10.) Then every man will go to his own home in greater peace and joy because Jesus will be the supreme World Emperor. We should be careful to take Him with us wherever we go. If we neglect to entertain Him, then we will forfeit life's best Friend. Let's be like the disciples who, on the road to Emmaus, said to Jesus, *"Abide with us: for it is toward evening, and the day is far spent"* (Luke 24:29).

I fear no foe, with Thee at hand to bless;
Ills have no weight, and tears no bitterness.

Where is death's sting? Where, grave, thy victory?
I triumph still, if Thou abide with me.[50]

RELATIVE QUALITIES OF SOCIETY AND SOLITUDE

Before we leave the double truth before us, there is a more general, fuller aspect of it that we should consider. First of all, both of these conditions are in the plan and will of God, whose aloneness and yet accessibility are both prominent in Scripture. One of the purposes of creation was to support human society. After God created Adam, He said, *"It is not good that the man should be alone; I will make him an help meet for him"* (Genesis 2:18). And to the couple He said, *"Multiply, and replenish the earth"* (Genesis 1:28). So God gave the lonely man a woman, thereby making a family out of solitude. (See Psalm 68:6.) But the necessity of solitude is also recognized. There are times when man must eat his morsel alone. (See Job 31:17.) Jesus had to tread the winepress alone, and during the days of His flesh, He was often found alone. (See Isaiah 63:3.) It was when the prophet Daniel was alone during the dark hours of the night that he received the secret of heaven. (See Daniel 2:19.)

Man finds it hard to avoid extremes, even in the questions of society and solitude, both of which have their dangers as well as their delights. We read a great deal these days about population explosion, or too many people for the earth to maintain. In civilized lands, the people are grouped into kinds of societies. As Christians, we have communal and national obligations that must not be neglected. It is perfectly true that "man was formed for society." It is just as true that he was formed for seasons of

---

50. Henry F. Lyte, "Abide with Me," 1847.

solitude to combat the materialistic influences of society. The Master who told us *"go ye into all the world"* (Mark 16:15) also urged us to *"come apart…and rest a while"* (Mark 6:31). Percy Bysshe Shelley preserves the balance in these lines—

> I love tranquil solitude,
> And such society
> As is quiet, wise, and good.[51]

William Cowper could write of

> Society, friendship, and love,
> Divinely bestowed upon man.[52]

But Andrew Marvell, poet of the sixteenth century, declared,

> Society is all but rude
> To this delicious solitude.[53]

"Man seeketh in society comfort, use and protection," says Bacon; but deeper spiritual blessing can be derived from solitude. Although we are part and parcel of the world of human beings in which we live, we must avoid the danger of becoming so immersed in the claims and clamor of society that we lose those finer qualities that seasons of silence before God alone can bring.

> The world is too much with us; late and soon,
> Getting and spending, we lay waste our years:
> Little we see in Nature that is ours;
> We have given our hearts away, a sordid boon![54]

---

51. Percy Bysshe Shelley, "Song," lines 37–39.
52. William Cowper, "The Solitude of Alexander Selkirk," lines 17–18.
53. Andrew Marvell, "The Garden," lines 15–16.
54. William Wordsworth, "The World Is Too Much with Us; Late and Soon," lines 1–4, 1806.

We can also err in withdrawing from society. The pendulum can swing too far in the other direction. Monks and nuns endeavor to shut themselves in from a world of human beings, and in some cases, they take upon themselves vows of silence. God not only said to Elijah, *"Hide thyself"* (1 Kings 17:3) but also, *"Go, show thyself"* (1 Kings 18:1). The child of God must learn to balance private meditation with public manifestation. Bacon reminds us that "the worst solitude is to be destitute of sincere friendship."

Without doubt, to turn from the world with all its pressures and perils to wait upon God in the silence of our chamber is to experience what Wordsworth calls "the bliss of solitude."[55]

> O the pure delight of a single hour
> That before Thy Throne I spend,
> When I kneel in prayer, and with Thee, my God,
> I commune as friend with friend![56]

Cynically, Bacon could write, "Whosoever is delighted in solitude is either a wild beast or a god." But being mortal beings, we can experience what Wordsworth suggests in "A Poet's Epitaph":

> And impulses of deeper birth
> Have come to him in solitude.[57]

Let us neither neglect nor despise the solitudes of life, for spiritual solitude is the mother country of the strong. John Milton, whose blindness excluded him somewhat from society, tells us in *Paradise Lost*,

---

55. William Wordsworth, "I Wandered Lonely as a Cloud," line 22.
56. Fanny Crosby, "I Am Thine, O Lord," 1875.
57. William Wordsworth, "A Poet's Epitaph," lines 47–48.

> For solitude sometimes is best society,
> And short retirement urges sweet return.[58]

Schiller, the German writer, warns us, "Abide not alone, for it was in the desert that Satan came to the Lord of Heaven Himself." Yes, but He also triumphed gloriously over Satan in the solitary desert, and angels came and ministered unto Him. God is able to feed His people even if they *dwell solitarily in the wood*" (Micah 7:14). Jesus was often found alone, but He was never lonely—"*I am not alone…he that sent me is with me*" (John 8:16, 29). Certainly we are in a world of men with all its responsibilities, cares, and sorrows; but Jesus said that though we are *in* the world, we are not to be *of* it. Like Him, we, too, must seek the solitary place where God is near, for it is in this way that we gather spiritual wisdom and strength to influence society. "*When even was come, he went out of the city*" (Mark 11:19) to converse with heaven. We cannot do better than conclude this meditation with a paragraph from Percy Ainsworth's great work *Paul's Hymn to Love*:

> The profoundest hours of life for any man are his silent hours. With the many he may be grave or gay, but he cannot realize himself with any fullness; with the few, and most of all with just one another, the meaning and message of life grow deeper; but it is left to solitude and silence to sound the deepest notes of his nature and chronicle the most profound experience of his soul. We can therefore easily understand how it comes to pass that the evangelists pause on the verge of Christ's silences. We must pause there, too. We cannot go farther than they, nor would we try to do so. But if in silence life finds its farthest meaning and most inward fulfilment, we can

---

58. John Milton, *Paradise Lost*.

but wait here on the verge of these silent hours in the life of Jesus, if maybe some gain of good may be ours.[59]

The solitary hours of Jesus were not an escape *from*, but preparation *for*, life. He won in silence the power to succor all who were baffled and beaten by the sins of a satanically controlled society. In the hours we are alone with God, the same passion to "rescue the perishing and care for the dying" is intensified in our hearts.

59. Percy Ainsworth, *St. Paul's Hymn to Love*, 1919.

CHAPTER 12

BURDENS WE SHARE AND BURDENS WE BEAR

"Bear ye one another's burdens, and so fulfil the law of Christ."
—Galatians 6:2

"Every man shall bear his own burden."
—Galatians 6:5

Although the two passages Paul gives us on bearing others' burdens occur in the same paragraph and are closely related, at first look, they seem to contradict each other. However, both verses are complementary.

There are burdens we share with others. These mutual burdens help us to relate to others. "A fellow feeling makes one wondrous kind."[60] By bearing the burdens of others, we actually lighten our own personal burden, as has been expressed—

Is thy burden hard and heavy?
Do thy steps drag wearily?

---

60. David Garrick, *Prologue on Quitting the Stage in 1776.*

> Help to bear thy brother's burden;
> God will bear both it and thee.[61]

Part of the burden of personal responsibility is to share the loads of others. If we shut ourselves up in selfish isolation, we *"sin against Christ"* (1 Corinthians 8:12). If our brothers in Christ are in need and we do not show compassion toward them, how can the love of God be in us? (See Matthew 18:5–6; 1 Corinthians 8:9–12; 1 John 3:17.)

There are burdens we must bear alone. No one can share them with us. Each person has his own problems to face and solve. A German proverb says, "Let every man carry his own sack to the mill." There may be times when we feel as if our own load is too heavy. C. H. Spurgeon says, "Each one thinks his lot the worst; but he is mistaken. If he thought himself the worst of the lot, he might be right." There is much truth in Horace's saying, "What anyone bears willingly he bears easily."

There are burdens we cast upon God. He not only carries His own redeemed children but also their individual cares and trials. (See Psalm 55:22.) The proverb puts it succinctly, "God giveth the shoulder according to the burden." Poet Ovid is credited with a similar thought, "The burden which is well borne becomes light." The only right way for the believer to carry a burden is to roll it upon the Lord.

THE BURDENS WE SHARE

In Galatians chapter 2, it is apparent that the first verse is connected to the example of Christ bearing the burdens of others in the second verse. There we are exhorted to manifest brotherly love toward those who fall from grace, realizing that

---

61. Elizabeth Charles, "Is Thy Cruse of Comfort Wasting?" 1859.

we ourselves are capable of the same lapse. In all meekness, we must seek to win back, or restore, those who are overtaken in a fault. We are not to disregard them but recover them for the Master. It was an old custom to provide for niches on bridges for travelers to rest their loads. Every Christian should strive to be a niche on the busy thoroughfare of life where the weary and heavy laden can rest their loads. *"We then that are strong ought to bear the infirmities of the weak, and not to please ourselves"* (Romans 15:1).

The exhortation *"Bear the infirmities of the weak"* is explicit. We are not to be self-centered, looking merely on our own burdens; we should also observe the burdens of others. (See Philippians 2:4.) Looking after number one is not the law of Christ but of the devil. If we close our ears and hearts to the needs of others, we live in vain. Selfishness gives birth to an ugly brood—greed, callousness, suspicion, death. We reveal the sympathy of Christ when we think of the "other little ships" who are weaker and whose struggle against adverse forces is more intense.

How can we make the most of our humble occupations as burden bearers? Whenever we enter our chamber to pray and plead for backsliders and lost souls, we help to bear and remove their burden. Praying in the Holy Spirit deepens our sense of need to reach those living in sin, and constrains us to function as intercessors for the transgressors.

When we go out into any form of service, seeking the salvation of others, we continue the blessed work of the cross. Old Testament prophets often spoke of *"the burden of the Lord"* (Jeremiah 23:33); we, too, are called to share His burden for lost souls.

When we meet despondent hearts (and only God knows how full the world is of them) and bring to them the consolations of the gospel and the unfailing promises of God, we lighten their load and share their burden.

When we cross the dark paths of the sorrow-stricken and speak comfortably to them, seeking to reveal something of the sympathy of Him who wept over the death of the one He loved, we follow His steps.

When we give of our love and substance to the needy, making it easier for them to live, we reflect the spirit of Him who, although He was rich, became poor for our sakes. (See 2 Corinthians 8:9.) As we have opportunity, we are to do good. (See Galatians 6:10.)

But alas, we are too selfish. We keep the sunshine bottled up in our own hearts instead of letting it shine, unhindered, to enrich impoverished lives in the world. We care little of whether the needy live or die, whether souls are saved or damned. We live in our own small world, taken up with and magnifying our own cares, trials, and needs. Rivers of living water do not flow out of our lives to refresh the thirsty souls.

But coupled with the exhortation *"Bear ye one another's burdens"* (Galatians 6:2) is the command *"Fulfil the law of Christ"* (verse 2) or, as Arthur Way translates it, *"Fulfil in this way Messiah's Law of Love"* (verse 2 WAY). In the essential things, Paul ever drives us back to the example of Christ. We are not to please ourselves, *"even [as] Christ pleased not himself"* (Romans 15:3). In life and death, He bore others' burdens. Our Lord is renowned as the great Load Lifter and Burden Bearer of a weary world, and His example is great motivation for us to bear the burdens of others. May grace be ours to pray more and criticize less, to love more and hate less, to bear more and blame less.

Such a particular ministry is but the continuation and expansion of Christ's ministry of bearing the infirmities of others. Paul exhorts us to *"warn them that are unruly, comfort the feebleminded, support the weak, be patient toward all men"* (1 Thessalonians 5:14; see Romans 15:1–2). The New Testament describes some of the burdens of others that Christ willingly bore.

THE BURDENS CHRIST BORE

1. THE BURDEN OF SORROW

Almost daily He was moved with deep compassion over the sorrow and grief of others. He shared the anguish of Mary and Martha over the death of their brother Lazarus, for He loved all three of them. We read that *"Jesus wept"* (John 11:35) at their anguish.

> There is no place where earth's sorrows are more felt,
> Than up in heaven.[62]

Jesus is touched by our infirmities even today. And since all hearts hunger for sympathy, we can act as consolers and speak of the healing balm of Gilead for the grief-stricken hearts.

2. THE BURDEN OF SICKNESS

Matthew tells us that the healing ministry of Jesus was the fulfillment of Isaiah's prophecy, "[Jesus] *himself took our infirmities, and bare our sicknesses"* (Matthew 8:17). Isaiah's term translated *"griefs"* (Isaiah 53:4) is the same word Matthew uses for *"sicknesses."* There are those who affirm that when Jesus died at Calvary, He bore not only our sin but our sicknesses, and

---

62. Frederick W. Faber, "There's a Wideness in God's Mercy," 1854.

that, therefore, because there is healing in the atonement, we should claim by faith physical as well as spiritual healing. But the unvarying testimony of New Testament writers is that He died only for our sins. Bearing sicknesses is what He did during His life, and He "bore them" in that He sympathized with the sufferers and banished all their diseases. And He is still "the sympathizing Jesus," as the hymn puts it.

> In every pang that rends the heart,
> The Man of Sorrows had a part.[63]

Are we fulfilling this law of love, or can it be that our outlooks are selfish, narrow, isolated, and circumscribed? How we need larger hearts, clearer and fuller vision, and more willingness to help others! Think of the many people in your neighborhood—the lonely, physically disabled, and housebound—whom you can visit and thus share, in sympathy and kindness, their burdens. Endeavor by God's grace to go through life lifting the loads of others, so that at the end of the day you will hear the divine Burden Bearer Himself say, "*Inasmuch as ye have done it unto one of the least of these my brethren, ye have done it unto me*" (Matthew 25:40).

3. THE BURDEN OF SIN

At Jerusalem, Jesus shed His tears over the sins of the city; at Calvary, He shed His blood to save the people from their sins. John the Baptist proclaimed Him as the One who came to bear the sins of the world. (See John 1:29.) Peter's testimony was, "*Who his own self bare our sins in his own body on the tree*" (1 Peter 2:24).

> O Christ, what burdens bow'd Thy head!
> Our load was laid on Thee;

---

63. Attributed to Michael Bruce, "Where High the Heavenly Temple Stands."

Thou stoodest in the sinner's stead,
Didst bear all ill for me.
A victim led; Thy blood was shed,
Now there's no load for me.[64]

The Savior left no part of the burden for us to bear, but took it all and made it His own. Although sinless, He was made sin for us. While we cannot emulate His vicarious sacrifice for sin, we can manifest an undying passion to bring the sinful to Him who alone can save. Grace can be ours to "weep o'er the erring one, lift up the fallen."[65] Oh, for Calvary hearts! Paul resorted to many means to save some. What an untiring soul winner he was! Christ had lifted his load of sin on that Damascus road, and he was constantly telling others of Him who was mighty to save and strong to deliver.

BURDENS WE BEAR ALONE

Bear ye one another's burdens.   (Galatians 6:2)

Every man shall bear his own burden.   (Galatians 6:5)

We now pass from mutual responsibility to individual obligation, from outer service to inner accountability, from the world around to the world within. It is interesting to note that in the above verses, Paul uses two different Greek words for our English word "*burden.*" In verse 2, the Greek word for "*burdens*" signifies any weight pressing heavily on either the mind or body of another, such as toil, suffering, and anxiety. We can help one another bear these burdens. In verse 5, the word "*burden*" implies a peculiar load that no one can share with us, one that

64. Anne R. Cousin, "O Christ, What Burdens Bow'd Thy Head."
65. Fanny Crosby, "Rescue the Perishing," 1869.

is allied to individual and moral responsibility. *"Every one of us shall give account of himself to God"* (Romans 14:12). Conybeare and Howson comment:

> [Paul's] meaning is, that self-examination will prevent us from comparing ourselves boastfully with our neighbour; we shall have enough to do with our own sins, without scrutinising his.

This word is associated with one's personal affairs and is used in many ways. For instance, it is applied to:

1. The freight of a ship or vehicle. (See Acts 27:10.) Any vessel is designed and consigned to carry a certain amount of freight or cargo. So says the proverb "Every man shall carry his own cargo."

2. The soldier who must carry his own accoutrements and provisions. *"For every man shall bear his own burden"* (Galatians 6:5).

3. The burden assigned to man or beast. The margin of the Revised Version gives the word *load*. Of the tea-carriers in the East, the saying is used, "Every man shall carry his own load"—a load that cannot be shirked or shifted to another, nor escaped or evaded.

The words of Paul seem to carry a nameless shadow. There are many who are fettered in the flight heavenward because of some personal burden. It may be inherited tendencies toward evil. They are victims of an evil heritage. Early environment has left its mark on their desires and habits. Grace, however, can counteract all hereditary traits and make us more than conquerors. Christ can lift this burden for us.

It may be a battle against temptation. These we fight alone. Our friends may think us free from the enemy's subtle snares, but they are unaware of the conflict raging within to maintain purity of life. Yet the Burden Bearer Himself knows and understands.

It may be a struggle against temper. We are ready to fly off the handle and say and do things that cause sorrow to those nearest to us, and for which we are ashamed and sorry afterward. Such impetuosity is a real personal burden many otherwise kind hearts have to bear.

It may be the realization of sin and pangs of an awakened conscience. We know that past sins have been graciously forgiven, but their effect is still with us and will be with us till the grave. There are those who carry this particular burden—their sin is ever before them.

It may be a hidden grief over a skeleton in the cupboard—a wayward child or one deformed and deficient.

It may be personal cares or pain and infirmity we have to bear alone.

How true it is that each heart knows its own bitterness! Behind pleasant countenances and happy exteriors, there may be a burdened heart. There are individual responsibilities we must carry that do not become any lighter as the days pass. Moffatt gives us the translation, *"Everyone will have to bear his own load of responsibility"* (Galatians 6:5 MOFFATT). Whether we live in a castle or a cottage, we cannot transfer our own sorrow, trial, mental anguish, or obligation on another. Whether in riches or rags, each person must carry his own load. But the comforting thought is that Jesus trod His winepress alone and carried His own cross. Thus, as we tread our lonely road, we must watch for the blood marks of One who bore burdens no other could share.

No matter who we are, in regard to our deepest life, we have a barrier that even our most intimate friends cannot help carry, an inner shrine into which they cannot enter. Like Job, there is a morsel we must eat alone. (See Job 31:17.) Solomon, the wisest man who ever lived, had everything his heart desired but was still lonely—

> Not e'en the dearest heart, and next our own,
> Knows half the reason why we smile or sigh.

But our Great High Priest, who is ever touched with the feelings of our infirmities, understands what we cannot share with others and offers to shoulder the burden.

THE BURDENS WE TRANSFER TO GOD

The psalmist has a most encouraging word for the burdened heart: "*Cast thy burden upon the LORD, and he shall sustain thee*" (Psalm 55:22). Is it not blessed to know that, whether our burdens are mutual or personal, we can transfer them all to Him? If our burden is one we have to bear alone, there is a shoulder waiting to share it, hence the words "*thy burden.*" From the context of this psalm, it would seem as if this particular burden was that of a deceitful friend—the heaviest load of all. (See Psalm 55:21.)

1. THE LIGHTENING OF THE LOAD

There are two ways by which a load can be lessened. One is by diminishing the actual weight of the load. The other is to strengthen the one that is bearing the burden. God is able to do both. Moses complained about the burden of the government of

Israel, saying, "*I am not able to bear all this people alone, because it is too heavy for me*" (Numbers 11:14). So God provided seventy elders to share the responsibility. "*They shall bear the burden of the people with thee, that though bear it not thyself alone*" (Numbers 11:17). But Paul did not receive the same aid for his painful thorn in the flesh. Three times he prayed for its removal or a lightening of the load, but the weight was not reduced. Instead, God increased Paul's strength to bear his burden. He said unto him, "*My grace is sufficient for thee: for my strength is made perfect in weakness*" (2 Corinthians 12:9). The apostle was daily sustained to carry his affliction. God shouldered both the bearer and his burden.

2. THE BLESSING OF THE BURDEN

> *Cast your cares on the* LORD *and he will sustain you.*
> (Psalm 55:22 NIV)

While a few Bible versions give us the word "*care*" for "*burdens*" in Psalm 55:22, the margin of the King James Version gives us the word *gift*, and the Revised Version margin says, "[the burdens] that he hath given thee." Is this not blessedly suggestive? "Cast thy gift upon the Lord." A burden is a gift! It is hard to think of the burden we are carrying as a gift—a blessing, a benefit. Yet it can be so!

> This heavy thing, it is His gift,
> His portion, thee to bless;
> Give it Him back; what He shall lift
> No more on thee shall press.[66]

What do we know about the sanctification of a sorrow, the blessing of a burden, the delight springing from a disappointment,

---

66. Handley C. G. Moule, "Cast Thou Thy Care upon the Lord."

the glory of a grief? Many of us would not be what we are today had it not been for the wonderful way God has transformed a burden into a blessing. A proverb says, "No one knows the weight of another's burden," but there *is* One who knows and cares. Scripture is reassuring: *"Blessed be the Lord, who daily bears us up"* (Psalm 68:19 RSV). The literal translation in the margin of Psalm 37:5 and Proverbs 16:3 is "roll thy way and thy works upon the Lord." Each exhortation has its accompanying promise. The French translation of Peter's call to "cast all our care upon God" (see 1 Peter 5:7) gives the idea of the unloading of a cart by removing the pins which fasten the backboard and tipping it so that the contents spill over.

"Blessed be ballast," the sailor shouts as a hurricane sweeps the ocean wild. Just so, many lives would drift if relieved of their ballast. They would be like frail vessels without freight to keep them steady on a storm-tossed sea. There is a fable that says, in essence, when God first made birds, He made them wingless. They were able to sing sweetly but had no beautiful plumage. Then He made wings for their backs, and they took them up with a sigh, for they were burdensome. But the wings grew fast, and as the birds tried to use them, they found that what they had deemed burdens became pinions. Their weights became wings, and what they began bearing ended in carrying them, enabling them to soar nearer heaven.

Have we learned how to transfer all our burdens to Him who bore our sins, allowing Him to transform them into blessings? Instead of treating a burden as a weight dragging us down, we must look upon it as a wing by which we can soar higher. We must pray that we never grumble at the load or fall beneath its weight, but that we prove how the ever-present Burden Bearer is able to make any burden sparkle as a gift.

Tell it to Jesus, He only can help you—
Mountains before Him will prove but a way;
Only to trust Him, for He will deliver,
See through the shadows a brightening day!

CHAPTER 13

TRIUMPHS AND TEARS

"When [Jesus] was come nigh [the city]...the whole multitude of the disciples began to rejoice and praise God with a loud voice for all the mighty works that they had seen; saying, Blessed be the King that cometh in the name of the Lord: peace in heaven, and glory in the highest."
—Luke 19:37–38

"When [Jesus] was come near, he beheld the city, and wept over it."
—Luke 19:41

The vivid account of our Lord's triumphal entry into Jerusalem is to be found in each of the four Gospels. Evidently, the incident vividly impressed the minds of the writers, each of whom recounts it in his own style. The last Sunday in the season of Lent is known as Palm Sunday, the day when the lifelong sorrows and humiliation of Jesus was relieved by one brief hour of glory and triumph. Such a jubilant appearance fulfilled Zechariah's inspired vision of the King of Zion entering the city riding on a donkey. As the hosannas rent the air, a great multitude spread their garments for Him to ride over; the way was decorated with branches cut from the majestic palm trees.

In his *Commentary on Matthew*, Richard Glover says of this royal welcome,

> Fine feelings breed fine manners. There is something courtly, beautiful, poetic in the welcome given here. Sir Walter Raleigh laid his velvet cloak on the ground for Queen Elizabeth I to tread on, so they carpet the pathway for Him with their cloaks; some of these cloaks, doubtless, rich and beautiful.

Hymns of praise in honor of Christ's works of mercy greeted Him as He rode through the city. *"Hosanna to the son of David"* (Matthew 21:9) is the Hebrew equivalent of *"God save the Son of David"* (verse 9 WEY). Yet what a strange King He was! The ass He rode on was not His own but was borrowed from one of the peasants; and instead of swords—the symbol of kingly power—there were only palm branches.

The whole episode suggests a series of impressive contrasts. Christ came as the King of Glory, yet He rode on an ass no one else had ridden on. In ancient times, this was the mark of kingship. Then, over against the acclamations of the populace, we have the anger of the priests, who felt their influence was being destroyed. (See Matthew 21:15.) Behind their sore displeasure was jealousy that there were no praises and plaudits for them. C. H. Spurgeon says, "If the multitude had been saying, 'Oh these *blessed* Pharisees!'...there would not have been a man among them who would have said, 'Master, rebuke thy disciples.'" These enemies of Christ could not bear to hear Him praised. How true to life this is! If there is someone we do not like, or are jealous of, it angers us to hear them praised. Christ did not try to dampen the popular enthusiasm His presence evoked at this time. This was the absolute opposite to His usual experience. He allowed the outburst of praise because He knew it was the distinct, voluntary fulfillment of the Messianic prophecy.

HIS TRIUMPH

This was our Lord's only day of earthly triumph; the rest was yet to come. The day of His transfiguration was unearthly in that it witnessed the drawing aside of the curtain of His inherent glory. The day of His triumphal entry into Jerusalem was akin to the appearance of a mere earthly conqueror, and to the disciples it seemed as if the prophetic hope of an earthly king was fulfilled. So He was hailed as the Son of David who would restore the kingdom to Israel. Thus the cry rent the air, *"The King of Israel"* (John 12:13)—the same greeting the angels sang over Bethlehem: *"Peace in heaven, and glory in the highest"* (Luke 19:38). But their aspiration was carnal in that they looked for a king who would cast off the Roman yoke and reign as a temporal deliverer. It would have fit their idea of a conquering king had He ridden on a war horse, revealing might, rather than on an ass, a sign of meekness. How disappointed the disciples were when they saw the King crucified as a felon on a wooden gibbet! *"We trusted that it had been he which should have redeemed Israel"* (Luke 24:21). At that time, they did not understand that He could only reach His crown *via* the cross; that at His death, the diadem of universal sovereignty would be His.

Hosanna is derived from a Hebrew word meaning "save, we pray thee." Although the multitude who shouted this term of greeting was ignorant of this fact, the One they lauded was on His way to the cross to die for their salvation, so the term was apt. While "hosanna" is a one-word prayer, it has vast meaning, for it is prayed by sinners who would be saved from sin and by saints who would be kept from sinning. An Arabian proverb advises, "Hold all the skirts of thy garment extended when the heavens are raining gold." Oh, that the lost could be prompted to hold out their garments to receive all the Savior has provided!

As to the palm tree that figures so largely in the royal welcome, the Arabs used to say it had as many uses as days in a year. The tree reached the height of dignity when its branches were used to wave a jubilant welcome to Him who made the trees. Nature is no infidel but has ever been the friend and ally of her Creator. The star led the wise men to the place of His birth. The sea closed its hungry mouth when He walked on the billows. The winds and waves obeyed His voice. The sun veiled its face as He hung upon the cross in agony and shame. The people sang their hosannas and surrendered their garments, and the best of trees waved Him on as He slowly journeyed through the crowds on the ass—an honor for such a dumb animal. Are we among the number that deems Jesus worthy of the highest praise? Are we among those who welcome Him with what we have?

HIS TEARS

It was but a short step from our Lord's triumph to His tears, from praises to pain. Try to picture the jubilant procession coming to a halt and the throng pressing in around Him on every side—only to see Him display His inner sadness in sobs. Surely He should have had tears of joy over the rapturous welcome accorded Him, but instead, the people saw tears of sorrow for the doomed city. While Matthew does not mention Christ's lament over Jerusalem, Luke does. (See Luke 19:41.) As the sight of the city came to view and all its glory burst upon the crowds, Jesus wept. The Jerusalem He had tried to woo and win had rejected Him, and so there came the sob of love rejected.

That display of tears while the triumph of the throng still rang in His ears has much to say of His love, as well as the terrible fate of the impenitent. His sobbing revealed that

> It was not vanity that moved His entry in triumph; that He could forget His own agony in thinking of others' approaching sorrow; that He sought not His glory, but men's salvation; that man, by impenitence can thwart God's mercy.

Christ never wept for Himself, and He did not want others to weep for Him. *"Daughters…weep not for me, but weep for yourselves"* (Luke 23:28). His tears were always shed over the sorrow and sin of the world. The thought of men dying in sin and entering into eternal darkness wrenched His heart and moistened His cheeks with tears. When He came to die, He sacrificed Himself without a murmur. His tears and death were for the lost.

What gave His death a sting was the knowledge that the merit of His sufferings would not save all; that although His sacrifice was sufficient to bear away the sin of the world, multitudes would continue to live and die in their sin. Thus, even in the midst of excited crowds acclaiming Him as Messiah, He was the Man of Sorrows who foresaw doom and desolation. His warnings had gone unheeded, and voices shouting their hosannas would soon change into malignant cries for His blood.

Calvary was visible from the Mount of Olives where He stood, and so overpowering were His painful sensations that He found relief in tears. *"He beheld the city, and wept over it"* (Luke 19:41).

Entering the city, Jesus immediately revealed that He was the Son of God with power and authority to purge the temple and to heal the sick and diseased. At the sight of the palm-waving crowd surrounding a man riding on an ass, many people asked, "Who is this?" Generation after generation has asked this same ignorant question, for men find it hard to classify Jesus, who has always been in a class by Himself. Those who were applauding Him replied, most strikingly, *"This is Jesus the prophet of Nazareth of Galilee"* (Matthew 21:11). They gave Him the most honored name they knew.

Once within Jerusalem, Jesus went first to the temple for a twofold purpose. First, he went to meet the true worshippers; and second, to meet those who were polluting the sanctuary. The people had called Him *"the King of Israel"* (John 12:13). The temple was the heart of Israel, just as Christ's true church is the heart of the world. Because the well-being of all else depends on the well-being of His house, it must be cleansed of its thieves and preserved for its supreme purpose—worship. All His temples must be cleansed, and often, He suddenly appears to refine them by fire. "He cleanses His church with fires of persecution; He cleanses the *heart-temple* by the chastisements of His love."

Within the precincts of the temple were the blind and the lame, whom the priests of the temple were not able, or willing, to relieve. The Great High Priest, however, healed them all. Witnessing the purification of the temple and the relief of the afflicted, the religious leaders asked, *"By what authority doest thou these things? and who gave thee this authority?"* (Matthew

21:23). Men are sustained in what they say or do by different aspects of authority.

+ *Stature*. Like Saul, who was head and shoulders higher than others, they are tall and commanding.

+ *Money*. We often say, "Money speaks," and often, it is able to give its possessors great power.

+ *Learning*. In many respects, "Knowledge is power," especially in the realm of the sciences.

+ *Lineage*. A prince has more authority than a pauper. Too often, this privilege has been abused.

+ *Impudence*. A good deal of bluff often gets people into responsible positions, but like soap bubbles, they soon burst.

+ *Physical force*. Rulers strive to maintain authority with their armies and weapons of war.

+ *Friends*. Influence can open many doors. We all know from experience that to be successful, it is not *what* you know but *who* you know.

But the source of Christ's authority, which was ever cropping up in His ministry, is different from all other sources of authority. His diploma of authority bore the seal of His deity. It was because of who He was that He was able to act as He did. If Jesus was less than God, then His professions were preposterous, His promises delusions and, therefore, incapable of fulfillment. But He declared that all power in heaven and on earth was His (see Matthew 21:23), and He proved it. *"Destroy this temple"* (Mark 14:58; John 2:19), he said, referring to the threat of His enemies to kill Him; and His resurrection revealed that He was indeed the Son of God having all power and authority.

The Pharisees could prevail nothing against Jesus, for *"the world is gone after him"* (John 12:19). The question is, Have we gone after Him? Have we raised our hosannas? Do we recognize Him as our Prophet, Priest, and King? Is the temple of our lives clean? He does not want the empty cries of passing enthusiasm and the hollow, empty songs of those who praise Him one day and cause Him to weep the next. He yearns for those who love and own Him as Savior and who are ever ready to do His will. May we never give Him occasion to grieve over us, as He wept over the so-called Holy City of Jerusalem!

CHAPTER 14

SO NEAR YET SO FAR

"Thou art not far from the kingdom of God."
—Mark 12:34

"Almost thou persuadest me to be a Christian."
—Acts 26:28

"My soul had almost dwelt in silence."
—Psalm 94:17

The three verses introducing this twin truth have one thing in common. They all describe an experience that was on the verge of realization, but which did not materialize. Together they illustrate the well-known proverb "There's many a slip 'twixt the cup and the lip."

The intelligent reply of the scribe to Christ's announcement of the greatest commandments led Him to say, *"Thou art not far from the kingdom of God"* (Mark 12:34). He was so near—yet so far from such a glorious goal. But many travelers have perished in sight of home. A Danish proverb says it well, "'Almost' never killed a fly." The solemn fact is that a person almost saved can die and be lost forevermore. The classic example of the advantage yet peril of close proximity is found in King Agrippa's response to Paul's recital of his dramatic conversion. The king said, *"Almost thou persuadest me to be a Christian"* (Acts 26:28). Let us look at this heart-moving confession.

Chosen to stand and testify before kings (see Acts 9:15), Paul became, next to Christ, the most outstanding, magnificent character not only in the New Testament but in the whole of Christian history. No other saint has arisen as illustrious in whole-hearted devotion to the Savior's cause as this man, the Apostle to the Gentiles. As a prisoner in bonds, Paul exemplified the blessing of adversity. God has a work that only imprisoned lives can accomplish. There was no other way by which the gospel could reach rulers like Felix, Festus, Agrippa, and Caesar except through a notable prisoner. So, like Joseph before him, Paul went from witnessing in a prison to witnessing in a palace. If we find ourselves in a tight corner, or in a limited, irksome sphere, let us take heart, for this may be the very platform upon which God can display His grace and power.

Agrippa's response is most arresting, coming as it did from a proud heathen monarch. Some writers affirm that when the king uttered the statement *"Almost thou persuadest me to be a Christian"* (Acts 26:28), he did so in a tone of contempt rather than sincerity; that the king's words were not an expression "of a half-belief, but of a cynical sneer." Further, while the King James Version favors retaining the word *"almost,"* other translators reject it, contending it is not in the Greek text. Marvin Vincent said that the words, then, are ironical, and the sense is, "You are trying to persuade me off hand to be a Christian."[67] Dr. C. I. Scofield commented on the Revised version of this text, *"With*

---

67. Marvin R. Vincent, *Vincent's Word Studies*, 1886.

but little persuasion thou wouldest fain make me a Christian" (Acts 26:28 ʀᴠ):

> The answer might be paraphrased: "It will require more than this," etc., or, "A little more and you will make [me a Christian], etc."

But accepting the text as it stands in the King James Version, we can develop these three thoughts:

1. The Noblest of Ambitions: "To be a Christian"

2. The Gentlest of Means: "Thou persuadest me"

3. The Nearest of Responses: "Almost"

THE NOBLEST OF AMBITIONS

We often hear the remark, "What's in a name?" Well, it all depends upon the name, for some names are rich in their association. "Christian" suggests the noblest, grandest life here and the assurance of a most blessed hereafter. All who are Christians, not in name merely but in life and service, belong to the aristocracy of heaven. There is no life comparable to that of a Christian, embracing as it does all that is pure, lofty, and attractive. To be a Christian after the New Testament pattern is to be like the best Man who ever lived and whose name is embodied in the term *Christian*. Since much misunderstanding, however, has gathered around this honored name, it is imperative to ascertain what is really meant by being a Christian.

A Christian is not necessarily one born in a Christian country. This was a mistake many heathens made when British traders came to their land and robbed them of natural products and rounded up the natives as slaves. Britain had the reputation of being a Christian country, but she was far from Christian in her empire expansion. There is no country on earth that is positively Christian. What a paradise the world would be if all the nations followed Christ!

A Christian is not one brought up in a Christian home. Too many people assume they are in the fold of the Good Shepherd because of their godly heritage. But grace does not run in the blood. Nothing can substitute for a personal relationship to Jesus Christ. Certainly the influence of godly parents in the home makes it easier for a child to become a Christian, but their religion is no guarantee for the salvation of their children. The only way to become a Christian is by personally receiving Christ as Savior.

A Christian is not all who are connected with a Christian church. All Christians should be associated with a church that functions after the New Testament pattern, but there are multitudes who are members of churches who are not members of the true church, which is Christ's body. One of the errors of the church is the fallacy that by infant baptism a child becomes a member of the church. It is association with a Person, not a place, that saves. It is to be feared that the majority of churches today do not declare how people can become and behave as Christians. Yet the supreme task of the church is to go into all the world and make disciples, or followers, of Christ.

A Christian is not one who practices Christian principles. Of course, if a person is a true believer, he will endeavor by God's grace and power to live as Christ lived. But one can do that Christ did—pray, read the Bible, go to church, and seek to be religious in life—yet not, fundamentally, be a Christian. It is possible to be religious but not Christian. Judas, a professed disciple, went from the Communion table to the grave to a lost and miserable eternity. To be godless means to be minus God. Many religious people are Christless simply because Christ is not their personal Savior and the Lord of their lives. Jesus said to those who called Him "Lord," who ate in His presence and taught others about Him in the streets, *"I know you not"* (Luke 13:25, 27).

What, then, is a Christian? As the converts of Wesley were called Wesleyans, so a Christian, a Christ-one, is called a follower or slave of Christ—a Christian. The term *Christian* occurs three times in the Bible, and the context of each reference provides a profitable study. (See Acts 11:26; 26:28; 1 Peter 4:16.) A Christian is one who thoroughly identifies with Christ in life, deed, thought, and word. He is one who is *in* Christ for salvation, *like* Christ in character, *for* Christ in witness, and *with* Christ in companionship.

> Christian, rise and act thy creed;
> Let thy prayer be in thy deed;
> Seek the right, perform the true,
> Raise thy work and life anew.[68]

THE GENTLEST OF MEANS

Although commentators tell us that the term *"persuadest"* is not in the original, we are happy the translators of the King James Version used it, because persuasion is more effective than force. The word *persuade* means "to speak winning words." Paul did not try to coerce Agrippa against his will or desire to become a Christian. As the apostle recounted how God had saved his

---

68. F. A. Rollo Russell, "Christian, Rise and Act Thy Creed," 1893.

soul, "persuasion hung upon his lips,"[69] and the king was drawn, not dragged, to testify to the power of Paul's appeal. Charles Churchill, poet of the seventeenth century, wrote of "the persuasive language of a tear," and Paul could use even this kind of persuasion, for he told those Ephesian elders how, for three years, he never ceased to warn them day and night, with *tears*, of the perils facing them. (See Acts 20:31.)

Throughout the Bible, persuasion is used both in a right and a wrong sense. Cruden says the term means "to convince, to assure, to advise, to deceive, to pacify, to provoke."

1. THE FORM OF PERSUASION

Persuasion is of a threefold nature—heavenly, hellish, and human—and it is employed by God, the devil, and man.

THE DIVINE METHOD

"*I know, and am persuaded by the Lord Jesus*" (Romans 14:14). In matters of self-abnegation and personal purity, Paul, prompted by Christ, sought to woo and win believers to a life of holiness. "By persuading others, we convince ourselves," and as Paul saw the saints yielding their lives more fully to the Lord as the result of his loving appeal, he was more firmly convinced of the divine truth he proclaimed. Under God, many of the prophets and apostles had the "tongue to persuade," as Edward Hyde could say of Hampden. How lovingly and tenderly Jesus tried to persuade those Jerusalem sinners to shelter beneath His wings—but they would not!

THE SATANIC METHOD

The devil is a past master in the art of persuasion. In some mysterious way, God allowed an evil, lying spirit to

---

69. Laurence Sterne.

possess the prophets, inspiring them to persuade Ahab to go to Ramoth-Gilead where defeat and death awaited him. (See 1 Kings 22:20–22.) *"Thou shalt persuade him, and prevail also"* (1 Kings 22:22). The devil does not present himself with tail and horns and pitchfork. Having accumulated wisdom through millenniums, he knows how to beguile, deceive, and seduce souls, leading them to destruction. In subtle and pleasing ways, he sets up his attractions against the Savior's. It was through satanic persuasion that sin originally entered the world. In *Othello*, Shakespeare has the lines,

> O balmy breath, that dost almost persuade
> Justice to break her sword![70]

THE HUMAN METHOD

The description given of another is certainly true of Paul: "Persuasion tips his tongue whene'er he talks."[71] He could say, *"Knowing therefore the terror of the Lord, we persuade men"* (2 Corinthians 5:11; see Galatians 1:10). He *"persuaded* [the saints] *to continue in the grace of God"* (Acts 13:43; see verses 18:15; 19:8; 28:23). But those who hated Paul's witness were persuaded to stone him and leave him as dead. (See Acts 14:19; 18:2; 19:26–28.) The apostle believed that every man should be fully persuaded in his own mind as to the facts of the gospel. (See Romans 14:5.) Can we not apply the lines of Shakespeare in *King Henry VIII* to the great apostle?

> He was a scholar, and a ripe and good one;
> Exceeding wise, fair-spoken, and persuading:
> Lofty and sour to them that lov'd him not;
> But to those men that sought him, sweet as summer.[72]

70. William Shakespeare, *Othello,* 5.2.17–18.
71. Colley Cibber.
72. William Shakespeare, *King Henry VIII,* 4.2.57–60.

Are we among the Lord's persuaders, endeavoring to woo the lost to receive and follow Him? As businessmen use persuasion to sell their products, do we encourage those who are spiritually bankrupt to seek the pearl of greatest price? Swift would have us "gently pity whom [we] can't persuade."[73] The tragedy is that the majority of people around us appear to be so dead to both heavenly and human persuasion but so open and responsive to satanic seduction. They are more charmed by the devil's approach than by the Savior's. When the rich man in hell tried to persuade Abraham to free him from torment, that he might go and warn his five brothers to repent of their sins and thus escape the pangs he was enduring, the answer came, *"Neither will they be persuaded, though one rose from the dead"* (Luke 16:31). Jesus rose from the dead and is alive forevermore, yet countless numbers are not convinced and remain in their sin.

2. THE FOUNDATION OF PERSUASION

From the narrative in which Paul's moving appeal to King Agrippa is set forth, we find that persuasion did not rest on mere sentiment or on an emotional basis and appeal, but on a strong, firm foundation. At the back of the united persuasion of the Savior and the saints in seeking the lost, there must be faith in those convincing truths urging them on to win the lost.

THE RECORD OF EXPERIENCE

As it was with Paul, so it is with every preacher and individual working for the salvation of others. Behind our entreaty, there must be a personal experience of what Christ is able to accomplish. If we are to persuade those we contact to turn to Him, we must have proof of His saving grace and power in our

---

73. Jonathan Swift, "The Swan Tripe Club in Dublin."

own life. Nothing can convict like conviction, and men cannot easily resist the power and appeal of experience. Lack of experience in the pulpit is responsible for indifference in the pew. No preacher can be effective who tries to present a Christ beyond his own experience. If he cannot say, *"Come, see a man, which told me all things that ever I did: is not this the Christ?"* (John 4:29), he is not qualified to preach about Him. (See Acts 26:1–23.)

THE RECORD OF CONSCIENCE

How pointed was the apostle's appeal when he said, *"The king knoweth of these things, before whom also I speak freely"* (Acts 26:26). Agrippa knew that what Paul was saying was true. The true persuader has as his ally the conscience of those he seeks to win. The king knew all about Herod, eaten by worms, and so realized in his own heart what Paul's God was able to do. God has not left Himself without witnesses, even in the most abandoned soul, and thus, under the truth of another's testimony, the inner heart of the sinner testifies to the truth presented.

THE RECORD OF TRUTH

What a challenge Paul flung at Agrippa when he said, *"King Agrippa, believest thou the prophets? I know that thou believest"* (Acts 26:27). Beneath the crust of indifference, apparent unconcern, and seeming contempt, there was secret faith—something persuasion could work on. In a land of Bibles, churches, and Christians, sinners know the Word's description of their deep need and the awful consequences of their rejection of the Savior is true. The mental belief they have, however, must become a saving faith. Thus, in the method of persuasion, the three voices of experience, conscience, and truth are combined with the three voices of the Trinity.

THE NEAREST OF RESPONSES

There is a Danish proverb that says, "'Almost' kills no man"; a German saying puts it "'Almost' never killed a fly"; but the solemn fact is that some people are *almost* saved...yet die lost forever. The old adage "There's many a slip 'twixt the cup and the lip" has much truth in it. *Almost* is a sad yet awe-inspiring word. In Scripture, history, and experience, it is associated with heart-moving incidents. The word, as it occurs in the Bible, provides a preacher with a telling message. We are left in no doubt as to where we are and how far we can go in spiritual things. The psalmist was among the number who was of a clean heart but who confessed, *"As for me, my feet were **almost** gone; my steps had well nigh slipped"* (Psalm 73:2). Yet when he was *"almost gone"* (verse 2) he was delivered: *"Thou hast holden me by my right hand"* (verse 23).

1. ALIEN

The sinner has to come a long way before he can find himself almost persuaded to become a Christian. He is alienated from the life of God. (See Ephesians 4:18.) Not only is he dead in sin (see Romans 8:10), but he is an enemy of God (see Colossians 1:21). *Alienated* means "belonging to others, foreign." *Enemy* implies one who is not only inwardly sinful but outwardly hostile and antagonistic. Created by God, they yet serve the devil. Meant to be holy, they live in sin. Destined for heaven, their faces are set hellward.

2. ALMOST

This haunting term comes from a root word meaning "to be near." Agrippa was near to the kingdom. *"A little more and you will be making me a Christian"* (Acts 26:28 BBE). He was near...yet so far. In his mind, the king was on the point of conviction; in his heart, on the point of persuasion; in his will, on the point of decision. But we have no record that he heard the *"little more"* from the apostle that was needed to make him a Christian. Therein lies the greatest peril of him who is brought face-to-face with the claims of Christ—to come so near to the door of heaven, then to turn away toward everlasting darkness, with the very nearness of bliss only adding to remorse in hell. Thus, an "almost persuasion" can become an "altogether perdition." Nowhere is the Holy Spirit as easily and fatally repelled as at the point where it would only require a grain of sand to turn the scale. The truth of all this is summed up in a solemn gospel hymn by P. P. Bliss, which has been so greatly used of God in the leading of sinners to take the final step:

> "Almost persuaded" now to believe;
> "Almost persuaded" Christ to receive;
> Seems now some soul to say,
> "Go, Spirit, go Thy away,
> Some more convenient day
> On Thee I'll call."

> "Almost persuaded," come, come today;
> "Almost persuaded," turn not away;
> Jesus invites you here,
> Angels are ling'ring near,
> Prayers rise from hearts so dear;
> O wand'rer, come!

> "Almost persuaded," harvest is past!
> "Almost persuaded," doom comes at last!
> "Almost" cannot avail;
> "Almost" is but to fail!

Sad, sad that bitter wail—
"Almost, but lost!"[74]

3. ALTOGETHER

Paul's response to Agrippa's confession that he was on the verge of decision was immediate and pertinent—"*I would to God, that not only thou, but also all that hear me this day, were both almost, and altogether such as I am, except these bonds*" (Acts 26:29). The margin gives the rendering: "Both in a little, and in much." When the apostle said, "*Altogether such as I am,*" he meant that he had crossed the boundary line and was a Christian, as he had made clear in his testimony to Agrippa. He was not *almost* but *altogether* saved. "*Altogether born in sin*" (John 9:34), all who accept Christ as their personal Savior are made altogether His. On that Damascus road, Paul was not almost persuaded to become a Christian. In response to the risen, glorified Lord's tender persuasion, he immediately surrendered himself completely to the One who had called him. It is to be hoped that you are among the number altogether saved and secure.

4. ABUNDANT

Paul did not desire Agrippa to be barely or merely saved but to have the abundant salvation he had experienced for so long. Jesus said that He came that we might have not only life but life more abundant. (See John 10:10.) This is the climax of the Christian life on earth. The word *abundant* means "above the ordinary measure," and it was included in Paul's "*altogether.*" It is to be feared that few of us have life above the ordinary measure. Ours is not the salvation to the uttermost Christ has provided for us. (See Hebrews 7:25.) We are no longer "*not far from the kingdom of God*" (Mark 12:34); no, we are in it. But we are not

---

74. Philip P. Bliss, "Almost Persuaded," 1871.

just in it; we stay there, with little desire to go on unto perfection. Are we in—fully in? And are we bringing others in? If we are fully saved, our persuasion will be more effective when we seek to warn sinners that, if they reject the uttermost salvation, no matter how near they were to accepting it, theirs will be the endurance of the uttermost wrath of God. (See 1 Thessalonians 2:16.)

> O fill me with Thy fulness, Lord,
> Until my very heart o'erflow
> In kindling thought and glowing word,
> Thy love to tell, Thy praise to show.[75]

---

75. Frances R. Havergal, "Lord, Speak to Me."

CHAPTER 15

THE BAG AND THE BOTTLE

"My transgression is sealed up in a bag,
and thou sewest up mine iniquity."
—Job 14:17

"Put thou my tears into thy bottle: are they not in thy book?"
—Psalm 56:8

Though we acknowledge that the Bible is a book for the whole world and contains a universal message, seeing it recognizes no distinction or race, we must not forget that it has an Eastern setting. It was written in the East by men of the East and is thus largely colored by Eastern imagery, customs, and ways. Such a fact accounts for many of the unique illustrations of Eastern ways and habits. And this is one reason why it is difficult for us with our Western ideas and associations to fully appreciate the figures of speech the Bible employs.

Of course, such a method of presentation indicates God's loving condescension. He ever strives to bring spiritual truth down to our level. Here, for example, are two metaphors we desire to combine simply because they are vitally connected with our spiritual experiences. Job gives us a bag for our sins and transgressions; David, a bottle for our sobs and tears. *"My transgression is sealed up in a bag, and thou sewest up mine iniquity"* (Job 14:17). *"Put thou my tears into thy bottle: are they not in thy book?"* (Psalm 56:8).

THE SIN BAG

To understand Job's bag analogy, it is essential that we look at the customs that prevailed in his time. Scholars tell us that money was brought to the treasuries of the princes, carefully counted in certain sums, deposited in bags, and then sealed until needed. Furthermore, we know that bills of indictment or condemnation were kept in sealed bags to be used against the guilty when needed. Possibly, it was the former custom Moses had in mind when he wrote, *"Is not this laid up in store with me, and sealed up among my treasures?"* (Deuteronomy 32:34).

The thought Job presents is that our sins and transgressions are counted, hoarded, and sealed—"sewn up" (see Job 14:17)—in a bag until the day of final settlement. God will not forget, miss, or lose one single sin of the sinner. As an Eastern prince would rip open a bag to count his treasures, so God open our "sin bags" on the day of reckoning. Transgressors must reap what they have sown. And such a "sin bag" speaks of two things: first, the condemnation of the sinner; second, the comfort of the saint.

1. THE CONDEMNATION OF THE SINNER

Such a forcible illustration ought to strike fear into the heart of the sinner who is apt to forget his sin. Here he is reminded that God's hand sews up his transgressions and keeps the bag. As sin is committed, it is thrown into the bag and can never escape divine guardianship. At the great white throne, the time of final settlement, the Lord will empty the bag filled by the sinner himself.

2. THE COMFORT OF THE SAINT

But what is despair for the sinner constitutes delight for the saint. In the "sin bag," there is comfort for the saint. God, in His grace, has put all our sins in His bag and has sewn it up. And no one can break into it and take our sins out; they are sealed and covered forever. But where is the bag? Well, such a question need not concern us. Has the bag not been dropped behind His back? (See Isaiah 38:17.) God's hand counted out our sins and dropped them into the grave of Christ, into the pit of oblivion. What grace! Let us praise Him anew for the sacred, scarred body of Jesus which became the bag. Our sins were sewn up in His heart. Knowing no sin, He yet became sin for us. (See 2 Corinthians 5:21.) Listen, friend, where are your sins? Are they in the bag awaiting judgment? Or are they in a bag at the bottom of the sea of God's forgetfulness?

THE TEAR BOTTLE

We are given a sweet, tender inside look into God's sympathetic nature in David's mention of God's tear bottle. David urges God to put His tears into a bottle and record them in His book. What a bold and expressive metaphor this is! Bottled tears express the tenderness of God. But the use of the tear bottle is explained in different ways.

It may refer to the traveler preserving water, milk, or wine in a leather bottle for a journey across the barren desert. The psalmist prays that God will remember his trials, travail, travels, and tears caused by his forced banishment from home. Pursued by Saul and almost in despair, David crosses the frontier and takes refuge in the city of Goliath. But he is quickly recognized and, resorting to a subterfuge, feigns himself mad, yet his eyes were on the Lord who had counted his tears.

Another explanation of the tear bottle affords a further application. If a friend took ill or was in trouble, neighbors would visit him and have a tear bottle close at hand. As tears rolled down the cheeks of the sufferer, they would be caught by the visitors and preserved in a bottle as a memorial of the sufferer's grief and anguish. And David enjoins God to remember his sighs and sorrows, to bookmark and bottle up his sobs. Somehow the psalmist is consoled by the thought that his toils and tribulations would not be forgotten.

Tear bottles also contained the tears of mourners. As tears rolled down the cheeks of sorrowing friends, they would be soaked up, squeezed into a bottle, and then preserved with the greatest care. Usually the bottle was buried in the tomb as a token of genuine sympathy. Since this time, they have been found in ancient tombs. All of this suggests God's compassion and care for His own.

Hezekiah was consoled by the assurance that God had seen his tears, Paul was mindful of Timothy's tears, and God treasures our tears. If our sins are in His bag, then we can be sure that our tears are in His bottle. Our losses, sorrows, pain, adversities, and graves are known to Him. There is no place where earth's sorrows are more felt than in heaven.

1. GOD REMEMBERS OUR TEARS

Tears shed over sin are precious to the Master whose feet were washed with the tears of a penitent soul. Bernard of Clairvaux put it, "The tears of penitents are the wine of angels." God takes note of tears produced by deep contrition over sin. But there is so little weeping for sin!

God also remembers the tears shed by those who suffer for the cause of Christ. And He will surely reckon with those who produce such tears. Tears shed for His sake glisten as pearls. The psalmist's feeling is comparable to that of Constance in Shakespeare's *King John*:

> His grandam's wrongs, and not his mother's shames,
> Draws those heaven-moving pearls from his poor eyes,
> Which heaven shall take in nature of a fee;
> Ay, with these crystal beads heaven shall be brib'd
> To do him justice, and revenge on you.[76]

Yes, God will never forget the tears shed over our separations. Tears over the partings of life are treasured up and transformed into "heaven-moving pearls." As beautiful rainbows are made up of drops of water, so God bottles our tears to transmute them into songs. Tears are to give way to triumph, sorrow to singing, pain to pleasure, graves to glory, and crosses to crowns. What we must pray for is deliverance from the tragedy of a lost sorrow. We must strive to get the utmost blessing out of our tears. Our tears must become our telescopes, giving us a clearer vision of our blessed Lord.

2. GOD REMOVES OUR TEARS

That which the hand of God presently bottles will be banished before long. Weeping, which is liquid pain, will vanish.

---

76. William Shakespeare, *King John*, 2.1.168–172.

No eyes are wet with tears in heaven, for *"God shall wipe away all tears from their eyes"* (Revelation 21:4). The tears Jesus shed over the sin of Jerusalem, the separation at Bethany, and the sufferings of Gethsemane and Calvary are bottled up. The Father hasn't forgotten them. He will turn His Son's tears into lustrous gems and give Him ample reward for His cross.

Our blessed Lord, whose eyes were often wet with tears, left behind two possessions associated with the bag and bottle: His blood and His napkin.

HIS BLOOD FOR OUR SINS

There was no blood in Christ's resurrection body. How could there be, when He gave it all at Calvary? The life of the flesh is in the blood, and it was Jesus' own life that He gave. *"A spear pierced his side, and forthwith came there out blood and water"* (John 19:34). And the blood *destroys* the bag. All our sins may be placed in a bag, but one touch of the precious royal blood obliterates both the bag and its contents. John Bunyan describes Christian carrying a heavy bag laden with sin. On the trudges with his load until he reaches the foot of a cross. Immediately, the bag fell off his back, and he sings,

> Must here be the beginning of my bliss?
>
> …
>
> Must here the strings that bound it to me crack?[77]

Then he gave three leaps for joy and went on his way singing. Has your bag fallen to the ground, and with it your sin?

---

77. John Bunyan, *The Pilgrim's Progress*.

HIS NAPKIN FOR OUR TEARS

In his description of the resurrection, John tells us that *"the napkin, that was about his head, not lying with the linen clothes, [was] wrapped together in a place by itself"* (John 20:7).[78] It will be noticed that the napkin was not with the other clothes but wrapped together in a place by itself. Surely we have a beautiful touch here. Why was this handkerchief carefully folded, and that by One who had wept much? Well, having borne our sin and conquered death, Jesus removed the chief cause of weeping. The handkerchief, then, could be folded up. Christ's discarded handkerchief is a foretaste of the coming time when all tears will be removed and rewarded. It speaks of the glorious certainty that all our pains and pangs will be cast into eternal oblivion.

Beloved, we are still in the vale of tears; our handkerchiefs are in constant use. God, however, marks our falling tears. His heart is touched with our grief and, sympathizing with us, He waits to bring blessing out of our bleeding.

> He knows, He loves, He cares,
> Nothing the truth can dim.
> He gives the very best to those
> Who leave the choice with Him.

What we must not forget is the truth that God's bottle is *only* for those whose sins are in the bag. We cannot have the consolation of the gospel here and eternal bliss hereafter unless we are cleansed by the blood of the Lamb. Tears are not dried in hell. There are no dry eyes in the abode of lost souls. There the bag is ever full of sins and the bottle runs over with tears. But

---

78. The word *"napkin"* used for our Lord's headcloth is the same term translated *"handkerchiefs"* in Acts 19:12.

if Christ is our Savior, the sin bag has been dealt with, and He stands ready as the Consoler to soothe and succor our aching hearts as we linger amid the shadows.

CHAPTER 16

BEAUTY FOR ASHES

"To give unto them beauty for ashes, the oil of joy for mourning,
the garment of praise for the spirit of heaviness."
—Isaiah 61:3

The book of Isaiah is wonderfully rich in symbols and metaphors, for the prophet was gifted in using illustrations of striking beauty and prophetic tenderness. In chapter 61, Isaiah has painted the portrait of the ideal messianic Deliverer and Consoler, with special reference to the return of the Jews from Babylonian captivity to full kingdom blessing.

In the poetic words of this verse, there is a foregleam of Jesus, the Man of Sorrows, presenting Himself as the transformer of sorrow and the provider of joy to those deep in grief and defeat. Not only was He anointed to banish the dark things of life but also to create blessings out of those sorrows. And what a blessed transmuter of sorrow Christ is!

As can be seen from the wonderful prophecy before us, Isaiah combines a triad of two contrasting yet complementary truths, proving how the God of all comfort works for His children who are bruised and battered by the storms of life. He is ever active in applying the consolations of the gospel to them.

BEAUTY FOR ASHES

It was usual in times of great mourning to lie in ashes and then be raised out of the dust and made beautiful. The ashes of lamentation would be removed from one's head and the bridal diadem put in its place. *"Thou hast turned for me my mourning into dancing"* (Psalm 30:11).

OIL OF JOY FOR MOURNING

Oil makes the face shine—a sign of beauty in the Eastern culture of Isaiah's day. Sorrow, on the other hand, was thought to disfigure the countenance and make it unlovely. In times of mourning or grief, oil for the toilette was not applied, seeing that its use was a sign of health and gladness. The oil of gladness is a divine promise and provision. (See Hebrews 1:9.)

GARMENT OF PRAISE FOR HEAVINESS

Beautiful garments were worn on thanksgiving days and during festive seasons. *"The spirit of heaviness"* (Isaiah 61:3) refers to the despondent spirit for which sackcloth is suitable, owing to its dark and heavy nature. Although we may have heavy hearts and secretly mourn, the eyes of others must see the garment of praise.

These, then, are the contrasted pictures suggested by the prophet's word. The mourner, with gray ashes on his disheveled hair, his spirit clothed in gloom like a black robe, is comforted as one comes to him and, with gentle hands, removes all of the ashes from his hair, trains a garland around his head, and anoints him with oil. The grief-stricken one lives again as the trappings of woe are torn from the body and it is clothed with a bright, festive robe.

And this is the miracle the Master is willing to accomplish in every sorrow-driven life. Let us now see how this Transformer can give us beauty for ashes, and how this symbol, so rich and tender, brings us very near to the Savior's heart of love.

BEAUTY OF GRACE FOR ASHES OF GUILT

Multitudes have proved that Christ is ready to give the beauty of forgiveness for the ashes of a deep-felt guilt over sin. Although the soul is seared with the foul and deadly wounds of iniquity and stained with the unspeakable anguish and remorse of remembered transgressions, the blood of Jesus can make the vilest clean. When Christ is received as Savior, He quickly changes the defiling ashes of guilt into the radiant beauty of a genuine and gladsome experience of sins being forgiven.

BEAUTY OF THE CHRIST-LIFE FOR THE ASHES OF THE SELF-LIFE

Ashes stand for humiliation. Kings placed ashes upon their heads as a sign of their penitence. Mordecai approached the queen in ashes. Job sat amid ashes.

Two avenues are open to the believer; namely, the road of Christ and the road of self. Over the one we carry the radiant beauty of Jesus; over the other we encounter the ashes of the old nature. Oh, how often do we realize the wretchedness of self-centeredness!

With blinding tears, we weep as we think of the many ashes of selfishness strewn upon the altar. Yet Christ waits to impart the beauty of His own unselfish life. (See Romans 8:2.)

BEAUTY OF VICTORY FOR ASHES OF DEFEAT

In the Old Testament, ashes represent the defeat of kings. Having lost in battle, they would return with torn garments and ash-laden heads. Victors wore a garland of flowers; the vanquished carried ashes.

Who among us never has sat on the ash heap of shameful defeat? Why, the best of us have made hasty decisions, plunging ourselves into perplexity, confusion, sorrow, and despair! We have yielded to besetting infirmities, causing us to fall before God in deep contrition of soul. We have fought hard and struggled desperately to conquer sin, only to reach the place of shameful defeat.

Are you a defeated soul? Well, here is One who can give you beauty for ashes, who can crown you with the blood-bought victory of Calvary! Paul knew all about ashes. This accounts for his cry, "*O wretched man that I am!*" (Romans 7:24). But he came to know that the Lord alone could brush the ashes of defeat from his brow and diadem him with victory. Thanks be unto God who gives us the victory!

BEAUTY OF COMFORT FOR ASHES OF SORROW

Ashes were also the symbol of grief; thus, when Job could cry no more, he sat down on the ashes. Women who had lost their treasures would sprinkle ashes on the threshold of the home; the act spoke of their inner emptiness and desolation.

Christ, however, transforms sorrow through His transformation of the mourner himself. The change is wrought in the sufferer. This Joy Bringer and Transmuter of grief into gladness produces the change by transforming not the sorrows but the bearer of them. The ashes may remain, and circumstances may not change, but out of them springs a fresh beauty, which surprises the sorrowing one. The facts of life remain untouched, for it is better and higher for lives to be changed rather than the sorrows attached to them. This transformation works in many ways.

1. JOY INDEPENDENT OF EXTERNAL CIRCUMSTANCES

When the dark clouds gather, we are thrice happy if we know how to turn away from external occasions of grief and sadness and rest in Him who is unchangeable. The secret of a deep, unchanging joy is the consciousness of Christ's sweet presence and the assurance of the strong love, sustaining hand, and infinite wisdom of a God who cares. This does not mean that we are less sorrowful but that we have appropriated the paradox *"As sorrowful, yet alway rejoicing"* (2 Corinthians 6:10).

Jesus does not offer to free us from all the ills that the flesh is heir to. His own tears sanctify ours. He means us to feel the bitterness and pain of sorrow; but while we suffer as humans, we are not to be lost in our grief. Opposite emotions must be harmonized. Songs and sighs must be companions.

2. UNDERSTOOD SORROW IS TRANSMUTED

Too often, we classify events in our lives into opposite categories, such as good and evil, prosperity and adversity, gains and losses, sunshine and shadow, fulfilled expectations and disappointed hopes. We must learn, however, to place them all in the one class of discipline and education. If *all* things work together for good, then the Lord can use opposite experiences for our growth in Christlikeness. If every joy and trial falls from above, then the same hand is able to work in and through all for our sanctification. The most unwanted circumstances are but tools in the divine hand for the shaping of character. And this is the only philosophy that can extract the sting out of a stab, wipe the poison from the arrow, and remove the bitterness from the cup.

3. SUBMISSION TO GOD'S WILL

Beauty of comfort for ashes of grief becomes ours when we discover the secret of God's direct or permissive will. Acquiescence in the will of God is the philosopher's stone, turning all grief into gold. It has been said that an accepted grief is a conquered grief; a conquered grief becomes a comforted grief; and a comforted grief is a joy.

If adversities are taken to the right place and borne in the right spirit, they will be quickly transformed. If wrongly received and borne, they will leave us worse than they found us. An affliction wasted is the worst of all wasted treasures. Oh, the tragedy of a lost sorrow.

There are those who confess that they would never have known the blessedness of Christ as Savior and Friend had it not been for the deep waters they crossed. They climbed to Him by the path of pain.

The time is coming, however, when every sorrow rightly borne will bring a greater degree of bliss and when every tear will flash as a diamond. Yes, and when all lessons have been learned, God will burn all the correction rods. But until the dawn of such a blissful day, may we have grace to sing:

He gives me joy in place of sorrow;
He gives me love that casts out fear;
He gives me sunshine for my shadow,
And "beauty for ashes" here.[79]

BEAUTY OF RESURRECTION FOR ASHES OF DEATH

Ashes are also the symbol of human frailty. Abraham said, *"I...am but dust and ashes"* (Genesis 18:27). The further significance of Isaiah's illustration, then, is that as ashes stand for mourning, sorrow, and death, beauty and joy await us at the hand of the Comforter. Soon He will give us the beauty of a glorified body for the ashes of a corrupt one. What a blessed exchange!

Is yours a desolate home? Have you been robbed of a radiant child, a strong-hearted husband, a beloved wife, a companion of a lifetime? Have those bodies you loved, embraced, and fondled gone to ashes? Do the words you heard at the graveside still linger in your memory: "Dust to dust, ashes to ashes"? Amid your loneliness, take fresh courage, for on some glad day, the ashes of your holy dead will be touched by Him who has power over death, and out of them will spring a glorified body like unto His own.

Before long, Jesus will return for His church, His blood-washed ones, and then they will experience the reality of exchanging the ashes of earth for the beauty of heaven, mourning for melody, and heaviness for unending happiness.

79. J. G. Crabbe, "Beauty for Ashes," 1889.

CHAPTER 17

ALONE YET NEVER LONELY

"Go ye therefore....Lo, I am with you alway."
—Matthew 28:19–20

F. W. Robertson of Brighton, England, whose masterful sermons ought to be read by every preacher, has a most unique chapter in one of his books on with the loneliness of Christ, in which he indicates that there are two kinds of solitude.

There is what he calls insulation in space, that is, separation caused by distance. Yet there is such a thing as inner consolation, seeing that sympathy can people our solitude with a crowd. A missionary in some lonely outpost is not lonely as he thinks of the loving, praying hearts in the homeland who constantly remember his needs.

Then there is isolation of the spirit, or loneliness of the soul. Paul was left alone in the crowded city of Athens. And one can feel lonely even in the heart of a crowd. F. W. Robertson goes on to show that there are two classes of people, and they meet this loneliness in different ways.

First, we have the self-reliant and self-dependent people, who are firm and unbending, and who, with strong determination, resolve to face their duty alone. The dread of unpopularity and reproach never influences them. They crave no sympathy for their isolation. Elijah, who found himself alone in the wilderness when the court deserted him, sternly faced the false prophets of Baal alone.

Then we have those who must have sympathy and friendship. They tremble at the thought of being left alone, not from any want of courage, but solely because of the intensity of their affection. Jacob was left alone and slept on his way to Padanaram, on the first night away from his father's home. (See Genesis 28:11.) The sympathy he yearned for, however, came in a dream. It is in this class that we can place the Lord Jesus Christ, who not only sympathized with others, but yearned for it himself. "*Will ye also go away?*" (John 6:67). A stern, hard spirit would never have responded the disciples as Christ did: "*I am not alone, because the Father is with me*" (John 16:32).

The Bible is a biography of lonely men and women. Solitude is the narrow gate through which the majority of heaven-born souls must pass.

+ *Abel* was murdered alone. As a man of sacrifice, he had to die the lonely death for his creed.

+ *Enoch* watched the threatening clouds of judgment alone. His vision and prophecy of the flood was unshared by others.

+ *Noah* dared to preach the gospel of righteousness alone, in a corrupt age. In his genealogy, he is spoken of as the only man perfect in his generation.

+ *Abraham*, obedient to the will of God, offered his beloved son of promise on Mount Moriah, alone.

+ *Jacob* wrestled with God alone. His name and nature were changed as "[he] *was left alone*" (Genesis 32:24).

+ *Joseph*, before he could act and reign as the savior of Egypt, had to suffer alone in the pit of rejection.

+ *Moses*, in order to give Israel a revelation of God, had to climb Mount Sinai and face God alone.

+ *Jews*, guilty of disobedience, were cut off from the nations, and for centuries, as a people, they have been isolated from other races.

+ *David* achieved his victory over Goliath alone. His confidence in God was unshared.

+ *Esther* cried, "*If I perish, I perish*" (Esther 4:16) as she sought the presence of the king by herself.

+ *Daniel*, in order to display the power of God, had to meet the hungry lions alone. And "*left alone*" (Daniel 10:8), he received the glorious vision of the divine program of the ages.

+ The *disciples* longed to teach the mysteries of the kingdom and had to get alone with Jesus.

+ *Paul*, before he could bring the gospel to Rome, the proud mistress of his time, had to defy Nero alone.

Likewise, Jesus is ever impressive in His solitariness. He had experiences He could never share with others. Because of who and what He was, He had to spend much time alone. The divine elevation of His character gave Him a loneliness unshared by men. When he was but twelve years of age, loneliness stabbed His heart. His parents could not understand His high thoughts and divine vocation. From His lonely soul came the question, "*Wist ye not that I must be about my Father's business?*" (Luke 2:49).

He also faced loneliness at His home in Nazareth, for those around Him did not believe in who He was. And yet His was not the solitariness of a lonely hermit. It was the solitude amongst a crowd. In "Guilt and Sorrow," Wordsworth wrote,

> And homeless near a thousand homes I stood,
> And near a thousand tables pined and wanted food.

Gethsemane was where Christ ate another morsel alone. There was no sorrow like His sorrow. He had to tread the wine-press alone. Every man must bear his own burden. There are some strange experiences we can never share with others. No stranger dares intermeddle with the agony of your soul.

Calvary found Jesus alone. His disciples had forsaken Him, and although two thieves shared the form of His death, He was alone in the object of His anguish. In that dark hour, He was made to bear the extreme limit of loneliness. He cried out, "*My God, my God, why hast thou forsaken me?*" (Mark 15:34).

> Alone, alone, He bore it all alone;
> He gave Himself to save His own,
> He suffered, bled, and died, alone, alone.[80]

CONSECRATION PRODUCED BY ISOLATION

To be wrapped up in ourselves; to become loveless, unsympathetic, cold, disobliging, and indifferent to the welfare and needs of others; to live in a little world of our own; is to produce

80. Ben H. Price, "Alone," 1914.

a fruitless solitude. People will leave us very much alone if we live for ourselves. On the other hand, there is a loneliness we cannot avoid if we are fully identified with the lonely Christ. The world has little sympathy for divine holiness. Spirituality is very disagreeable to unspiritual people. There is still reproach outside of the camp where Jesus is. So, my friend, you are in good company if you are being spurned, cut off, or made to feel that you are not wanted simply because of your allegiance to Christ. *"Marvel not, my brethren, if the world hate you"* (1 John 3:13).

He invites you to share His loneliness in a world in which He met rejection. This can be shown in several ways:

1. WE ARE CALLED AND BLESSED ALONE

I called him alone, and blessed him.   (Isaiah 51:2)

In the hour of regeneration, God deals with us alone. No two people's spiritual experiences are exactly alike. God deals with us all as individuals. Therefore, let us never try to force another into our own mold.

2. WE ARE LED AND GUIDED ALONE

The LORD alone did lead him.   (Deuteronomy 32:12)

Often, we are influenced by personal motives and considerations or the persuasion of others. Oh, to be led of God no matter how such divine guidance may conflict with our own plans or the desires of others.

3. WE SUFFER AND WEEP ALONE

He sitteth alone and keepeth silence. (Lamentations 3:28)

I watch, and am as a sparrow alone upon the house top.

(Psalm 102:7)

There are tears, sorrows, and separations we cannot share with others. Each enters his Golgotha alone.

4. WE MUST BE CONTENT TO SERVE ALONE

My sister hath left me to serve alone.   (Luke 10:40)

If others leave us high and dry because of our spiritual principles and methods, we must realize that such rejection is part of the price of our identification with Christ. Paul said, *"No man stood with me"* (2 Timothy 4:16). Divine companionship, however, was his: *"The Lord stood with me"* (verse 17).

5. WE HAVE TO PREVAIL WITH GOD ALONE

Jesus went apart to pray and remained there alone. (See Matthew 14:23.) It is He who urges us to shut the door and be alone with God. What do we know of this loneliness? Are we in the company of others too much? The fellowship of saints, blessed though it is, must never be substituted for deep, personal communion with Christ. Such solitude produces a fuller revelation. *"I was left alone, and saw this great vision"* (Daniel 10:8). And amid the solitariness of our witness, we prove that "one with God is always a majority."

THE BLESSEDNESS OF SPIRITUAL SOLITUDE

Alone, we are never lonely. It is the blessed privilege of every child of God to abide in living union with the living Christ, who could say, *"I am not alone, because the Father is with me"* (John

8:29). And how blessed it is to know that we have the joy of sharing heaven's companionship! The dread of isolation that the Savior experienced on Calvary when He cried, "*My God, my God, why hast thou forsaken me?*" (Matthew 27:46; Mark 15:34) will never be repeated by us, seeing that we have the promise, "*I will never leave thee, nor forsake thee*" (Hebrews 13:5).

We have the company of the Father: "*My Father will love him, and we will come unto him, and make our abode with him*" (John 14:23). We have the fellowship of the Son: "*Lo, I am with you alway*" (Matthew 28:20). We have the presence of the Holy Spirit: "*He may abide with you for ever*" (John 14:16). With such a blessed and blissful companionship, why should we be lonely or sigh for friendship? If the circle of our acquaintance is becoming narrower and our so-called friends drop us because of our witness, let us not mourn over our solitude. Victory will be ours if we can sing, along with May Grimes—

> A little sanctuary art Thou to me!
> I am always "at home" on land or sea;
> Alone, yet never lonely now, I prove
> The "hundredfold," Lord Jesus, in Thy love.[81]

Another has pointed out the road to conquest over solitude in these precious lines:

> Alone, yet not alone am I,
> Though in this solitude so drear;
> I feel my Savior always nigh,
> He comes the weary hour to cheer;
> I am with Him, and He with me,
> Even here alone I cannot be.

---

81. E. May Grimes, "A Prayer Sanctuary."

CHAPTER 18

SORROWS AND STARS

"He healeth the broken in heart, and bindeth up their wounds. He telleth the number of the stars; he calleth them all by their names."
—Psalm 147:3–4

One of the unique features of the Bible is its power to combine extremities. It contains a composition of opposites. For example, here are a few that could be traced with profit. The *provision* of God is proven by the fact that He can cover the heavens with clouds, yet provide the beast with food. (See Psalm 147:8–9.) The *Son* of God is spoken of as the mighty God and yet as a babe—a combination of wonderfulness and weakness. (See Isaiah 9:6; Luke 2:12.) The *abode* of God is in highest heaven and yet within the humblest heart. (See Isaiah 57:15.) What extreme dwelling places! The *saint* of God is in the heavenlies and is yet to be loyal as a servant of men. He is spiritual and secular; heavenly and homely. An old writer has said that Ephesians begins in the heavenlies but ends in the kitchen. (See Ephesians 1:3; 6:5.) The *nature* of God has a dual character, where majesty and mercy are happily combined. (See Psalm 147:3–4.) C. H. Spurgeon's comment on this last passage is:

[We must] read the two without a break, and feel the full force of the contrast. From stars to sighs is a deep descent! From worlds to wounds is a distance which only infinite compassion can bridge. Yet he who acts a surgeon's part with wounded hearts, marshals the heavenly host, and reads the muster-roll of suns and their majestic systems. O Lord, it is good to praise thee as ruling the stars, but it is pleasant to adore thee as healing the broken in heart!

What opposites are here happily wedded! Might and meekness, sovereignty and sympathy, glory and grace, stars and sighs, planets and pain, worlds and wounds, brilliant heavens and broken hearts!

THE DIVINE CHARACTER

A close study of the psalmist's manifold description of God will deliver us from a mistaken, distorted, one-sided view of the divine character. We have, in the first place—

1. A TWOFOLD DESCRIPTION OF GOD

He is revealed as the Maker of heavens and the Mender of hearts. Paul exhorts us not to mind high things but condescend to men of low estate. (See Romans 12:16.) God, however, can mind high things and *yet* condescend to men and matters of low estate. On the one hand, we have His greatness, in order that we might be subdued by His mighty power, on the other hand, we have His gentleness, in order that we might submit and surrender to His claim. Lofty transcendence and loving tenderness, then, go hand in hand. God is here seen as the majestic yet merciful One. What a descent from a world of splendor above to the earth of sighs below! Why, this is the story of a Man who, although rich, yet for our sakes became poor! (See 2 Corinthians 8:9.)

2. A TWOFOLD DANGER OF MAN

One common danger of man is to think of God as being far too remote, distant, and detached to evince any concern about us humans. He is like "a happy land" we sing about, "far, far away."[82] He is too infinite to be interested in our earthly lot and lives.

The other danger is to make God too cheap, common, and familiar. We overhear preachers refer to Jesus as a "good sport." Such cheap descriptions are most unbecoming of Him who is the King of Glory. Familiarity of this kind breeds contempt.

If we are taken up exclusively with the thought of the greatness of God as the Architect of the heavens, then we fail to realize His personal care and concern. If, on the other hand, we cheapen Him, forget that He is the lofty One, then we lose sight of His power to act in the great things of life.

A truly spiritual mind combines and harmonizes God's greatness and His grace. Balance is preserved between His loftiness and His love. Each side of His character is given its rightful place. Faith sees Him as the God at hand yet afar off. (See Jeremiah 23:23.) And both aspects of His character meet in Christ, who became the God-man. Deity and humanity flowed in the veins of Him who was ever kingly yet kind.

THE DIVINE COMBINATION

Guided by the Holy Spirit, the psalmist brought the stars and broken hearts together, for although they appear to be

82. Andrew Young, "There Is a Happy Land," 1838.

extremes, they are nevertheless alike. And it is indeed delightful to trace the resemblance of the two.

1. BOTH ARE NUMBERLESS

Stars are without number. (See Genesis 15:5; Hebrews 11:12.) On a clear night, hundreds of stars can be seen by the naked eye. Herschel, with the aid of a powerful telescope, counted 116,000 stars in less than an hour. If we could explore the regions of the sky with a perfect instrument, we might discover one billion stars and beyond an unnumbered host. Thus is it with the sighs of a groaning world. Why, the world is like a vast hospital, with every home a bed! Who can count the broken hearts, sighs, tears, groans, and graves? If we have the stars today, the sorrows will come tomorrow. All may be bright, merry, and peaceful in our circle today; but the very next day, the blinds are drawn, and hearts are crushed and avalanched with unexpected trials.

2. SOME OF BOTH ARE UNDISCOVERED

The magnitude of the heavens is beyond all human calculation and conception, and perhaps beyond the grasp of angelic comprehension. Astronomers are always discovering fresh planets and locating new stars. A gigantic telescope is now being prepared that will penetrate regions of space up to this time unsearched. Thus is it with crushed hearts—the majority of them are hidden from the gaze of man. Their number and causes are secret. The greatest sufferers are the unparaded ones. Smiling faces and outwardly contented lives hide aches and pains and tragedies unheard of. The world will never know how many broken hearts are carried by silent martyrs.

3. BOTH ARE COUNTED BY GOD

Man is unable to count the stars above and the sighs below, but God is able to tell the number of both. He is omniscient in both realms. He who numbers the stars beyond computation is also able to count the hairs of the head. It makes no difference to Him whether it is stars or sobs, constellations or crosses, suffering and bruised hearts, or the starry and brilliant heavens; with God's perfect arithmetic, He is able to count both. So, take courage, faint heart; the world may not know your grief, but God can count all the tiny stars of sorrow twinkling in the sky of your life.

4. BOTH ARE CALLED BY NAMES

God has names for all the stars, some of which are given in Scripture. (See Job 9:9.) Many of them have been named by man. And the naming of the stars by their Creator speaks of a personal interest. What a precious truth this is! He knows the stars by name. Are you not of more value than many stars? You have His Word, *"Fear not...I have called thee by thy name"* (Isaiah 43:1). He knows the street you live on, the number of your house, and the many cares within it. He is one of your circle, or longs to be. He singles you out and lavishes His love upon you as if you alone needed it. He knows! He loves! He cares!

5. BOTH ARE THE COMMON POSSESSION OF ALL

When a poor old woman saw the sea for the first time, she exclaimed, "Thank God for something there's enough of!" Well, God has not been stingy with the stars. And rich and poor alike enjoy them. No one will ever have a monopoly of the heavenly forces. Greedy men corner the necessities of life, but power will never be theirs to fence off the stars and call them their own. Taxes are demanded for all we have below; the stars, however, are still free of tax. It is just so with our griefs, heartbreaks, sin, and graves. No respect is paid to position, wealth, and honor. Suffering comes alike to prince and pauper, saint and sinner.

6. BOTH DIFFER IN MAGNITUDE

Paul reminds us that *"one star differeth from another star in glory"* (1 Corinthians 15:41). Astronomers agree with this fact, for, as they can prove, the brilliant stars studding the sky differ in size, light, and importance. So it is with the sorrows of man—they vary in their nature and number. Conviction of sin, disappointed hopes, heredity, separation, and death are greater for some than for others. It would seem as if some people get through life without a care, while others are loaded with adversity.

7. BOTH PROCLAIM MAN'S LITTLENESS AND FEEBLENESS

Gazing out upon the immensity of the heavens, as the psalmist thought of the sun, moon, and stars, the work of God's fingers, he could not help but exclaim, *"What is man, that thou art mindful of him?"* (Psalm 8:3–4). Why, some of the stars are billions of miles from the earth, so far that if a ball could travel at five hundred miles per hour, it would not traverse the distance in 400,500,000 years, or over seven hundred fifty times the period since creation! Thus it is with the problems of life that are so baffling to our finite understanding. Some of God's providential dealings are just as inexplicable as the mysteries of the stars. We cannot understand the full reason for so many "gimlet holes to let the glory through," as a child called the stars. In the same manner, we must wait for the breaking of the day for an explanation of the many tears we shed.

8. BOTH PRAISE GOD

Earth has no "Hallelujah Chorus" equal to what the heavens produce. Praise Him, ye stars! (See Job 38:7; Psalm 148:3.) How they glorify their Creator!

> Forever singing as they shine,
> "The hand that made us is divine."[83]

It was so with Him who came as the Light of the World. Jesus, who will yet be seen as the Bright and Morning Star, could sing and carry a happy heart. (See Psalm 40:8; Mark 14:26; Numbers 24:17.) Can we glory in our tribulations? Have we songs in the night? Or can it be that sorrow has silenced our song? Have we learned how to fashion a ruby crown out of a rough cross? At midnight, in a dark, damp dungeon, and with bleeding backs, Paul and Silas could sing praises to God! Praises in a prison? Yes, this is what God can do for trusting souls.

9. BOTH ARE FASHIONED BY GOD

God made the stars. They represent the work of His perfect fingers. Man is proud of his achievements, but he has yet to fashion a star. The order, beauty, and magnitude of the stars likewise reveal a mastermind. There was method behind their creation. Thus it is with one's cares and trials. Sometimes it is easy to sing but difficult to believe the words

> Every joy or trial falleth from above,
> Traced upon our dial by the Sun of Love.[84]

It is not hard to believe that God sends our joys. We readily accept the good things of life from His loving hands. But to accept the fact that He also permits our sighs and crushing

---

83. Joseph Addison, "The Spacious Firmament on High," 1712.
84. Frances R. Havergal, "Like a River, Glorious," 1876.

blows in order that our life may become more godlike—that is somewhat difficult. And yet the trial of faith can result in praise. The darker the night, the more dazzling the stars. "Not a single shaft can hit till the God of love sees fit."[85] But the shaft does hit; it is sent forth by the hand of One who cares and who seeks through sorrow to promote His own glory and our eternal good. There is always the "Nevertheless afterward" of chastisement. The noblest life is often the product of sanctified tribulation.

THE DIVINE CONSOLER

The God of the stars is the One we need for our broken hearts. Earthly physicians may be able to heal bruised bodies. Broken hearts, however, are beyond their repair. It is because God is the Maker of stars that He can mend our sorrow. The greater includes the lesser. To God, great things are small, and small things are great. His power as the Creator is available as your Comforter. He can adapt Himself to your need.

Yes, and the broken in heart are placed before the stars. Suffering souls are the Lord's first thought. He is more concerned over the salvation of human lives than the shining of heavenly luminaries. He thinks more of souls than stars. Calvary proves this! The stars cost Him His breath—He spoke and it was done. But souls cost Him His blood—Christ died for us!

> 'Twas great to call a world from naught;
> 'Twas greater to redeem.[86]

Two thoughts emerge from this last aspect of our meditation.

---

85. John Ryland, "The Sovereign Ruler."
86. Samuel Wesley Jr., "The Lord of Sabbath Let Us Praise," 1736.

1. THERE IS NO PHYSICIAN LIKE THE CREATOR

If He knows how to keep the stars in their courses, He understands your case and can manage it. Having fashioned your heart, He knows the balm to apply, seeing that it is His mission to heal. (See Isaiah 61:1; Luke 4:18.) Are you broken in heart? Then look into His face and pray, "O God of the stars, heal these scars of mine! Creator of suns, prove Yourself to be the Cleanser of sins and the Comforter of sorrows!" He will not fail you.

2. HE CAN HEAL THE BROKENHEARTED BECAUSE HIS OWN HEART WAS BROKEN

The Creator became the Crucified One. Jesus traveled from stars to scars. This is why the Lord is so precious. (See Psalm 69:20.) He had to bleed before He could bless. The fingers that helped to fashion the stars were ultimately nailed to a cross. But, having been hurt, He can heal. He has healed many broken hearts. Is He mending yours? You have His promise of His being near to your crushed spirit. (See Psalm 34:18.)

Do you doubt the interest of the almighty One in your life? Have you learned that His greatness guarantees His graciousness; His sovereignty, His sympathy; His power, His pity; His kingliness, His kindness? Is the Lord your healer? Do you allow His majesty as you see it in the star-spangled sky to awe and solemnize you? Have you discovered that He is near enough to soothe and satisfy your aching heart and to save your precious soul? If not, turn to Him now!

What can it mean? Is it aught to him
That the nights are long and the days are dim?
Can he be touched by the griefs I bear,
Which sadden the heart and whiten the hair?

About his throne are eternal calms,
And strong, glad music of happy psalms,
And bliss unruffled by any strife.
How can he care for my little life?

And yet I want him to care for me
While I live in this world where the sorrows be.
When the lights die down from the path I take,
When strength is feeble and friends forsake,
When love and music, that once did bless,
Have left me to silence and loneliness,
And my life-song changes to sobbing prayers,
Then my heart cries out for a God who cares.[87]

87. Marianne Farningham, "He Careth."

CHAPTER 19

ROOTS AND STARS

"I am the root and the offspring of David,
and the bright and morning star."
—Revelation 22:16

To take note of the union of apparent contradictions and the meeting of extremes in the Person and work of our adorable Lord is a fascinating study. Qualities of diverse character are brought together in complete harmony in Him. The best life is, at its best, incomplete and fragmentary. Christ, however, combines the most opposing temperaments and reconciles the diversities of our being. And He can do this, seeing that He is not only a man but Man; that is, our Savior was everything that all men were meant to be. In an ideal character, He embraced all the noble attributes of the human race; all varying yet perfect ideals were blended in perfect unity within the perfect character of Jesus.

His glory is seen in the combination of gentleness yet strength and firmness He exhibited. Womanly graces and manly virtues were wedded into a blissful partnership. The eagle, known as the "king of birds," has not only a stern eye, firm beak, and strong talons that enable it to grip the rock, but also a soft, downy breast where the eaglets nestle for warmth and comfort and safety. Thus is it with Christ. He has kingly majesty yet queenly grace. He is strong yet sympathetic. He is lordly yet loving. And such a harmony of opposites suggests two truths.

1. JESUS IS WITHOUT NARROW LIMITS OF INDIVIDUALITY

When we think of Napoleon, we think of a warrior; of Columbus, a discoverer; of Abraham Lincoln, an emancipator; of Paul, energy; of John, love. Those who are most balanced usually have defects in their qualities. Jesus, however, does not draw some and drive away others due to any oddities, or peculiarities, such as a genius often has. Our Lord had no idiosyncrasies. He was perfectly whole, symmetrical, combining with a remarkable equality all the traits of human life. Therefore, He is adapted to all. He is the garment that fits everybody, yet fits nobody, seeing that He is distinct from all others.

2. JESUS COULD RECONCILE OPPOSITE OFFICES

Christ is the Shepherd, yet the Lamb; the Priest, yet the Sacrifice; the Vine, yet the Branch; the King, yet the Servant. He, Himself, tells us that He is the Root and yet the Bright and Morning Star. There is a world of difference between a root and a star. There is no natural unity between the two. In fact, they are utterly unlike each other. But Christ unites both objects in His own Being. Taken separately, the figures are rich in spiritual significance; taken together, they bring encouragement to our hearts; for in having diversity in Himself, such as roots and stars suggest, we can find all we need in Him who is both the

Root and the Star. Let us trace the teaching underlining this double metaphor.

LOCAL YET UNIVERSAL

The root is local; it is embedded in a single spot. It grows from a seed in certain soil and must stay where it finds nourishment. The star, on the other hand, is universal; it sheds its light and influence upon the world. Whether man is in a crowded city, a lonely glen, or amid the solitude of an ocean, he can lift up his eyes to heaven and be comforted by the shining Star.

Roots, then, grow in one place and have a fixed, definite locality. Stars, on the other hand, are the joy of all localities. Their brilliance is for the world. Thus it is with Christ, our Lord. Born in Bethlehem, He grew up in Nazareth, and in the days of His flesh, He never traveled beyond the Holy Land. Yet today He is the Light of the World. As a root out of a dry ground, He now has a universal radiance. Go to dark Africa, and you will find Him there; the frozen North and India's coral strand both hold His followers. Although in the days of His flesh, Jesus Christ, as David's Son and Lord, was rooted in the rich soil of Palestine and admired by only a few, He now shines with a light serene as the Bright and Morning Star upon millions of adoring souls.

And such a fact constitutes Jesus, the perfect One. Although He came of Jewish stock, He is not limited to the narrow bounds of nationality. We have racial peculiarities and prejudices. Take, for example, the Jew. Why, he is a Jew always and everywhere. But all nations accept Christ, seeing that He is *"the desire of all nations"* (Haggai 2:7). A solution for racial problems, then, is the presentation of Christ in His fullness. And once a nation receives Him, it sees Jesus through its own eyes. A further feature of the gospel is that Christ can be my personal Savior and Lord, despite the color of my skin and the peculiarities of my being.

UNKNOWN YET KNOWN

Looking again at the apocalyptic figures, we can discern a union between the secret and the seen; the hidden and the revealed. A root is an object concealed from observation. Whether just under the surface or deep in the earth, roots shun the light and exist in the darkness below. A star, however, is for all to see. On the brightest day, a buried root cannot be seen, but on the darkest night, the evening star twinkles brightly.

Christ is unique in that He combines the known and the unknown. *"The darkness and the light are both alike to thee"* (Psalm 139:12). As a root, He is hidden in glory and buried in your heart and mine. Yet He cannot be hidden. If He is hidden in our lives as a root, then through our lives, the radiance of His presence will be revealed in some way or other.

And, further, Christ is known yet unknown. While there is much that we can see of His glory and majesty and understand of His grace and power, He is still beyond human comprehension. There are mysteries in Him that man can never fathom, aspects of His character beyond human ken. We can walk in His light as He is the Star yet never penetrate the roots of His deity, wisdom, and fullness.

EARTHLY YET HEAVENLY

Roots and stars, belonging as they do to different worlds, suggest that Jesus is a citizen of both worlds. A root is a common child of earth and rest where the feet of toilers tread and lovers walk and children play. The root is the part of a plant fastened to earth. A star, on the other hand, has its dwelling in the solitary heights of heaven. It is beyond human reach. It is conspicuous among the glories of the sky.

Extreme locations meet in Christ. As the Root and Offspring of David, He came from the royal house. He was the Root of Jesse (see Isaiah 11:10) and the Root of David (see Revelation 5:5). Human descent and true humanity were His. He had a human mother; He required a baby's clothing and care; He toiled, suffered, and wept as a man. Like the tribe of Judah from which He came, He took "root downward." And yet amid His earthly life, He manifested the shining, lofty brilliance of deity. Although from heaven, He ever remained in heaven. (See John 3:13.) He was not so heavenly that He could be of no earthly use, nor too earthly to be of no heavenly use. He balanced both worlds in His adorable person.

Such a combination brings hope and comfort to our hearts, seeing that we need the continual assistance of this heavenly, earthly Friend. We are all like roots. The majority of us have to live out our days in some fixed spot. Some are planted, grow, die, and are buried within the same locality. Our days are filled with common duties and ministries of earth. Life develops, like a root, amid things of earth. Yet the glory of the commonplace can be ours. Our spirits can shine as stars; we can live in the heavenlies. A radiance not of earth can surround our life and path. Some are all root—of the earth, earthly. Others are all stars—they live in the clouds. Harmony, however, must reign between roots and stars.

Buried amid things of earth, we have by our side the Root and the Offspring of David. As the Man Christ Jesus, He is touched with the feeling of our infirmity. But as the Bright and Morning Star, He seeks to fill our common, ordinary life with light supernal. May He enable us to have more starry brilliance about our lives, counteracting thereby much of the earthiness that clings to us as roots!

HUMAN YET DIVINE

A further application of the opposite metaphors we are considering brings us to the truth of our Lord's dual nature. A root is planted by the hand of man, grows on the earth, and develops under the care of the gardener. Roots are produced by man. A star is of a different order. It is planted in the heavens by a divine hand. Stars are created by God.

In Christ, deity and humanity were fused together into the perfect whole. He was God in the flesh. In His condescension, He became the Root and Offspring of David. He commenced His human years with a cradle of straw and ended it in a well-spiced grave. No one can dispute the human, historic Christ, and there are some who know Him only after life in the flesh. To them, He is never more than a root.

But Jesus was God's Son as well as Mary's Child; He was the Mighty God as well as the Babe wrapped in swaddling clothes; the Star of heaven as well as the Root of earth. The star that the wise men saw and were guided by was the symbol of the starry deity of Him who was born a babe. To Jews, Jesus was only another Jew; but to the Spirit-anointed eyes of Peter, He was the Christ, the Son of the living God.

TEMPORARY YET ABIDING

The arresting figures of speech Jesus employed to describe Himself suggest transient and eternal qualities. Roots are a temporary thing. Seed is sown and gradually sends out its tiny roots; growing amid the darkness of the soil, it serves its purpose and then perishes and dies. (See Job 14:8.) Stars are different; they abide. The stars shining on Adam and Eve in beautiful Eden have shone also on billions of people since their time. Stars never change, although we certainly know them better now than we did before, for astronomers have opened for us the starry heavens.

Roots, then, come and go; but the stars go on forever. Roots are temporary; stars, permanent and perpetual. So it is with Christ. As the Root, He had a temporary manifestation, remaining only some thirty-three years on earth. He came, lived His life, crossed the stage of time, and then died. The place that knew Him ceased to know Him as the Man of Nazareth. But when men buried Him as the Root, He did not decay. He arose, and is alive forevermore. And before long, all the redeemed will behold Him as the Bright and Morning Star.

JEWISH YET CHRISTIAN

It would seem as if the two metaphors before us express the twofold relationship exhibited in the book of the Revelation. As the Root and Offspring of David, there is the assertion of Christ's connection with Israel in royalty. He came as the King of the Jews but was rejected as David's Lord and Heir. Yet the time will come when He will be seen as the promised Messiah, the King of Israel. When He returns to earth, Israel, looking upon Him who was pierced, will function once more as the long diverted channel of divine grace to the nations of the world.

As the Bright and Morning Star, Jesus is associated with His church. Before the tribulation and millennium eras, He will appear as the Star to His bride. As the Sun of Righteousness, He will arise upon Israel with midday splendor. But as the morning star appears before the midday sun, so Jesus will first appear as the Morning Star for His redeemed. The morning star is the harbinger of day. Now, from the heights, He watches His church toiling against contrary winds, but soon on some starlit morning, He will come again to take His own to the eternal land of light and love. But until the Bright and Morning Star bursts upon the darkness of the world, let us hitch the little wagon of our lives to Him who is the hidden Star. Then, although we live out our lives as roots on earth, we will yet shine as lights in the world, and thereafter shine as stars forever.

CHAPTER 20

GOLDEN LAMPS AND OLIVE TREES

"Behold a candlestick all of gold...and two olive trees by it."
—Zechariah 4:2–3

The entire ministry of Zechariah was exercised among the remnant of Jews after their seventy-year Babylonian captivity. God granted him wondrous visions, eight in all, calculated to meet the special need of the feeble, struggling colony at that time. Each vision was specially adapted to the trials and circumstances of the emancipated people. One must be careful to understand the primary application of the visions. Their value has a broader significance than their original purport, as we discover in the vision of the golden candlestick, the golden lamps, and the olive trees.

Some of the visions can teach us the great doctrine of justification by grace and righteousness through faith. Other visions teach of sanctification and power for service—life and light in the Holy Spirit. The fifth vision, which we will look at here in more detail, is vitally associated with some of the other visions, all of which are taken up with Joshua, the high priest, who was the one the Lord freely justified, gave a change of raiment to, and plucked as a brand from the fire.

THE OUTLINE OF THE FIFTH VISION

[Zechariah] *said, I have looked, and behold a candlestick all of gold, with a bowl upon the top of it, and his seven lamps thereon, and seven pipes to the seven lamps, which are upon the top thereof: and two olive trees by it, one upon the right side of the bowl, and the other upon the left side thereof.... Then* [the angel] *spake unto* [Zechariah], *saying, This is the word of the* LORD *unto Zerubbabel, saying, Not by might, nor by power, but by my spirit, saith the* LORD *of hosts.*

(Zechariah 4:2–3, 6)

It is essential to have before us a clear outline of the salient features of this remarkable fifth vision, or dream. The vision, being one, suggests perfection, completion. The number seven, the perfect number, is used three times in this vision—seven lamps, seven pipes, seven eyes. (See Zechariah 4:2, 10.) The two general divisions are:

1. THE GOLDEN LAMP

The various particulars given of the beautiful lampstand are worthy of study and have, as we will see, deep, spiritual significance. We know that the lampstand

+ Was made of all gold.

+ Was composed of seven lights or lamps.

+ Had a bowl, or reservoir, at its top to store oil.

+ Had seven pipes leading from the bowl to the seven lights.

+ Was fed continually with oil with no human aid.

In the wondrous, exquisite mechanism of this lampstand, there were no oil cans in ministering hands, no clumsy attendants. It was fed directly by the two olive trees as they poured the necessary oil into the bowl.

2. THE OLIVE TREES

The outstanding particulars of this section of the vision are clear.

+ *Position*. At the top of the lampstand, one tree was on the right side of the bowl and the other was on the left.

+ *Nature*. They were olive trees, producing golden oil (typical of fruitfulness in our witness for God).

+ *Branches*. There were two main golden pipes that fed the seven lamps.

+ *Number*. Two is the number suggesting unity in service and testimony. *"If two of you shall agree on earth as touching any thing that they shall ask, it shall be done for them of my Father which is in heaven"* (Matthew 18:19).

THE INTERPRETATION OF THE FIFTH VISION

There are three outstanding interpretations of Zechariah's vision that we can profitably consider.

1. THE HISTORICAL INTERPRETATION

The remnant of Israel was assailed by the strong and mighty king of Persia. An army with *"force and power"* (Ezra 4:23) came against them and put an end to their noble activities. In the progress of the word of restoration, they were arrested. Then this vision was sent to them to encourage their downcast hearts and to provide them with strength, consolation, and, eventually, victory.

In response to all of this, there was the echo of the divine throne in answer to man's rage, indicated by the phrase "not by force and power" (See Zechariah 4:6.) The forces battling against the Jews had left God out of their calculations. So, Zechariah awakes from sleep and, with his mental powers quickened, makes sense of the vision and records the vivid impression. Then he assures the harassed remnant of the secret victory they would have in Christ. Their source of power would not be outward or human but secret and divine.

As we follow more fully the historical interpretation of this seventh vision, we see these aspects:

THE GOLDEN LAMP

Without doubt, Israel, because of its Jewish service and polity, became the channel by which the revelation of God was given to the heathen world around. The lamp represents a type of Jewish theocracy. In past generations, this chosen nation was the depository of divine truth, life, and light. She showed forth God's salvation.

She was golden. She was divinely called and was God's own peculiar, precious treasure—a holy nation. She was wonderfully illuminated, guided, and sustained as miraculously as was the lamp Zechariah saw. She existed to give light to other nations, from whom God had separated her.

THE TWO OLIVE TREES

Scripture describes the two olive trees as *"the two anointed ones, that stand by the Lord of the whole earth"* (Zechariah 4:14).

The priesthood and the kingdom were the two institutions appointed as the instruments through which God caused His Spirit to flow in the old dispensation. Joshua and Zerubbabel symbolized these two institutions. Joshua the high priest represented the priesthood; Zerubbabel the king represented the kingdom. The two figures are mentioned together because they embodied the united service and testimony of the anointed Priest and Prince, whose effectiveness was brought about by holiness and power. Further, although their supply of sustenance was unseen, they, as God's channels, were seen. While God can act independently, He deigns to use men to convey His salvation to other men. While He alone can save souls, He seldom saves them without using human instruments.

2. THE PROPHETIC INTERPRETATION

The visions of Zechariah are rich in their prophetic significance, and in the fifth vision, we have a prophecy of the last days of Gentile dominion. The golden lamp stand speaks of the remnant who seeks to shed light abroad during the dark days of the tribulation period. The two olive trees can stand for the two witnesses (see Revelation 11:3–13)—the counterparts of Joshua and Zerubbabel. These two are marked by power. (See Zechariah 4:6 and Revelation 11:3–4.) But the pair also points forward to the kingdom age, the millennial era that Zechariah mentions. (See Zechariah 6:12–13.) Then the golden lamp will be prominent, and the whole earth will be filled with light and glory. The two olive trees personify Christ who will be a Priest upon His throne.

3. THE SPIRITUAL INTERPRETATION

As we come to apply the truth of the vision to our own hearts and lives, may unction be ours to comprehend the deep spiritual truth it has for us.

THE GOLDEN LAMP

The universal church was created by the Lord to function as He does as the Light of the World. Individual members of the church must shine as lights in the world. Their duty to witness is clearly expressed: *"Let your light so shine before men"* (Matthew 5:16).

The lamp was made of solid gold, a precious metal that is an emblem of deity. We have been made partakers of the divine nature. We can never act as light bearers if the divine Light is not within us.

The lamp was the only light of the temple. As there were no windows, natural light could not enter. All light comes from God. The Bible, inspired and illuminated by the Holy Spirit, contains the only authentic knowledge of God, salvation, eternity, and ourselves. The light of reason, philosophy, and learning are windows created by man.

The lamp was simply a light bearer. It did not produce light; it only bore it. We dare not reveal our own wisdom, goodness, and power. As lamps, we exist for one thing, namely, to manifest the all-sufficiency of the Savior.

The lamp's seven golden pipes can typify the opening up of all the avenues of our being to receive the divine supply of oil. The lamp's two main golden avenues speak of prayer and faith by which we can appropriate all God has for us. The lamp's reservoir suggests a heart which does not hoard the oil but makes use of it as it is received. If we try to economize on any blessing or gift of God, it soon disappears. We must use it or lose it. If we would be always fresh and full, burning and shining lights, then we must keep on using what is given. When we give to our capacity, God not only replenishes the supply in His own wonderful, secret way but enlarges our capacity to use even more.

THE TWO OLIVE TREES

Here we come to the sources of supply. The two living trees, whose ripening fruit continually pressed out by unseen hands or without pressure of man, remind us of Christ and the Holy Spirit.

The Lord Jesus is on the right side, the heavenly side of our spiritual life. Paul reminds us that we are seated with Him in heaven. The Holy Spirit is on the left side, the earthly side of our life and witness. He is the direct agent between our hearts and the Lord's.

The two branches, the princely pair of advocates, point to the advocacy of Christ in heaven with the Father and the advocacy of the Holy Spirit from the Father, who is within us that we do not sin. If we do sin, the blood of the Advocate on high pleads the efficacy of His blood on our behalf. All that God gives to us comes through these two divine channels. With an Advocate on each side of us, how can we, as the children of God, be lost? It is from the Savior and the Spirit, these two who are one yet distinct, that the believer draws both his salvation and spirituality. All the golden oil of grace is supplied by these two anointed Ones who stand by the Lord on earth.

The lamps were filled with oil, and oil typifies the Spirit who gives light as well as life. His personal indwelling is our golden oil. In the Hebrew, the two anointed Ones are given as sons of oil. We have the oil of our Substitute in heaven and the oil of the Spirit in our heart.

There is no mention of the lamps' source. They were fed in an unseen way, without human conveyance. Just so, there is nothing whatever human about our spiritual supply. It is all of grace, lest any man should boast. (See Ephesians 2:8–9.) The lamps always shone because of the silent, secret supply of oil.

The fire on the ancient Jewish altar had to be kept burning constantly. If the pipes of our being are always open to the unperceived flow of oil, our light will never go out.

The lamps were fed by two pipes. Ask in faith and you will receive. Believing prayer and unwavering faith are the two pipes we must keep open. On the right side is prayer—perfect contact with Him who dwells above. On the left side is faith, which leads us to prove Him on the earthward side.

THE STRENGTH OF THE VISION

Daniel speaks of being strengthened by the vision he received. Likewise, Zechariah's vision strengthened him and led him to victory. It is profitable to look at the good that came out the vision and then relate it to our own lives as we appropriate the oil, the source of a Spirit-filled life.

1. THE REMOVAL OF OBSTACLES

How full of spiritual truth is the command *"O great mountain…become a plain"* (Zechariah 4:7). Often in Scripture a mountain is figurative of colossal difficulties. Zechariah uses it to describe a great and mighty nation; one, however, that God is able to humble. He can bring the mighty down from their seat. All of us have mountains of difficulties, but they can all flow down at His presence. Prayer and faith can remove mountains. Our mistake is that we try to climb them. But in the authority and power of God, we can command our mountain to become a plain. *"Be thou removed"* (Matthew 21:21; Mark 11:23). The word to Zerubbabel was, *"Not by might, nor by power, but by my spirit, saith the Lord of hosts"* (Zechariah 4:6). The Spirit, of course, manifests might and power. But it is different in quality from the might of man and the power of the flesh. The forces we are to harness are not earthly but heavenly.

2. THE GLORY OF GOD

What triumph there is in the phrase *"He shall bring forth the headstone thereof with shoutings, crying, Grace, grace unto it"* (Zechariah 4:7). The headstone, or capstone, is a sign of the completion of a building. We are complete in Him who is the Head of His church, and we cannot do anything but cry grace unto Him, and by the Spirit, magnify Him in our lives.

3. THE COMPLETION OF SERVICE

In connection with Zerubbabel's restoration of the temple, we read, *"His hands shall also finish it"* (Zechariah 4:9). In spite of demons and men, adverse circumstances and earthly forces, there will be no broken columns, no unfinished roof. God knows how to deal drastically with those who interfere with a Spirit-inspired building operation. Human effort, impulse, and ambition can be weak and unstable. It is only through the Spirit's energy that we will be able to say with the Savior, *"I have finished the work which thou gavest me to do"* (John 17:4).

4. THE WORKS OF RIGHTEOUSNESS

Although the rebuilding might progress slowly, the people were not "to despise the day of small things" (see Zechariah 4:10), for although the work was slow, it was sure. *"They shall... see the plummet"* (verse 10). A plummet is a symbol of righteousness. A builder places his plumb against the wall to see if it is upright and perfect. Our lives are to be straight and our labor upright. There must be nothing crooked, out of plumb, in our ways and methods. We must build on scriptural foundations and shun compromising to the ways of the world.

5. THE USE OF FEEBLE INSTRUMENTS

It would seem as if there is a reference to the feeble, depressed condition of the returned captives as they faced the gigantic task of rebuilding the temple. The words are set in the form of a prohibition: "Let none despise the day of small things." (See Zechariah 4:10.) What an assuring message this is for our weak and timid hearts! God often takes the weak things to confound the mighty in accomplishing His purposes.

6. THE CLEAR SKY

What comfort there is in the statement "*The eyes of the* Lord, *which run to and fro through the whole earth*" (Zechariah 4:10). Nothing is hidden from Him. The week of seven days has been called "The seven eyes of Deity"—one eye for each day. This teaches the perfect oversight and providence of God on every day of the week and every week of the year, no matter where we may travel through the earth. "*Thou God seest me*" (Genesis 16:13). For the Spirit-filled person, life is one of clear skies with the eyes of the Lord ever upon him.

CHAPTER 21

PEACE AND SWORDS

"On earth peace."
—Luke 2:14

*"Suppose ye that I am come to give peace on earth?
I tell you, Nay; but rather division."*
—Luke 12:51

"He that hath no sword, let him sell his garment, and buy one."
—Luke 22:36

"Put up thy sword into the sheath."
—John 18:11

The verses quoted appear to be contradictory, but a brief consideration of them removes the apparent discrepancy. Suppose we look at them in order, viewing them in the light of their contexts.

PEACH ON EARTH

In the Revised Version, this second clause in the angelic chorus is joined to the third and reads, *"On earth peace among men in whom he is well pleased"* (Luke 2:14 RV) or, "Among men of good courage," as the words are translated in the margin. The birth of Christ did not bring much peace to the earth in His own time. The designation Prince of Peace is a prophetic one and refers to a coming age, when *"the government shall be upon his shoulder"* (Isaiah 9:6) and there will be no end *"of the increase of his government and peace"* (verse 7). Since man's fall into sin, the mass of mankind has been at enmity with God and with one another, and the scourge of war has continued through the centuries. Christ's first advent did not correct this sorry state.

Generally, the multitudes are not *"men with whom he is pleased"* (Luke 2:14 RSV), nor "men of good pleasure." (See Romans 8:7; Titus 3:3.) The poet has reminded us that "war must be while men are what they are."[88] Samuel Butler, poet of the sixteenth century, expressed it:

> Bloody wars at first began,
> The artificial plague of man,
> That from his own invention rise,
> To scourge his own iniquities.[89]

1. I AM NOT COME TO GIVE PEACE ON EARTH

The initial mission of the incarnation was to open up the way whereby the sinner, at enmity with God, might be at peace with Him. This Jesus accomplished by His death and

---

88. William James Bailey, *Festus*, 1839.
89. Samuel Butler, "Satire upon the Weakness and Misery of Man."

resurrection when He became our peace and provided for all who were estranged from God because of their sin. *"For it pleased the Father that in* [Christ] *should all fulness dwell...having made peace through the blood of his cross"* (Colossians 1:19–20). But when He said, "I came not to give peace on earth" (see Luke 12:51), Jesus was referring to the inevitable divisions that accepting Him as Savior and Lord would produce. He emphasized this fact when He spoke of the five people in one home who were divided because of His claims. *"A man's foes shall be they of his own household"* (Matthew 10:36). The gospel is represented as a decomposing, dissolving force that causes separation and disunion in families, fostering discord between the nearest and dearest relations.

Such an unhappy division is not directly caused by His coming, but it is an inevitable consequence. The cause of such is the corruption of human nature, the enmity that is excited by purity, and the opposition that righteousness provokes. When a family member in an ungodly home is saved and goes all out for Christ, friction, animosity, and division result. These divisions remain unless or until the rest of the family is converted.

2. HE THAT HATH NO SWORD, BUY ONE

As we are to find, these words of our Lord are to be taken figuratively, not literally. In John's gospel, we read that Christ rebuked Peter for using a sword to defend Him. (See John 18:11.) The Master plainly taught that He did not want His servants to fight as men of the world do, for His cause should never be promoted nor defended by the use of material force or arms. (See John 18:36.) Paul reminded us that *"the weapons of our warfare are not carnal"* (2 Corinthians 10:4). The noble words of Whittier fittingly express the Christian attitude—

In God's own might
We gird us for the coming fight,
And, strong in Him whose cause is ours
In conflict with unholy powers,
We grasp the weapons He has given—
The Light, the Truth, and Love of Heaven.[90]

We now come to examine more fully the import of our Lord's seemingly contradictory demand about weapons of war. Have you bought your sword yet? Jesus told His disciples that He came not to send peace but a sword, and that if they had no swords, they were to sell their garments and buy such instruments of war. (See Matthew 10:34; Luke 22:36.)

Sell your garments and buy swords. Surely these are strange words to come from the lips of the Prince of Peace through whose influence and evangel the world will yet beat its swords into plowshares! Of course, we are not to take our Lord's word about garments and swords as literally as the disciples did when "*they said, Lord, behold, here are two swords*" (Luke 22:38). Responding to the offer of material weapons, the Master said, "*It is enough*" (verse 38), implying thereby not that two swords were sufficient to fight with but that He had something else in mind, which His disciples failed to understand.

The reply of Christ was spoken in irony. When we desire to waive a subject, we say, "It's enough!" It is used in this way in this narrative. "It is a sigh of the God-man," a powerful writer reminds us, "over all violent measures meant to further His cause." His disciples wanted to trust in swords; they believed that the time would come when they would sorely need them. Christ's rebuke of Peter, however, proves that He did not require swords in His defense. "*Put up again thy sword into his place: for*

---

all they that take the sword shall perish with the sword" (Matthew 26:52). All of Christ's assembly must know that He does not save with sword and spear. (See 1 Samuel 17:47.)

The inference of the passage is very clear to the spiritual mind. Our Lord is simply saying that the days are coming when His disciples will find themselves in daily conflict with worldly forces. Before long, they will have to fight against the wild beasts of hatred, envy, trial, apostasy, and antagonism of a Christless world. In this conflict, they will require all the strength they can command, and He will be there with them, urging them to be ready to endure hardship as His good soldiers. His word about selling garments and buying swords warns them to be fully prepared for the terrific onslaught awaiting them after His ascension. There are two thoughts emerging from our consideration of our Lord's militant message: the foes we face and the cost of the sword.

THE FOES WE FACE

It is clear that the Master is warning His people that the life to which He calls them is not a picnic but a war. He came not to send peace but a sword! There are those in theological circles who cry, "Peace at any price!" And the price they pay is a sinful silence regarding their position in fundamental matters. But for the true believer, there can never be any peace in an atmosphere of Modernism. Because of his allegiance to the Lord, he must be willing to be stripped of all that he holds dear and, standing with the sword of truth in his hand, use it effectively against all his foes.

Beloved, we are not true to the Captain of our salvation if the element of battle is lacking. How can we, how dare we, be silent when there is waging a daily war against seen and unseen foes? Oh, when will we discover that life is not about sitting down in a comfortable drawing room, joining in a fashionable parade, or aimlessly sauntering down the street of time; life is about daily struggling and engaging in warfare against sin and Satan. There's a war to be won, and it's time we all enlisted! There are foes to face, a sword to wield, scars to wear, and a crown to win.

1. THERE ARE EXTERNAL FOES

At the end of his warfare, Paul, that doughty fighter and warrior, could triumphantly exclaim, *"I have fought a good fight"* (2 Timothy 4:7). And if we would come to our end with the same paean of victory, then we must know the full strength of the foes we face.

ADVERSE CIRCUMSTANCES

It is a struggle to win success and to gain a position of comfort and influence. Multitudes of young people realize that life is a battle. It is hard work though and through, especially at first, when one's feet begin to climb the ladder. If young people desire to succeed in these competitive days, they must be willing to sacrifice many legitimate things for a sword. There is no royal road to success. Men are not carried to the skies on flowery beds of ease. The biographies of the famous are full of stories of hardship, poverty, and trial willingly endured for the sake of success.

> The heights by great men reached and kept
> Were not attained by sudden flight,
> But they, while their companions slept,
> Were toiling upward in the night.[91]

---

91. Henry Wadsworth Longfellow, "The Ladder of St. Augustine," stanza 10.

THE REBELLIOUS WORLD

Our present world is under the domination of a usurper. The devil is the god of this world. Since the fall of man, the world has been a vast battlefield; the climax of the battle was reached at Calvary. When Christ died, He gathered together all the power of sin, death, and Satan and spoiled his principality. The cross robbed hell's rebels of their vaunted authority. By His death, Christ struck a blow that shattered the enemy's kingdom. And faith appropriates that victory!

The world, however, is still hostile to God; it is no friend to grace. The friend of the world is the enemy of God! So, if we are hated by the world, we are not to marvel. For the child of God, the world offers tribulation. He is treated as the offscouring of all things. Go out and live for God as you should, and you will soon become a target for a satanic world to fire at. Opposition will come to you from avowed foes, hostile friends, and cynical critics. As you earnestly contend for the faith, you will learn what it is to valiantly resist rebellious forces, even in the religious world.

2. THERE ARE INTERNAL FOES

Every man's heart is a veritable battlefield upon which bloodless conflicts are waged against the evil propensities of the old, natural life. Each of us forms a combination of the angel and the beast! Noble aspirations and dark passions are in deadly combat within. The flesh lusts against the Spirit; the Spirit fights against the flesh. And these inward spiritual conflicts tremendously influence our lives. Defeat within means defeat everywhere! Internal defeat means external disaster and eternal loss. The Grecian philosopher, we are told, compared man's inner life to a chariot in which two horses stood side by side. The one was a good horse, nobly trained, and answered to the slightest touch of the rein. It was ever obedient to the will of the driver. The other was a bad horse, ill-disciplined, and was always bent on the defeat of the skill and purpose of the charioteer as he sought to guide the chariot.

Such a philosophy illustrates the warring principles of good and evil. If we are led and controlled by the firm, victorious hand of Christ, progress is ours. The wild steed can never be self-conquered. To our shame, we know what it is to be borne along by the bad horse. Dragged down and humiliated, however, we come to sing, *"Thanks be to God, which giveth us the victory through our Lord Jesus Christ"* (1 Corinthians 15:57)!

3. THERE ARE INFERNAL FOES

We are slow to realize that the struggle we are engaged in is a greater one than that in which the objective is money or fame or victory over circumstances. Success in the good fight we are in means winning an incorruptible crown. We have enlisted in a holy war against unholy forces. The keenest conflict is within the spiritual realm. Satan, demons, and evil influences are the subtle foes we wrestle against. (See Ephesians 6.) And such a conflict is becoming keener and tenser, as the devil knows his time is running out. Owing to the liberation of apostate forces, the warfare of the believer is more intense than it was fifty years ago. Christian soldiers today need a sterner resistance and keener vigilance than the warriors of the past century.

THE COST OF THE SWORD

Coming to the weapons the Lord would have us wield against our foes, we understand, of course, that the sword He refers to is not a glittering one such as Peter used in defense of his Master. Spiritual victories can only be achieved by the use of spiritual weapons.

> The cause of God is holy,
> And it useth holy things.

Although battles on the spiritual battlefield are bloodless, they are not without sacrifice. The seriousness of the conflict is shown by the sacrifices it demands, and the cost by the weapons of truth, faithfulness, and holiness that are wielded. By our Lord's mention of a sword, we are to understand the effective witness in life and service that honors Him. The selling of our garments symbolizes the price we must pay to be such a witness.

1. THE SYMBOL OF DISOBEDIENCE

The first reference to garments is found in Genesis 3:7, where our first parents sewed fig leaves together and made themselves aprons. The presence of clothes, then, is an evidence of sin. Had there been no disobedience, there would have been no garments. Before they sinned, Adam and Eve were naked yet not ashamed. Clothed with the garment of innocency and the light of purity, they were beautiful to behold. The glory of God covered their bodies, but it vanished, as it did from the temple in Israel's day. Disobedience destroyed this covering of glory, and with nakedness confronting them, our first parents made garments to cover the body.

To sell a garment, then, means that we must part with all phases of disobedience. We can never win through unless we are prepared to part with all antagonism to God. Fighting power can never be ours if we continue to disobey the Lord. The cost of a sword is absolute yieldedness to the will of God.

Furthermore, to go without garments means to be in a condition of nakedness. Perhaps we are not victorious simply because we are too well clad with the garments of self-righteousness and self-glory. Fancied greatness robs us of our sword. If we would be victorious in life, then we must realize our spiritual nakedness. Well might we pray, "O Lord, teach me how to sell the garments of self-effort, self-will, and self-pride. I am so haughty, so conceited over what I know and can do. Strip me in order to fight Your battles."

2. THE SYMBOL OF LUXURY

Think of the wealth that is lavished on clothing our bodies. Clothing seems to be all many deluded souls live for. You can tell a man by the clothes he wears. If he is immaculately dressed, you can assume he occupies a high position in life. Fine feathers make fine birds—but not fine soldiers. Flowing garments are a hindrance to fighters, as young David proved. He realized that victory did not depend on his show but on having the right weapons, so he parted with Saul's garments.

And if we would claim a kingdom for the Master, we must learn how to dispense with life's luxuries. Many things may be harmless and legitimate in themselves; lawful yet not expedient for good soldiers of Jesus Christ. If we would help other baffled and beaten souls less strong to win through, we must willingly abstain from what impedes their progress.

Christ emptied Himself. And the price of a sword of victory is the surrender of some garment of luxury. Think of the joys and pleasure our Lord had in heaven. Yet He renounced them all in order that He might teach us how to wield the sword of the Spirit.

3. THE SYMBOL OF COMFORT

Those who wear soft clothing are in king's houses, but John the Baptist did not associate with such people. The fact that he was a separated man was revealed in the clothes he wore and in the place he lived.

People do not wear clothes primarily to be attractive, although some might; they wear them to protect themselves from climate of our country—to keep out the cold and rain and snow. Children who are ill clad evoke our sympathy. Comfortable clothing, then, is a valuable asset. The prophet speaks of durable clothing (see Isaiah 23:18), and durability should be considered more important than mere fashion.

The application at this point is not far to seek. Selling the garments means that we must be prepared to part with many comforts for Christ's sake. What things are gain must be counted as loss! (See Philippians 3:8.) Perhaps your defeat can be traced to the fact that you are too comfortable. Have you ever made yourself uncomfortable for His dear sake? Do you know what it is to sacrifice comfort for His cause? The Good Samaritan did without the comfort of riding. He gave his beast to a half-dead sufferer and willingly walked over the Jericho road. We have learned a wonderful art if we know how to do without many things for Christ's sake.

Alas, it is here that we can trace the weakness in Christian service. We live too much in the center of ourselves. We have lost the meaning of that blood-red sacrifice. We consider our own ease and comfort too much. True, we are soldiers—but fireside ones; the element of battle is lacking.

The garment of comfort was the one Jesus sold. This is why we read about Him being wearied by His journey and of His having nowhere to lay His head. If the Christless multitudes around are to be won for God, then there will need to be fewer comfortable soldiers in His army.

> We are not here to play, to dream, to drift;
> We have hard work to do and loads to lift;
> Shun not the struggle: face it, 'tis God's gift.[92]

4. THE SYMBOL OF RESPECTABILITY

The garment is also the badge of propriety and respectability. Clothes form a necessary covering because of sin. A person insufficiently clothed is an outrage to public decency. Modern modes of dressing often shock one's propriety. Nudism is a satanic device whereby immoral forces are strengthened in the world. What great need there is to emphasize the Pauline injunction regarding the wearing of modest apparel!

The vital application, however, is not far to seek. There are times when, in the battle of righteousness, we are compelled to cast away the garment of propriety. For the truth's sake, we may be deemed improper! We must be ready to sacrifice the respectable, well-ordered ways of society and denomination, and adopt an attitude somewhat contrary to accustomed decorum. And surely the time has come when it is necessary to shock some people into grace. To turn the world upside down will mean scrapping religious pride and ecclesiastical fussiness. Hugh Price Hughes once declared, "We Christians must make ourselves a public nuisance until we have put down every other nuisance."

Generations ago, British sailors used to strip to the waist when they went into action against a foe. And stripping in the spiritual conflict makes for victory! The time for tearing off the garment of respectability, which is often another name for snobbery, has come. The tragic need of the lost world and of an

92. Maltbie D. Babcock, "Be Strong," 1901.

apostate church demands that we stand out as fools for Christ's sake. We have become too stiff, cold, regular, proper, and proud to fight the Lord's battles. One has a great vision of the possibilities of victory in all kinds of service if only the Lord's people are willing to die to their reputation as the Master Himself did. Defending the truth may mean the surrender of a church, a denomination, or a career. Devotion to conscience and principle may occasion much impoverishment. But if our hands are to grip the sword, then our garments must go.

Let us hear the conclusion of the whole matter. To do battle is our duty and will be until we reach heaven where all is bliss. While here in the fight of faith, we must be ready to renounce all those things, habits, and desires that hinder a fuller victory. We are impressed by the example of the divine Captain Himself, who literally sold His garments and went naked to His cross. Had He remained in the seclusion of heaven with the insignia of royalty, how tragic our lot would have been. Our blessed Lord, however, allowed the brutal soldiers to gamble for His vesture in order that He might wield the sword of power. Calvary meant nakedness and shame, but with it came a mighty victory over sin, death, and hell. May He enable us by His Spirit to pay the price of power, no matter how high that price may be!

CHAPTER 22

ISRAEL AND THE CHURCH

*"Thy two breasts are like two young roes that are twins,
which feed among the lilies."*
—Song of Solomon 4:5

"Thy two breasts are like two young roes that are twins."
—Song of Solomon 7:3

Although nowhere in the Song of Solomon can one find a reference to God or any other divine name—a feature it shares with the book of Esther—it has ever been deemed sacred by the Jews, who placed it among the holiest of their sacred books. The Chaldean Targum, the oldest Jewish commentary on the Song of Solomon, says, "The songs and hymns which Solomon the prophet, king of Israel, delivered by the spirit of prophecy, before Jehovah, the Lord of the whole world" and then proceeds to explain the book as the divine allegory of God's dealings with Israel. An ancient Hebrew expositor wrote,

Far be it! far be it! that the Song of Songs should treat of earthly love; for had it not been pure allegory, and had not its excellence been great, it would not have been numbered with the holy books; nor on this head is there any controversy.

This Song was included in the Septuagint version of the Bible around 200 BC and was received as a sacred book without exception. It is included in the list of sacred books by Josephus, and was quoted as having divine authority by the early church. Without doubt, it forms part of the divine oracles to which the Lord set His seal when He said, *"Search the scriptures...they are they which testify of me"* (John 5:39). Thus, as Professor Stowe expresses it, "If a fact can be established by testimony, it is established by testimony, that the Song of Solomon was a part of the Hebrew canon in the time of Christ." If this idyll of love were removed from the Hebrew Bible, the Song would not retain its significance. St. Bernard, who reveled in the book, said, "It [is] the Song of Songs, because other songs must be sung first, and this as the fruit of all the rest; grace alone teaches it; experience alone can learn it."

The Christian fathers described the writings of King Solomon as a ladder with three rungs. The book of Ecclesiastes is natural, the book of Proverbs is moral, and the book of Song of Solomon is spiritual.

Historically, the Song describes the relationship of Jehovah to His earthly people, Israel. Prophetically, the Song speaks of the time when Israel is reunited to Jehovah. (See Hosea 2:14–20.) Spiritually, the Song pictures union and communion between Christ and believers. (See 2 Corinthians 11:2.) The imagery is that of the love of the bridegroom for the bride, and is a type of the love of Christ for the redeemed.

In parabolic imagery, this mystic song of love proves that Solomon had no equal in the art of allegory—Jesus excepted, for He was greater than Solomon and *"never man spake like this man"* (John 7:46). A writer of a past century wrote,

> If you would be holy, read the Psalms; if you would be wise, read Proverbs; but if you would learn Love's language, and understand all action of love to establish real lasting communion, read the Song of Songs and breathe the fragrant air that surrounds the utterances of the King of Love to His Bride.

Such an understanding of the book's spiritual significance is necessary, no matter what part of it you consider. When you approach the Song of Solomon in light of its orientalism and symbols, then it is not a stumbling block, nor foolishness, nor incomprehensible, as some unspiritual minds have deemed it to be. It is with this allegorical background in mind that we study the prophetic and spiritual aspects of the *"two young roes that are twins"* (Song of Solomon 7:3).

Among the animals of creation, the loving hind and the pleasant roe, with their graces, speed, lustrous eyes, and stateliness, were chosen by Solomon, as well as many Oriental poets, to illustrate human strength, beauty, and attractiveness. The two narratives we are considering set forth the union and communion existing between the Lord and His church; the twin roes are definitely applied to them. It would seem as if we have a double portrait. The bridegroom draws a heavenly portrait as he extols the bride, describing her beauty from the head down. (See Song of Solomon 4:5.) Then He draws an earthly portrait as he describes the bride from the feet up. (See Song of Solomon 7:3.) Beneath these combined passages, which contain truths somewhat delicate to handle, are deep, heart-stirring truths for meditation.

PROPHETIC APPLICATION—ISRAEL

What must be borne in mind is the fact that although Solomon was inspired by the Holy Spirit to compose the Song of Solomon, which the church has taken as symbolic of Christ and His church, His bride, he, as the ruler of Israel, knew nothing about the church that Christ was to build. Thus, the first and most prominent application of this book is to Israel. The two breasts and two young roes are emblems of Israel, called by Jehovah, His wife.

1. DEVELOPMENT

The two breasts indicate the formation of the heart and affections, as well as full moral and physical development. The connection between the spouse (see Song of Solomon 4:5) and the *"little sister, and she hath no breasts"* (Song of Solomon 8:8) is marked and instructive. Some commentators see in the latter a reference to those in Ephraim or the ten tribes of Israel who had no breasts—no heart's affection—and who were not fully developed. In the former reference, Judah is depicted, for the two tribes had fuller love for Jehovah and a deeper moral and spiritual development. It was from this remnant, so full breasted, that our blessed Savior came.

As for the twin roes, they can typify the unity of mind and heart in restored Israel. The nation, divided after Solomon's death, will be united as one harmonious family, and her Lord will say of her, "Israel, my glory!" (See Isaiah 46:13.) Applied to ourselves, we can ask the heart-searching question, "Are we fully developed spiritually and morally, or are we like the little sister with no source of satisfaction and nourishment for others around?" Do crying souls turn to us in vain for the rich, warm milk of sympathy, love, and cheer? Well might we pray, "O Lord, make us full, double-breasted Christians!"

2. NOURISHMENT

Breasts represent the means of growth and sustenance. They gather and give, and are a blessing to others. It will be so with Judah and Ephraim when, fully reunited with Israel, they become the means of spiritual nourishment to the nations. Isaiah prophesied about the day of kingdom blessing when those around will *"be satisfied with the breasts of her consolations"* (Isaiah 66:11). Then, as the prophet states it, she will *"milk out, and be delighted with the abundance of her glory"* (verse 11).

Applied to the Lord and ourselves, the figure is arresting and comforting. Would that we had the necessary spiritual perception to discern all that is involved in the divine title El Shaddai. (See Genesis 17:1.) *Shad* is a Hebrew word meaning "breast" and is used in Scripture to mean a breast of a woman or of a beast. The prefix *El* implies "strong." Thus, God is saying, "I am the strong, breasted One," and He is presented through-out Scripture as the Life Giver, Nourisher, and Satisfier who pours Himself into all who believe. A fretful, unsatisfied babe is not only strengthened and nourished by its mother's breasts but also satisfied, quieted, and refreshed. It is so with Him who is our El Shaddai, who not only strengthens us but satisfies us. He both feeds us and rests us. What Solomon said of the wife and mother can be slightly altered to describe God's all-sufficiency: *"Let* [Him] *be as the loving hind and pleasant roe; let* [His] *breasts satisfy thee at all times; and be thou ravished always with* [His] *love"* (Proverbs 5:19). May we ever be found at the secret source of every precious thing, ever seeking pleasure, strength, and succor in Him who has promised to comfort us even as a mother comforts her children!

SPIRITUAL APPLICATION— THE CHURCH

The Jews of old, as well as the early Christian fathers, applied the twin breasts in various and interesting ways. They were said to illustrate the Bible with its Old and New Testaments—two satisfying breasts producing full spiritual nourishment. They were said to represent the two tables of the Law, with the Ten Commandments divided into two fives covering life godward and manward, all of them designed to foster spiritual growth. They were used to illustrate twin ordinances under Jewish law—the Passover and circumcision; and the two ordinances of the church—baptism and the Lord's Supper, the inseparable twins in the believer's life. They were applied to the two commandments our Lord emphasized, namely, to love God and to love our neighbors. (See Luke 10:27.) If looked at as such, John declared that one breast is useless without the other. (See 1 John 4:20.) How contradictory it is to profess love for God and yet hate our brother! They were made to typify preachers and teachers who, as having *"two breasts as twin roes,"* are spiritual nurses, feeding both saints and sinners with the sincere milk of the Word, that they may grow thereby.

They were held by many expositors to represent the twin graces of faith and love, which is a most reasonable application. The church is set forth as a bride adorned in bridal attire, and her dress is akin to the soldier's defensive armor that Paul describes (see Ephesians 6:11–18), upon which the two breasts are shielded by the breastplate of the warrior. *"Putting on the breastplate of **faith** and **love**"* (1 Thessalonians 5:8). Faith and love, then, are the mailed breasts of the soldiers of Christ and the twin roes of the bride of the Beloved. A woman once praised

Jesus for His works, saying, *"Blessed is the womb that bare thee, and the paps which thou hast sucked"* (Luke 11:27). He replied, *"Yea rather, blessed are they that **hear** the word of God, and **keep** it"* (Luke 11:28)—those who hear it with the ear of faith and keep it with the heart of love. These twin breasts are ever before us in Scripture: *"Faith which worketh by love"* (Galatians 5:6). *"Faith, and a good conscience"* (1 Timothy 1:19). Faith without love is hypocrisy. Love without faith is legality.

Is there any spiritual significance in the repeated term *"twins"* used in this verse: *"Two breasts are like two young roes that are twins"* (Song of Solomon 4:5)? Indeed, there is. Twins are born together, grow up together, and are one in feeling and sympathy. What one feels, the other suffers. Often, the correspondence is remarkable. Is this not true also of the noble pair of twin brothers, faith and love? If one increases without the other, the lack of symmetry is noticeable. If one virtue sickens, the other pines alongside it. One is not healthy without the other. They are a well-matched pair of twins when they develop together. If one is injured, the other suffers the same wound. If faith in God is damaged, love is impaired. If faith dies, love cannot live. No one can believe in God without loving Him, and vice versa.

There is also a deep, spiritual truth for our hearts in the sphere where the twin roes find their sustenance—they *"feedeth among the lilies"* (Song of Solomon 2:16). Notice that it does not say that they feed *on* the lilies but *"among"* them. The lilies Solomon had in mind afforded no suitable food for flocks and herds. These lilies grew in incredible numbers, were luxurious, and because of their high, broad leaves, retained their moisture. Wherever they were found, one would also find rich pasture. Consequently, such a place was a favorite haunt of hinds and roes. The lilies guided the way to nourishing herbage.

If the twin graces of faith and love are to grow, it is imperative for them to feed among God's lilies—the pure and holy provisions of His grace and Word and spiritual fellowship. These twin breasts can supply rich milk only as they feed among the lilies of divine promises. We can further note that the first twin of faith attracts attention in heaven, because faith looks upward and pierces the unseen, and has a keener perception than the roe's far-seeing eye. Nothing can feed faith like constant fellowship with Him who is the Lily of the Valley. The second twin of love is never found without her twin sister. If faith looks heavenward, love looks out upon the earth with the gentleness of the eye of the lovely, and loving, roe. Love for the saints and for sinners is allied to faith in God through Jesus Christ our Lord. As seen by Him, faith and love are the two breasts of the believer, or twin sisters, each one being dear to the other.

Our faith reposes in Jesus, and our love goes out to Him and to others. The world, impressed with our unwavering faith in God and our undying love for Him, comes to admire our love and learns to respect our faith from which that love flows. Paul commended the believers at Ephesus for their "*faith in the Lord Jesus, and love unto all the saints*" (Ephesians 1:15). In his parting benediction, the apostle wished for the Ephesians peace among themselves and also "*love with faith*" (Ephesians 6:23), the twins coming from "*God the Father and the Lord Jesus Christ*" (verse 23).

CHAPTER 23

WAGES AND GIFT

"The wages of sin is death, but the free gift of God is eternal life in Christ Jesus our Lord."
—Romans 6:23 (RSV)

No one can study the Epistles of Paul without discovering how he delighted in using contrasts, or opposite truths. Expressing the divine message in pairs seemed to come easy to his well-trained mind. If we take Romans, for example, we find it almost completely composed of a series of contrasts or comparisons. In the verse we are considering, we have a striking illustration of a twin expression, as well as a summary of the entire epistle, which is made up of two parts.

1. God and His gift, or what we are in Christ and receive from Him

2. Satan and his wages, or what we are in ourselves and outside of Christ

Paul divided the world into two distinct classes or conditions: Those who are lost in sin (this covers almost half of Romans) and those who are saved from sin (this embraces the rest of the epistle). We have the power of one master, Satan, and his bitter bondage, along with the fatal penalty that continuing in his slavery involves. We have the benefactions of the other Master, Jesus Christ our Lord, and all the present and eternal gains service for Him bestows.

Setting forth truth in pairs in this manner is an effective way of teaching Scripture. *"Men loved darkness rather than light"* (John 3:19)—what opposites this phrase contains! In Paul's marvelous summary in Romans 6:23, we have a trinity of twins:

1. Contrast of masters—God and sin
2. Contrast of remuneration—wages and gift
3. Contrast of possessions—death and life

CONTRAST OF MASTERS

Sin and Satan are synonymous terms, for had there been no Serpent, there would have been no sin; no devil, no damnation; no enemy, no evil. Our Lord declared that *"no man can serve two masters"* (Matthew 6:24). These two masters are presented by Paul, and if we understand the exact nature of each, we may find it easier to decide which to choose and serve.

1. GOD, CHRIST JESUS OUR LORD

Jesus could say, *"I and my Father are one"* (John 10:30); if we serve one, we serve the other. What wonderful, delightful, and gracious Masters these are to serve! In secular work, we find our daily task congenial and lucrative if the character of our master is righteous and good. Our heavenly Lord is the best, most loving Master it is possible to have. He is not a hard taskmaster, a despot forcing us to labor with vigor and serve as slaves. He is our Creator, the Lover of our souls, the Friend that sticks closer than a brother, and the Originator of grace, salvation, and heaven.

2. SATAN

What a diabolical master the devil is! He is sin personified, the original source of corruption and violence in the world. Knowing that sin is the contradiction of the will of God, Satan is bent on making all men sinners by practice, as he made them by birth. He is the most extensive employer of labor in the world—there is never any unemployment in his satanic workshop. He can always find plenty of hands to do his hellish work. In his service, none is ever found on the dole. It was he who marred God's universe at creation and has ever been the parent of sin, not some or certain sins, but *sin* in its radical nature. Of course, he pays wages to his deluded slaves. He may not pay every week, but every sin committed by way of his instigation has its payday both here and in a lost eternity.

CONTRAST OF REMUNERATION

Before a person finally submits to a master or manager in business or industry, he needs to settle his salary. There would have been much less social problems in the past had masters shown greater eagerness to reward, and not to exploit, those who labored for them.

Paul gives us a remarkable contrast in the matter of remuneration: From one Master, we receive a most liberal and lasting present or gift. From the other, a miserable pittance, one we should fling at the devil with disgust, as Judas flung his mean pay for betraying Jesus at the feet of those who had tempted him to sell Christ for such a paltry sum.

1. WAGES

> For the wages of sin is death; but the gift of God is eternal life through Jesus Christ our Lord.   (Romans 6:23)

The term Paul uses here, *"wages,"* is a military one; it suggests the ration money paid to soldiers which was punctually given when they enlisted for war. (See Luke 3:14.) We find ourselves captivated by Arthur S. Way's translation of the passage we are considering: *"The pittance-wage that sin doled out to you was death; but the lavish bounty of God is life eternal, involved in your union with the Messiah, with Jesus our Lord—ours!"* (Romans 6:23 WAY).

Dr. Way gives us a most interesting footnote to this passage:

> There is possibly a military metaphor here :—the contrast between the soldiers' ordinary pay, the smallness and irregular payment of which gave rise to constant grumbling and occasional mutiny, and the donative, or largesse, of the emperor on his accession, which was sometimes (e.g. on the accession of the reigning emperor, Nero) for political reasons, very large.

Join forces with the devil, live for him and serve him, and he'll pay you—make no mistake about it. Not only that, he will pay you generously, in the unanswered achings of soul; in mockings of spirit; in a heart shut against the sunshine of God's love; in sin, sorrow, and shame; in a blasted life; in hatred for things holy; in eternal darkness and woe. Sin today, and you'll get your wages—the inclination of your heart to do the same tomorrow. Satan will give you a liberal installment for your slavery now, and he'll pay you the balance in hell; no, the balance will *be* hell. If, like the rich man, sinners groan and moan over their final pay envelope, their cruel taskmaster will always be on hand to say, "Be content with your wages!"

2. GIFT

God does not pay wages; He bestows gifts. Death is the wage of sin and comes by desert, but life is a gift and comes by favor. Sinners merit hell, but saints do not merit heaven, even though they are saints. The psalmist wrote, *"The Lord will give grace and glory"* (Psalm 84:11)—a well-matched pair. We have the grace; the glory is to follow, and it will be ours through grace. The Lord Jesus died for us that we might be with Him in glory. (See 1 Thessalonians 5:10.) One purpose of His ascension was to prepare a place in the Father's home for those He redeemed with His blood. What a contrast! Sinners work for wages. Saints become saints by taking a gift. Wages are the reward of activity; gifts are by appropriation.

We do not work for a gift. It would not be a gift if we had to do anything for it. Several years ago, a friend surprised me by saying, "Give me three pounds, and I'll give you a most service-able Christmas present." I demurred somewhat, for £3 seemed a lot to part with without knowing what my friend had bought for me. Still, because we were close friends, and I knew my fellow preacher would not trick me, I handed over the money. Then he produced a Christmas package that contained a most necessary article at the time, an electric razor for which he had paid over £6. Although he had called it a gift, it was not really a gift, for we had paid for it jointly.

But salvation *is* an outright gift, for we contribute absolutely nothing to receive it. We are saved by grace, which is the gift of God. (See Ephesians 2:8.) What God gives is the bounty of His love, not a hard-earned wage paid out by a just overseer of life. As Dr. Way puts it, "[We receive] *the lavish bounty of God*" (Romans 6:23 WAY). As the loving gift of the Philippians released Paul from the necessity of working for a tent maker's wage, so the acceptance of God's gift of eternal life liberates us from the bondage of sin and sets us free to serve Him.

The Revised Standard Version expresses it, "*The free gift of God*" (Romans 6:23 RSV). Was Paul guilty of tautology when he wrote of a "*free gift*," seeing that any gift is free; otherwise, it would not be called a gift at all? The term signifies the gift of grace, given independently of the merit of the receiver. This is why grace is described as unmerited favor. Ellicott's comment on Romans 6:23 summarizes the significance of the contrast:

> The natural antithesis [to gift] would be "wages;" but this would here be inappropriate, and therefore the Apostle substitutes "the free gift." In spite of your sanctification as Christians, still you will not have *earned* eternal life; it is the gift of God's grace.

If you have a dear one who loves you very much and whose character and conduct are most commendable, then the merit of the loved one shapes the value of your gift. Thus, in a way, mutual love buys the gift. But suppose the one you love turns from you almost in hate and becomes a prodigal; yet, in spite of his low life, you made him the recipient of the most costly gift you could buy. That would be a free gift, a gift not based on the merit of the receiver.

To God, we were prodigals, low, despicable, abhorrent, full of putrefying sores from the sole of the foot even unto the head. (See Isaiah 1:6.) Yet, apart from our corrupt nature, in response to our repentance and faith, He bestowed upon us His unspeakable gift, the Savior. We did not merit or deserve Him but simply received Him as the gift of God's love. *"God...gave his only begotten Son"* (John 3:16).

> Nor merit of thine own
> Upon His altar place;
> All is of Christ alone,
> And of His perfect grace.[93]

CONTRAST OF POSSESSION

The free gift bestowed upon unworthy sinners by the bountiful Giver is "life! life! eternal life!" The wages paid by sin is death. It does not say that death is the wage of some great specific sin but of all or any sin. A single sin, however insignificant it may appear to the sinner, brings death. *"Whosoever shall... offend in one point, he is guilty of all"* (James 2:10). What blind fools we are when we allow the richest possession that can be had—and that without money and without price—to pass us by. "Our paradises, if only we knew it, are cheap enough; it is our hells that are expensive."

1. DEATH

Moffatt translates Romans 6:32 as *"Sin's wage is death"* (Romans 6:23 MOFFATT). Death is due to sinners, as wages are due to a servant for his work. While man is loath to believe it, and would break the alliance if he could, God has bound sin and death inseparably together. We may try to put this fact out of sight, or reject the Bible's warning about the unrelieved midnight of remorse in a lost eternity as the result of sinning against

---

93. Lucy Ann Bennett, "Rest, Rest Thee, Weary Heart."

God, but the revelation of final doom has never been abrogated. God has no pleasure in the death of the wicked. None is as gracious and limitless in mercy as He who has made infinite provision for men, that they should not die lost forever. But, as in the days of the Savior, men still reject Him.

LEGAL DEATH

There are four aspects of death that sin procures, the first of which is legal death. *"In the day that thou eatest thereof thou shalt surely die"* (Genesis 2:17). What death is this? From the day that man first disobeyed God's command, the sinner has been severed from the covenant of God and has been under sentence. All who do not believe are condemned. They are *"condemned already"* (John 3:18), in the present tense, meaning "here and now." When hanging was the form of capital punishment, the judge would don a black cap before pronouncing the sentence of a guilty murderer. The condemned one would remain in the death cell for a specified period under the sentence of death. The sinner, likewise, is under sentence of death because the Judge has proclaimed, *"The soul that sinneth, it shall die"* (Ezekiel 18:4).

PHYSICAL DEATH

Paul says that through Adam's transgression, *"sin entered into the world, and death by sin; and so death passed upon all men, for that all have sinned"* (Romans 5:12). Physical death means the severing of the deathless soul from the body when the call comes. This aspect of death was not in God's original plan. The last enemy of man to be destroyed, then, is death. Every funeral and every graveyard is the evidence of sin. Had there been no sin, there would have been no cemeteries. If Adam and his descendants had remained sinless, the population of the world would have been solved by the Lord taking home all who were ripe for glory, as He did with Enoch and Elijah, both of whom did not taste death.

SPIRITUAL DEATH

When Paul wrote of those who had been dead in trespasses and sins (see Ephesians 2:1), he was describing those who were very much alive physically but dead spiritually: *"She that liveth in pleasure is dead while she liveth"* (1 Timothy 5:6). A lunatic is dead mentally but alive physically. The apostle says, *"Is dead,"* not "will die." When one consciously enters into practical sin, spiritual death begins and develops because the soul is severed from Him who came as the Life. Cut off from Him, the sinner is a child of the devil and a creature of death, although he remains alive physically and socially.

ETERNAL DEATH

Four times over in the Apocalypse, the solemn, dreadful phrase *"second death"* (Revelation 2:11; 20:6, 14; 21:8) appears. This is equivalent to the "eternal death" (see Matthew 25:46) of which Jesus spoke. This final aspect of death surpasses those we considered earlier. As eternal life involves the perfect develop-ment of the saint's spiritual faculties, eternal death implies the atrophy of such faculties. As far as any spiritual quickening or advance is concerned, he is dead forever. Such unrelieved doom is the last installment of sin's wages. Would that sinners could be found heeding the warning to *"flee from the wrath to come"* (Luke 3:7)!

2. LIFE

Is there any other gift comparable to the gift of life? *"The free gift of God is eternal life in Christ Jesus our Lord"* (Romans 6:23 RSV). The gift of God *"is"* eternal life—the present tense implies that the moment one quits his death-laden service of the devil and receives the Savior, his new life begins, and it flows on until it reaches the ocean above. The nature of this life should be stressed: it is *"eternal,"* or a life in which there is no death. Further, the transition from death to life is not a process. There is no sloping gradient, no ascending staircase with God and heaven at the top. It is not a gradual journey toward consummation. When a sinner receives Christ, who is life, he passes from death into life immediately. How long, after all, does it take to receive a gift from a friend waiting to present it?

Sinners work for hell; but heaven is not gained, it is given. Paul makes it clear that the life offered as a gift is not *something* but *Someone* who comes as *"the gift of God"* (Romans 6:23). The Revised Standard Version has it, **"In Christ Jesus our Lord"** (Romans 6:23 rsv), not "through Christ Jesus our Lord" He is the Life. *"In him was life"* (John 1:4). John's teaching is very clear and emphatic on this point: *"God hath given to us eternal life, and this life is in his Son"* (1 John 5:11) or, as it could be stated, "This life *is* His Son." Then comes the twin declaration, *"He that hath the Son hath life; and he that hath not the Son of God hath* **not** *life"* (1 John 5:12). Therefore, he must be dead. All God has so freely given is deposited in His Son, where it awaits man's appropriation. How blessed we are, then, when we take the gift and go on to praise and live for the bountiful Giver!

> Fill Thou my life, O Lord my God,
> In every part with praise,
> That my whole being may proclaim
> Thy being and Thy ways.[94]

---

94. Horatius Bonar, "Fill Thou My Life," 1866.

CHAPTER 24

WINGS AND HANDS

"Under their wings, on the four sides of them, were human hands."
—Ezekiel 1:8 (MOFFATT)

There is much in the visions of Ezekiel—one of the most original of the prophets—that strikes us as somewhat strange and monstrous. John Calvin acknowledged that he could not understand the visions of this prophet. And yet we may ask the Holy Spirit's aid in our effort to interpret one of these visions.

Ezekiel always sought to maintain the union between heaven and earth. Though he possessed a remarkably prophetic eye and poetic mind, which enabled him to soar into the open heavens and record all he witnessed, he always remained practical. He was a true "son of man," a title that is given to him over ninety times. With the sweep of an eagle's wing, he could rise far above the common experiences of life to the awful regions of unearthly sublimity; yet, again and again, the awe of what he saw in his flights was relieved by glimpses of some traits of human nature.

In his vision, Ezekiel found himself among those who were hearing about the penalty due them because of their sins. He was one of the captives in Chaldea when his remarkable visions came to him.

The first chapter of his prophecy contains a description, stated in figurative language, of the highest intelligences of the heavenly world. A conception of their qualities and attributes, the powers they possess, and the services they perform are conveyed to us in parabolic form. The symbolic creatures with living wings were the cherubim. They possessed a beautiful combination of heavenly and human features. (See Ezekiel 1:5–14.) Their animal forms denote subjection. Each head is representative of certain qualities: in the lion, boldness and courage; in the ox, enduring strength; in the eagle, vision and aspiration; in the man, free conscious intelligence. The numerous eyes indicate the wide range and varied character of their knowledge. The feet are also symbolic. Angelic beings are described as not only having wings but human faces, feet, and hands as well.

Note the significance of the characteristic features of hands under wings.

SYMBOLISM EZEKIEL'S CREATURES

1. WINGS

In abstract qualities, wings symbolize shelter. *"Hide me under the shadow of thy wings"* (Psalm 17:8). The wings of a dove symbolize love. Wings indicate untiring flight, strength, and endurance. Their supreme function is to soar. Watch a bird with massive wings rise from the carrion of earth upon which it has been feeding and, soaring up into the heights, vanish out of sight into the heavenly regions. Such is a type of our heavenly spiritual life. Faith and hope are the soul's wings. With them, we fly swiftly up to God. Wings, then, represent the deep, unseen life nourished by things divine.

2. HANDS

These are the human possessions with which we gather, hold, and use. With our hands, we labor and serve. They link us to the world we can see and touch and handle, just as wings draw us up into the world we cannot see.

Taken together, then, wings and hands imply the complete life of man. There are two sides we must hold in balance, the heavenly side and the earthly side. The spirit of man is like the wings, the invisible part connecting him with heaven. The body of man is like the hands, the visible part binding him to earth.

Having a living soul, man is yet made of dust. The beast belongs to the lowest sphere; it has no wings. Angels belong to the heavenly sphere; they have no human bodies. But man, the human creature, comes in between and partakes of both natures, for he has one nature that finds its sphere in that which is material and earthly and another that finds its realm in the unseen, the spiritual, the eternal.

THE IDEAL COMBINATION

Wings and hands suggest an ideal unity. We have not only wings for motion but hands for action, and we are never complete unless these two work in unison. The ideal life lies in the use and perfect blending of serving and soaring, the blending of the eternal and earthly.

Man is both a child of the soil and a child of the sky. We have a perfect illustration of this combination in our Lord, whose life was one of unfailing service below and unbroken communion with the Father above. He constantly used His wings; they were never folded. Yet He was the most practical of all men; His hands were never idle.

Some are all wings. They desire an ideal life in the restless exercise of the wings. Isolated from the ordinary, social, natural life of man, they seek the solitude of a cloistered cell.

Others desire the heavenly life. They are always flying on wings from one holiness convention to another. They are always up in the clouds. And there are many who long for the wings of a dove that they might fly away from all their cares, responsibilities, and trials, and spend their days in holy fellowship.

Some are all hands. They are on the other extreme. They seldom use their wings. They are all for this world. They give themselves up without reserve to things seen and earthly. They never pray, never soar, never turn aside from what is visible for fellowship with God.

Some are practical but not visionary. Others are visionary but not practical. We, however, must learn how to combine all these traits. Mary and Martha must dwell in one person. We must preserve balance between vision and vocation; worship and work; communion and commerce.

In the battle of life, we have wings for the light and hands for the fight. Not only must we mount up with wings, but we must walk and not faint. So with wings we soar from the mundane things of earth and develop the spiritual side of our nature. Then we must go back to the tasks of our hands, dispensing the wealth of heaven we have appropriated.

Now to understand the implication of the wings covering the hands:

1. DIVINE INSPIRATION MUST PERMEATE ALL HUMAN INSTRUMENTALITY

The wings were over the hands and yet connected with them. This is symbolic of the fact that human instrumentality was permeated with superhuman power.

Take the Bible—such a revelation could only be accessible through human channels. The thought of heaven had to be translated into the language of earth. God spoke to holy men. He gave them wings and caught them up to receive the revelation of Himself; but human hands had to write that revelation out.

Again, the wonderful instrument of the human hand is capable of vast achievements. It is a symbol of power and skill. But the greatest of all achievements of which this facile instrument is capable are made possible by God. The power of the hand is not of itself. God filled Bezaleel with the Holy Spirit; similarly, all the work we do with our hands, whether spiritual or secular, is useless unless winged by divine might. Human effort was never intended to stand alone. Wings must overshadow the hands. We are "workers together with God." (See 2 Corinthians 6:1.) The treasure is in earthen vessels.

2. DIVINE GLORY ACTUATES HUMAN ACTIVITY

Hands under wings intimate their right place, for the hand of service must ever be under the wing of faith. While we have to work with our hands in order to maintain our life, if we do everything for the glory of God, we will have the joy of His approving smile.

The unseen must control the seen. The heavenly must control the earthly, the spiritual the secular. Whether we eat or drink, or whatever we do, we can do all for the glory of God. (See 1 Corinthians 10:31.) And when in all our service we keep the hand under the wing, we are delivered from functioning as a mere timeserver. We rise to a noble dignity in labor.

Let us not be all hands, but let us cover them with our wings and welcome the glory of the Lord into the most commonplace duties of life. In the carpenter's shop at Nazareth, we see the toil of divinity revealing the divinity of toil.

3. DIVINE COMMANDS DEMAND HUMAN OBEDIENCE

Wings and hands are placed together, for they are meant to work together. Noble service requires swiftness and grace. Not only must there be eagerness to serve and delight in service but promptness, speed, and fleetness. Wings must carry out the work our hands find to do. Alas, we know what ought to be done; we see the tragic need of souls at home and abroad; we have the only remedy for the chaotic condition of the world—but we are wingless.

> It is love that makes the willing hands
> In swift obedience move.

4. DIVINE SERVICE REQUIRES HUMAN HUMILITY

Note that the hands were under the wings, that is, partly hidden or concealed. This suggests that all that is conspicuous in life and service must be hidden by that which is its true source.

Some are willing to serve, most when their service can be seen and known and blazed abroad. They like the world to see what they give and do with their hands. They never know the sweetness of bringing anything in secret to the Master's feet.

There is never anything anonymous about their giving. They need wings to cover up what their hands do.

Let us be active by all means, but let us never serve God with our wings plucked. If we live and serve only for self-glory, the work of our hands will bring no further reward, our labor no greater honor. But if our hands of service are covered with wings of humility, we will always enjoy the benediction of heaven. Wings and hands are meant to work together in our lives, and *"what therefore God hath joined together, let not man put asunder"* (Matthew 19:6; Mark 10:9).

CHAPTER 25

MIRRORS AND RIDDLES

"We see as yet the Vision glassed in a mirror—
it is a dark riddle—but then face to face shall we gaze.
Now my knowledge comes from seeing but a part;
but then shall I understand, as fully as I am understood."
—1 Corinthians 13:12–13 (WAY)

In Paul's comforting words to the saints at Corinth, he exhorted them to think of two worlds, the one above and the other below, separated by a very thin veil indeed. And as we can see, he used two words to describe these two worlds: *"now"* and *"then."*

"Now we see through a glass, darkly" (1 Corinthians 19:12). Here we have this earth plane with its interrogation; this present world of questioning, perplexities, and tangled threads.

"Then face to face" (verse 12). These words direct us to the heavens of explanation, the paradise of revelation where all the mysteries of earth are solved and everything inexplicable is unraveled—where we see light in His light. The apostle himself had learned how to balance these two worlds; he shows us how to set the gloomy *now* over against the glorious *then.*

THE WORLD OF MYSTERY

Paul uses two striking figures of speech to emphasize and illustrate the seemingly perplexing, baffling experiences of life: the mirror and the riddle. As Arthur S. Way translates it, *"We see as yet the Vision glassed in a mirror—it is a dark riddle"* (verse 12 WAY). Corinth was famed for its metal mirrors fashioned of silver and brass. Sometimes a mirror was produced that was somewhat blurred or warped, and a person looking into such a defective mirror would receive a distorted image of himself. We know what it is like when we look into one of those crazy mirrors and see ourselves elongated or broadened in an enormous size. Here Paul is saying that many of the events and experiences of life are reflected in a distorted mirror. Somehow, they do not seem to be right or just but twisted and out of proportion.

Further, we see things as a riddle, or as the Revised Version margin has, "dark riddle" or "puzzle." Who has not watched a child trying hard to piece a puzzle together, and, after a while, he becomes impatient and discards it, for the pieces do not seem to fit. Often we try, intelligently, to piece the different and disturbing trials and sorrows of life together, but somehow they do not form a perfect whole. The reason for this is obvious—some of the missing parts of the riddle are in the hand of God, and we must wait until we see Him face-to-face for a solution of life's problems.

1. THE VALUE OF MYSTERY

Does mystery have a ministry? We think it does. Mystery goes to make life what it really is. It is by those dark, inexplicable enigmas we meet with that we live. Mystery teaches us the value of God, from whom nothing is hidden. If there were no mysteries, then we would be as wise as God Himself. Mystery, therefore, teaches us the dimness of our vision and littleness of knowledge on the one hand, and the greatness of God's wisdom and power on the other. If we try to probe and unravel the seeming mysteries of life, we find ourselves in a maze of doubt and despair and in a condition of mental and spiritual dejection. We must accept the fact that there are mysteries and believe that God is all-wise and all-perfect. He does not make mistakes. When, ultimately, we see Him face-to-face and understand everything from His standpoint, then we'll bless the hand that guided and the heart that planned.[95]

2. THE VARIETY OF MYSTERY

Because of our mental limitations, there are many things that somehow perplex our finite, puny minds. In various areas of life, we see through a glass darkly.

Take the facts of our faith. We accept the existence of God, believe in Him, and seek to obey Him; yet those transcendent attributes of His are beyond our human ken. *"Touching the Almighty, we cannot find Him out"* (Job 37:23). Who, with all their natural and acquired wisdom, can fully comprehend the omniscience, omnipresence, majesty, and eternity of God? Is it not said that He is the God who hides Himself? (See Isaiah 45:15.)

Then take the mode of our redemption. Who can solve the mystery of Christ, the sinless One, who died for a world of sinners who were ruined by the fall? The same applies to the operations of the Holy Spirit. Who is able to diagnose and clearly define and trace His movements within the soul of man? No one can tell whence He comes and whither He goes in the work of regeneration. (Seek John 3:8.) We are just as baffled when it comes to the perfect conception of heaven.

---

95. "The Sands of Time Are Sinking."

Take the facts of life. As nature has her secrets hidden away in the flowers of the field and in the ways of birds and beasts, so our secrets are hidden. Every tear is a profound mystery. No one can tell us why we cry or why we laugh. Who can read his brother's mind or fully understand his own? There is One, however, who *"knowest* [us] *altogether"* (Psalm 139:4).

Does it not inspire confidence that He feels our every heartbeat and knows our every sigh? Elihu says that God *"giveth not account of any of his matters"* (Job 33:13). He does not need to, for *"he doeth according to his will"* (Daniel 4:35), and He knows what is best for His own.

> Every hour in perfect peace
> I'll sing, He knows, He knows![96]

Take the problems of war. When world wars and civil wars bring about so much bloodshed, devastation, and sorrow, we find ourselves very perplexed. Though born in hell, such carnage is permitted by God. Doubtless He overrules it for His glory. Why does a God of love allow the earth to be drenched with blood and saturated with the tears of those whose loved ones are killed? Have you never paused and cried, "O God, why do men make wars?" Why is this grim, gaunt monster of hell— the child of the devil who has been a murderer from the beginning—allowed to stalk the earth with bloodred hands? Why? This is one of the riddles that awaits a solution.

Take the burdens of life. Everywhere we meet the problem of pain and the mystery of misery. Distortions seem to abound. The philosophy of the book of Job revolves around the baffling experiences of life. We never consider it a mystery when the aged suffer physical infirmity. After weathering the storms and hurricanes of life, it seems natural for them to have aches and

---

96. Mary G. Brainard, "I Know Not What Awaits Me," 1869.

pains. Neither are we mystified when we see those who have lived for the satisfaction of the lusts and passions of the flesh suffer. They are only reaping what they've sowed. In their physical anguish, Nature is simply extracting her dues.

But how do we feel when we encounter those who are young and tender smitten with some terrible disease or disability or deformity by no fault of their own? Several years ago, I found myself in a godly home where the parents were perplexed over the providential dealings of God. Theirs was the anguish of seeing their first child practically an imbecile from birth with no hope of normality. Have you ever visited a home or hospital for handicapped children and looked on their ugly, twisted forms? Have you not cried in your heart, "O God, why?" Christians, because they are Christ's, learn to believe that such adversities draw them nearer to God and enrich their lives. But after every allowance is made, we are left with the question "Why do the innocent suffer?"

Take the glaring inequalities. Life is full of disparity and irregularity. Much that is common to our so-called enlightened and cultured society seems so unfair. Here is a rogue with no thought of God and with no desire to help his fellow man, rolling in wealth and altogether ignorant of the hardship afflicting so many. Yet alongside him is another who fears God, who is upright in all his ways and has a passion to uplift the needy; but he is poor and struggles to make ends meet. This was the mystery David must have had in mind when he wrote, *"Fret not thyself because of evildoers...because of him who prospereth in his way"* (Psalm 37:1, 7).

Why is a man who is so selfish at the core allowed to add to his gold store and consume all his possessions on the gratification of his own sinful and selfish desires, while near at hand is another who, although he has so little of this world's goods, strives to give the Lord His tithe? Of course, we know the Bible says that the little money a righteous man has is of greater value than that of the wicked, but we are still left with inequality. Furthermore, why is a man who is so decrepit and vicious allowed to live on, while a neighbor who is so godly is suddenly stricken down? Again, why is it that many godly parents have the sorrow of seeing their children grow up to be godless, wayward adults? There are many homes today with such heartache. We may find comfort in singing

> O blessed life! the mind that sees,
> Whatever change the years may bring,
> A mercy still in everything,
> And shining through all mysteries.[97]

But while faith may find relief in such a song, we are still left with these baffling inequalities of life that God permits. He bids us wait for the answer to life's riddles in His "nevertheless afterward."

Take the enemy of death. Death is always a mystery. That is why we stand in silence in the death chamber or around an open grave. Although Euripides said, "Learn that to die is a debt we must all pay," the question arises why some are called upon to pay the debt when they have scarcely begun to live. We never think of death as a mystery when the aged are taken from us. Having journeyed beyond the allotted span of time and encountered the storms of life, the Pilot comes and guides them into His haven of rest.

But are we not mystified and perplexed when the very young are cut down? We expect the full bloom to wither and die; but when a bud is nipped by a blasting frost, how sadly disappointed

97. William Tidd Matson, "The Blessed Life."

we are. Loving hearts are heavy with grief when children, whose lives are so full of promise, are taken to be with the Lord. And even though they learn to say with sweet resignation, *"The LORD gave, and the LORD hath taken away; blessed be the name of the LORD"* (Job 1:21), the riddle remains unsolved. Why does God permit the cradle to be emptied and the home to be robbed of its precious sunbeam? The answer is beyond our present comprehension.

When we reach glory, it may be that we discover that if God had spared many of these dear children, they would have grown up to live godless lives that would have brought their dear parents down to the grave in shame and despair; and so, in His mercy, He translated them. Foreseeing their future, He gathered them home while they were innocent and pure. For there are worse experiences than that of having a baby in heaven, as many dear mothers have learned as they've watched a child of another home nursed and fondled, allowed to live—only to grow up a criminal and end his days in prison. Therefore, as we meditate on the varied experiences of life, so bewildering to our finite minds, we find consolation in the Master's assertion, *"What I do thou knowest not now; but thou shalt know hereafter"* (John 13:7).

THE PARADISE OF REVELATION

Paul knew how to balance the two worlds of here and hereafter. Over against the world of mystery, he places the paradise of revelation, when we will see *"face to face"* (1 Corinthians 13:12). Paradise will unravel all our perplexities, and glory will soothe our griefs. I recall visiting a home in which the mother was most gifted with her needle. She handed me a piece of cloth she had been working on for a considerable time. It was given to me the wrong way up, and all I could see was a strange medley of colors—nothing but a series of knots and twisted threads; no order, no beauty, nothing whatever to excite admiration. Then I turned the cloth over, and on the other side I was amazed to see the tracing of a bunch of lovely flowers. It took all the knots, the twistings, and the mixture of colors to form this beautiful piece. The weaving of the cloth of life is something much like this.

> My life is but a weaving
> Between my Lord and me;
> I cannot choose the colors
> He worketh steadily.
>
> Oft times He weaveth sorrow
> And I, in foolish pride,
> Forget He sees the upper,
> And I the underside.
>
> Not till the loom is silent
> And the shuttles cease to fly,
> Shall God unroll the canvas
> And explain the reason why.
>
> The dark threads are as needful
> In the Weaver's skillful hand,
> As the threads of gold and silver
> In the pattern He has planned.[98]

May grace be ours to live in patience, judging nothing before its time. (See 1 Corinthians 4:5.) Once we are in the paradise of

---

98. Benjamin Malachi Franklin, "The Weaver," 1950.

revelation, we will see behind a frowning providence a smiling face. William Cowper has reminded us that, here and now:

> Blind unbelief is sure to err
> And scan His work in vain;
> God is His own interpreter
> And He will make it plain.[99]

This is the hope Paul holds out in his declaration, *"Then shall I know even as also I am known"* (1 Corinthians 13:12). The partial is to give way to the perfect. Beyond this life, with its language of riddles, lies all the necessary answers, and a complete unfolding and understanding of the seeming mysteries of life. Present chastisements will then yield the peaceable fruits of righteousness. It may be that these lines are being read by a grief-stricken heart. Tears, sorrows, losses, and disappointments have been yours, and you feel that God has made a terrible mistake in the ordering of your life—that if you had been the planner, things would have been different. But because God is all-wise and all-loving, you must believe that He knows what is best for those who are His. When you are finally with Him, and may read the meaning of your tears, you will wonder why you ever doubted His permissive will.

> Then in the kingdom bending
> Before our Savior's feet,
> Life's dark enigmas ending
> In hallelujahs sweet.

At times, it may be hard to believe that *"all things,"* even the most untoward experiences of life, *"work together for good to them that love God"* (Romans 8:28). What we have to learn is to trust Him where we cannot trace Him. Job, more than any other man, was beset by the seeming mystery of God's dealings with him. Yet he had great patience in his severe trials and came to triumphantly declare, *"Though he slay me, yet will I trust him"* (Job 13:15).

Not now, but in the coming years,
It may be in the better land,
We'll read the meaning of our tears,
And there, sometime, we'll understand.

We'll catch the broken threads again,
And finish what we here began;
Heav'n will the mysteries explain,
And then, ah then, we'll understand.

...

Why what we long for most of all,
Eludes so oft our eager hand;
Why hopes are crushed and castles fall,
Up there, some time, we'll understand.

God knows the way, He holds the key,
He guides us with unerring hand;
Some time with tearless eyes we'll see;
Yes, there, up there, we'll understand.[100]

---

100. Maxwell N. Cornelius, "Sometime We'll Understand," 1891.

CHAPTER 26

LOSING AND FINDING

"He that findeth his life shall lose it:
and he that loseth his life for my sake shall find it."
—Matthew 10:39

"He that loveth his life shall lose it; and he that hateth
his life in this world shall keep it unto life eternal."
—John 12:25

"He saved others; himself he cannot save."
—Matthew 27:42

The paradoxical declaration about losing and finding life is the only saying of our Lord's that is recorded, with slight differences, by all four evangelists. It seems as if it was uttered on four separate occasions.

First, it forms part of the Master's instructions to the twelve apostles as He sent them forth to preach the gospel and heal the sick. (See Matthew 10:5, 39.)

Second, He said it just after He first announcement His own approaching suffering and death, to prepare His disciples for the days of tribulation awaiting them. (See Matthew 16:25; Mark 8:35; Luke 9:24.)

Third, it forms part of one of His apocalyptic discourses and is based on the warning of sharing the same fate of Lot's wife, who literally lost her life while she tried to save it. (See Luke 17:33.)

Fourth, it was used when the Greeks desired to see Jesus, and He saw in them a foretaste of the Gentile harvest, which would owe to His death as *"a corn of wheat"* (John 12:24). In this way, He led His disciples to spiritual gain through temporal loss. (See John 12:25.)

In addition to the different circumstances under which the saying was spoken, we have varying applications of truth suggested by the slightly different wording by the writers.

In Matthew 10:39, the present tense is changed to the past in the margin of the Revised Version, whereas in Luke 17:33, the future tense is used. As you can see, the context of both passages is related to the future judgment.

The word *"will"* in Matthew 16:25, Mark 8:35, and Luke 9:24 is translated *"would"* and *"shall"* in the Revised Version. This signifies a desire to serve and a willingness to lose life, respectively.

In Matthew 10:39 and Luke 9:24, the words *"for my sake"* are used, indicating the reason for the sacrifice. In Mark 8:35, there is the addition *"and the gospel's,"* corresponding with Mark 10:29.

In John 12:25, the words *"loveth"* and *"hateth his life"* are used, reminding us that while self-preservation is the law of nature, self-sacrifice is the law of grace.

THE PRINCIPLE

The seemingly paradoxical statement of losing to find expresses a law of human nature that is abundantly illustrated in many realms. Every day, we are reminded that finding is often losing, and losing is often finding. If a farmer hoards all his grain instead of sowing part of it, he will never reap a harvest. If a businessman refuses to invest his capital, he will never succeed in his business. If the student grudges time and toil, he will never attain to high standards. No matter what our profession or ambition may be, self-denial is the price of success. Goals are never reached without labor and suffering. We must be prepared to lose much we would like to do in order to achieve our aim.

That the same principle holds true in the vegetable kingdom can be gathered from John's mention of losing and finding, where our Lord speaks of Himself as dying as *"a corn of wheat"* (John 12:24). But through dying, He brought forth much fruit. A garden or a field constantly preach that life proceeds from death or finding from losing, and the higher we go in the scale of life, the more apparent this principle becomes. When it comes to humans, self-preservation is generally preferred to self-privation. They are not prepared to renounce in order to receive: "A man there was, though some did count him mad, the more he cast away the more he had."[101]

THE EXAMPLE

Our Lord, who enumerated the principle of losing to find, was Himself the highest exemplification of such universal law. Because He was willing to humble and empty Himself, He

101. John Bunyan, *The Pilgrim's Progress.*

became highly exalted. (See Philippians 2:5–11.) He reached His crown through the cross. One of the most blessed characteristics of His earthly ministry was the living out of the truth He taught. He practiced what He preached. His message went through the crucible of experience and was woven into the very texture of His life. He not only said that a man should never look back once he placed his hand on the plow, but He also exhibited a determination to finish a God-given task in spite of demons and men. Thus, as He died, He cried, *"It is finished"* (John 19:30)! He not only urged men to forgive, but at Calvary, He forgave His very murderers.

So, in more senses than one, *"the Word was made flesh"* (John 1:14). Christ was the living embodiment of the truth He taught. In Him, and by Him, the spoken Word became living flesh. He was a perfect, living epistle, and this is no more evident than in what He said to His disciples about losing one's life in order to find it. He not only preached about self-sacrifice, He performed it. His precepts became practice. This is why His sayings are so arresting and so powerful; He was the living illustration of them. It is in this connection that we take the jibes of the religious leaders who plotted His death—*"He saved others; let him save himself"* (Luke 23:35) and *"If thou be the king of the Jews, save thyself"* (verse 37)—and place them alongside His declaration, *"Whosoever will save his life shall lose it"* (Luke 9:24).

1. HIMSELF HE CANNOT SAVE

Recognizing man's freedom of will, Christ left the choice of losing or saving one's life to the individual. The surrender of one's self-life for a nobler one is a voluntary one. The powerful message of the cross is that although Christ was chosen by God to die, He could have saved Himself. He could have saved His life in the past counsels of eternity when God disclosed to Him

His plan for man's redemption. Jesus might have been unwilling to come into the world as the Lamb slain from before the foundation of the world. He could have refused to pay the awful price of our deliverance from sin; but He pleased not Himself. He was willing to lose His life that multitudes might find eternal life. So, forfeiting all self-interest and self-glory, He became the Babe.

Jesus could have saved Himself from the cross while on the Mount of Transfiguration, where He discussed His prophesied death with Moses and Elijah. Perfect in creation and in probation, He was ready to be perfected in glory and could have returned there with the two ancient prophets. If Enoch was translated without tasting death, how much more worthy was Jesus, the Son in whom the Father was well-pleased, of escaping death. But at that mount, we witness the great renunciation, for down came the Master to lose His life in order to find it in a more wonderful way.

Jesus could have saved Himself the anguish of those last days and the shame and ignominy of Calvary on that day when the people were bent on making Him their king. Seeing in Him God's Anointed One, they hailed Him as their Messiah. He was the One the common people heard gladly. By His words and works, He captured the popular imagination, and was idolized. He could have multiplied His miracles and thereby increased His fame, power, and influence, ushering in His kingdom without a bloody death. But He knew that the only way to the throne was by suffering on the tree; and although He was a king, He lost He was willing to die as a criminal.

Jesus could have saved Himself from all the hardships and privations of His physical limitations. Think of all His tears, groans, weariness, hunger, thirst, sorrow, and rejection! Why, because of all He was in Himself as the Lord of Glory, He could have passed through the world without a groan or care. He who dried the tears of others could have saved His own eyes from weeping. But during His brief but dynamic ministry, He constantly lost His life, lavishly expending it on others. Willingly He broke His alabaster box of precious ointment at the feet of humanity. His constant unselfishness revealed that

A life of self-renouncing love
Is one of liberty.[102]

Jesus could have saved Himself from the brutal and bitter end, the gruesome spectacle of the cross. It was not the Roman nails that fastened Him to a wooden gibbet. As the Son of God, He had power to summon a legion of angels to His aid. Yes, He could have descended from the tree when taunted to do so, for He made that tree and the spikes that fastened Him to it. But He humbled Himself, even to such a terrible death.

The first part of that jibe, *"He saved others,"* was true. Because He did not save or spare Himself, He was always saving others. He died daily to self-ease and self-interest, and He was always at the service of the blind, sick, diseased, distressed, hungry, and bereaved. He could not save Himself and others at the same time. So, the last part of the derision—*"Himself he cannot save"*—is true also. He could have saved Himself, but He willed to live and die for others.

2. HIMSELF HE HAS SAVED

No one else has found life through losing it in the measure that the Master did. Because He lost His life, in both living on earth and dying on the cross, He saved it eternally, for He is *"alive for evermore"* (Revelation 1:18). He sees His lost life in the

---

102. Anna L. Waring, "Father, I Know That All My Life," 1850.

myriads of those washed in the blood He freely shed for them. The seed that fell on the ground and died has produced a multitude of harvests. Had He loved His life and kept it, He would have lost the exaltation of the

> Ten thousand times ten thousand, and thousands of thousands; saying with a loud voice, Worthy is the Lamb that was slain to receive power, and riches, and wisdom, and strength, and honour, and glory, and blessing.
>
> (Revelation 5:11–12)

Had He gone back to glory from the Mount of Transfiguration instead of from Mount Calvary, He would have gone alone, and heaven would have been empty of the vast number of men who now extol His worth. He was willing to climb the steep ascent back to heaven through peril, toil, and pain, but in the redeemed in heaven and on earth, He sees the travail of His soul and is supremely satisfied.

THE OBLIGATION

The apostle Peter would have us remember that Jesus, in His self-renouncing life, left us an example that we should follow. (See 1 Peter 2:21–23.) Jesus Himself said it was enough that the servant be as his master. (See Matthew 10:25.) But are we practicing the losing and finding He exhorted us to practice? *"Give, and it shall be given unto you"* (Luke 6:38) was one of His precepts, and it is only as we forfeit ourselves that we find our true selves. As Richard Glover expresses it—

> We never have a life till we give it up to our Savior. Withhold life from Him, and it ceases to be anything worthy of the name of life. Keep back your heart, and it

is never your own. Give up your heart, and your heart is yours, full of power of enjoyment and self-enrichment. The unselfish alone are truly rich: "Blessed are the poor in spirit": they have "the kingdom of Heaven." Do not save yourself from sacred pain and gracious trouble, or you lose your true self, your power of right feeling and gracious purpose. So, they who are over-anxious to save their bodily life lose the life of their souls; while they who sacrifice their lives for Christ find the life of the immortal soul forever. Buy not gold too dear; but part with all that keeps you from Christ, or give all He asks of you.

Our Lord had much to say about the elementary law of self-denial in Christian living. *"If any man will come after me, let him deny himself, and take up his cross, and follow me"* (Matthew 16:24). The cross for the believer is the denial of self. Willingly, Christ gave Himself up for our salvation, and He calls us to self-renunciation for the spiritual benefit of others. *"As he is, so are we in this world"* (1 John 4:17). But we are loath to lose our self-life still more every day in order that needy hearts may be enriched. We tend to forget that self-preservation ends in self-destruction, that self-seeking is self-losing, and that, on the other hand, self-sacrifice results in self-exaltation.

Each of us has a lower life, which is animal, earthly, and transient, as well as a higher life, which is spiritual, heavenly, and eternal. In the cultivation of the lower life, we tend to exclude the higher, but when we strive to nourish the higher life, we further all that is truly worthy in the lower.

If we live only for the earthly and transient, that which we anticipate as gain will turn out as irreparable loss. If, on the other hand, we live for heavenly things, the apparent loss of what we treasure will prove to be unspeakable gain. It is only in the surrender of our life that we save it; in losing it, we find it. If we would be the means of saving others, then we cannot save ourselves. Unless blood tincture is mixed with service, it will not prove fruitful for the Master. It is only as we "lay in dust life's glory dead"[103] that

> From the ground there blossoms red
> Life that shall endless be.[104]

103. George Matheson, "O Love That Wilt Not Let Me Go," 1882.
104. Ibid.

CHAPTER 27

GRACE AND TRUTH

"Grace and truth came by Jesus Christ."
—John 1:17

"Full of grace and truth."
—John 1:14

"Abundant in goodness [grace] and truth."
—Exodus 34:6

There is an old proverb that says, "Every couple's not a pair," but here are a couple of virtues that make a princely, well-matched pair. Although man's deepest need is grace through truth, by nature, he likes neither grace nor truth. He is satisfied neither with perfect justice nor perfect goodness. When John the Baptist came in truth and righteousness, he was hated, deemed too harsh, and rejected as one who had a devil. When Jesus came in grace and love, those who were professedly teachers of truth, but destitute of grace, taunted Him as being a friend of sinners. When the righteous requirements of God's law are preached, many are apt to say, "That is too straight; you must allow a little margin for human imperfection and slight deviation from truth." The stressing of rectitude of life and character may be thought by some to be legal preaching, but truth in the inward parts is what God demands. On the other hand, when the matchless grace of God is proclaimed, man's wisdom often cries out that it is toleration of evil and lawless license.

W. P. Mackay uses the illustration of an employer who goes to a convict's cell and says, "Now I know you, what you are and what you've done, every robbery you've committed, and that you are worse than you believe yourself to be. I am going to give you a chance to become honest. I'll trust you as night watchman over my valuable goods."

So the prisoner is released and takes up his post and proves faithful.

One day, some of his companions in crime threaten him to inform the jeweler of his past life unless he bribes them. But the trusted watchman asks, "What will you tell the boss about me?"

"Why, that you were ringleader of housebreakers," they reply.

"Ah," the prisoner says, "but my master knows all of that better than you do; he knows me better than I know myself, yet he trusts me."

This illustrates grace and truth. The jeweler is extending grace to the one-time convict on the ground of truth, because he fully knew what he was capable of.

Is this not the way God deals with us? He comes to us in grace, but He knows with whom He is dealing. He knows the whole truth about us. Nothing is hidden from Him with whom we have to do; yet in spite of having the whole truth before Him, He saves us through grace, gives us a new nature, and places us in the highest position in His service. It may aid us in our meditation of these twin virtues if we consider, first of all, their appearance twice over in the first chapter of John. These two essential features are ascribed to God in the Old Testament and characterized the Son of God when He changed the form of His preexistence and took upon Himself frail flesh to die.

Christ came from the Father, who was *abundant in goodness and truth*" (Exodus 34:6). The Hebrew word used here for "*goodness*" is *checed*, which can be translated "loving-kindness" or "grace." Then we read in the gospel of John that Christ was "*full of grace and truth*" (John 1:14). Some expositors translate this passage, "Glory full of grace and truth." Of this summing up of the character of the divine revelation, Westcott says,

> Grace corresponds with the idea of the revelation of God as Love (1 John 4:8–16) by Him who is the Life: Truth with that of the revelation of God as Light (1 John 1:5) by Him who is Himself Light.

The word *full* implies abundance, a plethora of the virtues mentioned. There was no half measure of grace and truth, no fraction, but the perfect completeness of both. This is why they flow as a never-ending stream to us poor sinners, that we may rejoice in the blessings they bring. Furthermore, they are mentioned together because they are central to our salvation.

GRACE

What is grace? Godet describes it as

The divine love investing the character with affableness towards friends, with condescension towards inferiors, with compassion towards the wretched, with pardon towards the guilty; God consenting to *give Himself*.

The word *grace* springs from the same root, meaning "to rejoice"; and this primarily signifies that which gives joy or pleasure. As a divine virtue, it denotes the free, spontaneous, absolute loving-kindness of God toward men, and so it is contrasted with debt, law, works, and sin. Alas, sinners find it hard to believe in such unadulterated, unmixed grace. Yet this was the gospel Paul preached, as did Martin Luther: "Full, free justification by grace through faith without the deeds of the law."

There are those who seem to feel that they have to help God save them from sin's penalty; those who argue, "Do the best you can by the help of your own innate grace, and if you fail, divine grace will step in and take over." But the first thing the grace of God does is bring to the sinner the salvation he needs but cannot attain. (See Titus 2:11.) Man's deliverance from the tyranny of sin is *all* of grace, lest he should boast. (See Ephesians 2:9.) Grace, then, is an undeserved benefaction a person receives as he repents and believes and indicates sin and guilt on his part, which this grace removes by pardon, justification, and adoption into sonship. This free and unmerited gift is the first central gift of pardon, and through grace, we can receive even more gifts. Further, by receiving initial grace, capacity becomes ours to receive more grace. "*Grace for grace*" (John 1:16). And there is never any end to the grace of God. Godet says,

Its horizon stretches out in an infinite expanse before the eyes of faith, and as the believer travels towards it, it recedes into a distance that is just as infinite as ever.

The well has no bottom, but the mercy of God permits the believer to sit beside it and drink of its refreshing waters.

Grace led my wandering feet
To tread the heavenly road;
And new supplies each hour I meet
While pressing on to God.

Grace all the works shall crown
Through everlasting days;
It lays in heaven the topmost stone
And well deserves the praise.[105]

TRUTH

In Scripture, truth is often paired with grace because they are intertwined. They are twins, born of God. We have grace in truth and truth in grace. In his sinful ignorance, man does not know the truth about an all-loving, all-gracious God. He may believe many things about His creative works, but how a thrice-holy God can receive him as a sinner and clear him of his guilt is a truth he cannot understand. Why, he does not know all the truth about himself. *Truth*, which is a word John repeatedly uses, is saving light. The word itself means "reality"—reality itself as well as any statement of it—and when it is joined to *grace*, it denotes the saving realities of God and Christ Jesus. Truth is the reality of God's will, His purpose and plan for our salvation, and every act of His in accord therewith. To quote Godet again:

---

105. Philip Doddridge, "Grace! 'Tis a Charming Sound."

Truth is the reality of things adequately brought to light. And, as the essence of things is the moral idea which presides over the existence of each one of them, *truth* is the holy and good thought of God, completely unveiled; it is *God revealed*. Through this attribute the incarnate Word also became anew what He originally was, the *Light* of men. (See John 1:4–5.) By these two essential attributes of Jesus' character—Life and Light—therefore, the witnesses of His life were able to recognize in Him the only Son coming from the presence of the Father. Their feeling was this: This being is God *given*, God *revealed* in a human existence.

The truth of God, then, consists in the revelation of His grace, and John, regarding them as distinct virtues, yet joins them together. Grace is God possessed; truth is God known. Then the apostle goes on to tell us that while *"the law was given by Moses...grace and truth came by Jesus Christ"* (John 1:17). The contrast is expressive. The Law Moses brought from the mount was distinct from himself; it was not part of him. What he received from God he relayed to Israel. But grace and truth came by Jesus Christ. The word *"came"*—literally, *became*—implies the historical manifestation of grace and truth in the Person and ministry of Jesus. Grace and truth were not only themes He preached; He was, in Himself, their perfection. As the incarnate One, He became the full embodiment of saving truth. Did He not declare, *"I am...the truth"* (John 14:6)? In the original, the article "the" precedes *"grace"* and *"truth."* Jesus was *the* grace and *the* truth, for he was the personification of both gifts.

CHAPTER 28

FAITH AND WORKS

"A man is justified by faith without the deeds of the law."
—Romans 3:28

*"As the body without the spirit is dead,
so faith without works is dead also."*
—James 2:26

"By works was faith made perfect."
—James 2:22

While at first sight it would really seems that Paul and James are diametrically opposed in their theological presentation of faith and works—Paul affirming that we are saved by faith alone; James declaring that faith without works is dead—careful consideration of their respective teachings, along with a comparison with other similar Scriptures, manifests complete harmony between the teachings of Paul and James. Personal dislike and a misunderstanding of James's practical application of the gospel to Christian living have led many to disparage James. Martin Luther, in his zeal to exalt justification by faith alone, rashly said that James and Paul contradicted each other, and he called the work of James "an epistle of straw, and destitute of evangelical character."

Such a statement is absurd. How could James be in disagreement with Paul, seeing that his epistle was probably the first book of the entire New Testament to be written, with Paul's epistles to the Romans and Galatians being written some years later? Not extant, then, when James penned his epistle, how could Romans be construed as a contradiction of James's teaching or his teaching a rebuke of Paul's magnificent dissertation of justification by faith? Further, as *all scripture is inspired by God*" (2 Timothy 3:16 RSV), the same Holy Spirit who inspired James to write his portion of Scripture likewise inspired Paul to pen Romans. And the Holy Spirit does not and cannot contradict Himself; neither did He allow those who wrote under His dictation to contradict each other. It is, therefore, impossible for one portion of Scripture to repudiate another.

When certain facts are kept in mind, it is seen that perfect harmony prevails between the two faithful apostles. Paul and James wrote to two different classes of people, endeavoring to combat two opposite errors prevalent at the time.

In Romans, Paul was writing to a church composed of Jews and Gentiles, and his purpose in the first three chapters was to show that all people are sinners and are in need of the salvation freely provided by Christ Jesus. The apostle was opposing the spirit of self-righteousness that is common to both Jew and Gentile and inherent in human nature. In his own unconverted state, Paul had tried to establish his own righteousness.

The apostle James, the half-brother of Christ, was writing to *"the twelve tribes which are scattered abroad"* (James 1:1). These were the *"thousands of Jews…which believe; and they are all zealous of the law"* (Acts 21:20). What he exposes in his epistle was that spirit of religious formalism to which those reared in Judaism were especially liable. They put on an appearance of righteousness before God, but they failed to live righteously before men. Although there was a mere intellectual assent to truth, theirs was a dead faith, seeing that it was without works, or the outworking of an inner salvation.

Alexander Maclaren said, "Paul is a preacher of faith, but of faith which works by love. James is the preacher of works, but of works which are the fruit of faith." In Romans, Paul deals primarily with the doctrine of justification before God, which has nothing to do with human worth or works, but is our position entirely through faith in Christ and His atoning death. James, on the other hand, deals principally with justification before men. He does not disparage true heart faith, as we will see, but emphasizes the fact that such a faith should reveal itself in an outward life of piety and good works. The one apostle deals with the positional aspect of the Christian life; the other, its practical side.

Paul and James use the terms *faith*, *works*, and *justified* in different senses but without contradicting each other's application.

Take *faith*. When Paul writes of faith, he has in mind the faith that saved. *"By grace are ye saved through faith"* (Ephesians 2:8). Such a faith was a living and active principle of the soul, manifesting itself in the love and trust of the heart and the obedience of the will.

When James refers to faith and links it to works, which he does several times, he implies a mere theoretical and intellectual orthodoxy that has no effect on character and conduct. Real faith is living and vital, but the dead faith the apostle speaks of is not a product of salvation. This lifeless faith may be associated with a profession of religion that results in no possession of life. It is a body without a soul.

Take *works*. When Paul uses the word *works*, if it is not qualified by the adjective *good*—as in *"See your good works"* (Matthew 5:16)—he is speaking of things done in a legal spirit to earn salvation. No sinner can work his way into acceptance by God.

When James refers to works, he uses the term to denote actions performed in a grateful spirit, as the natural result of a close relationship with God. The world cannot see our inner faith, but it can see our deeds; and it is by these deeds that we reveal the unseen faith motivating our everyday living.

Now take *justified*. When Paul, the master teacher of evangelical truth, writes of being justified, he uses it in a theological sense, indicating the initial acceptance of the believing sinner as righteous before God. When James writes of being justified, he uses it in a practical sense, as a person's actions are visibly manifested in the sight of others. Our standing before God, as those justified by faith, must be translated into our state here below. Acceptance by God must be reflected in our godlike actions before men.

The interesting thing to observe is that both Paul and James use the example of Abraham and Rahab to prove their separate points. In respect to Abraham, both apostles quote Genesis 15:6: *"He believed in the Lord; and he counted it to him for righteousness."*[106]

---

106. Compare Romans 4:1–5, Galatians 3:1–9, and Hebrews 11:31 with James 2:21–25.

Paul and James reveal harmony of thought, despite their differences in expressions, in other passages in their writings that deal with the same two themes we are considering. James fully recognizes the importance of true faith: *"Let him ask in faith, nothing wavering. For he that wavereth is like a wave of the sea driven with the wind and tossed"* (James 1:6; see also James 1:3; 2:5; 5:15). Paul insists upon the necessity of good works: *"Abound to every good work"* (2 Corinthians 9:8; see also Ephesians 2:10; Colossians 1:10).

Both Paul and James were equally emphatic in repudiating barren orthodoxy. The question James asks, *"What doth it profit, my brethren, though a man say he hath faith, and have not works? Can faith save him?"* (James 2:14) is answered by, *"Faith working through love"* (Galatians 5:6 RSV). Like James, Paul vehemently condemns mere outward profession—the shell but no kernel: *"They profess to know God, but they deny him by their deeds; they are detestable, disobedient, unfit for any good deed"* (Titus 1:16 RSV; see Romans 2:17–24). Thus, the two apostles "were not fighting face-to-face as opponents, but back-to-back as comrades defending the purity and integrity of the gospel they both loved." They are not contradictory but complementary. The faith Paul speaks of must result in works, and the works James mentions must spring from faith. It was William Cowper who wrote, "Unless profession and practice go together, a man's life is a lie." We can only be justified by faith; and our profession can only be justified by works. As the poetess Hannah More expressed it:

> If faith produce no works, I see
> That faith is not a living tree:
> Thus faith and works together grow,
> No separate life they e'en can know:

They're soul and body, hand and heart—
What God hath joined, let no man part.[107]

In the Twelfth Article of the Church of England, the relationship between faith and works in the Christian life as that of cause and effect is well expressed:

Albeit that Good Works, which are the fruits of Faith, and follow after Justification, cannot put away our sins, and endure the severity of God's judgment; yet are they pleasing and acceptable to God in Christ, and do spring out necessarily of a true and lively Faith: insomuch that by them a lively Faith may be as evidently known as a tree discerned by the fruit.

Faith and works, often thought of as root and fruit, caught the imagination of the spiritual poet who wrote:

Faith is the living, growing root,
Works are the ever rip'ning fruit;
Faith is the fountain far below,
Works are the streams which ever flow;
Faith is the furnace underground,
Works are the heat which spreads around;
Faith on firm foundation lies,
Works make the solid building rise.

---

107. Hannah More, "Dan and Jane."

APPENDIX

It is hoped that the foregoing samples of expounding twin truths of Scripture will serve to stimulate the preacher and student to develop this most profitable line of Bible study. If they do so, they will find that the Word abounds in matched, as well as unmatched, pairs of truth. For instance, here are a few suggested illustrations which one could expand upon:

—TWIN SYMBOLS: SUN AND SHIELD

The Lord God is a sun and shield. (Psalm 84:11)

—TWIN GIFTS: GRACE AND GLORY

The Lord will give grace and glory. (Psalm 84:11)

—TWIN RESPONSES: OFFERING AND SONG

When the burnt offering began, the song of the Lord began also. (2 Chronicles 29:27)

—TWIN DISPENSATIONS: LAW AND GRACE

The law was given by Moses, but grace…came by Jesus Christ. (John 1:17)

—TWIN CHARACTERISTICS: CHILDREN AND NO CHILDREN

Become as little children.
(Matthew 18:3) (Childlike humility)

Be no more children.
(Ephesians 4:14) (Childish immaturity)

—TWIN OBJECTIVES: PRESERVATION AND PERSEVERANCE

Preserved in Jesus Christ. (Jude 1:1) (Final preservation)

Watching…with all perseverance.
(Ephesians 6:18) (Perseverance of the saints)

—TWIN ATTITUDES: FOR AND AGAINST

He that is not against us is for us. (Luke 9:50)

He that is not with me is against me. (Luke 11:23)

—TWIN BENEFACTIONS: LIFE AND LIGHT

With thee is the fountain of life: in thy light shall we see light.

(Psalm 36:9)

—TWIN NATURES OF CHRIST: GOD AND MAN

Thomas Hardy speaks of "twin halves of one august event."[108] One of the most august events in world history was the incarnation of Christ, who came to earth, combining in His person deity and humanity:

God was manifest in flesh.   (1 Timothy 3:16)

The man Christ Jesus.   (1 Timothy 2:5)

—TWIN NATURES OF THE CHRISTIAN: OLD AND NEW

Born of the flesh…born of the Spirit.   (John 3:6)

Put off…the old man…put on the new man.
(Ephesians 4:22, 24)

Pursuing our line of study further, it will be found that many Bible characters are presented in pairs, and by their combination, they suggest truths of deepest significance and solemnity. Think of these doubles:

+ Cain and Abel
+ Abraham and Lot
+ Isaac and Ishmael
+ Jacob and Esau
+ David and Jonathan

Then there is much instruction to be gathered from words that occur only twice, both in the Hebrew and the Greek. A long list of these might be gathered. One can consult E. Bullinger's *Number in Scripture* and W. E. Vine's *Expository Words*. An illustration of this phase of meditation is in the word *apoprigo,*

---

108. Thomas Hardy, "The Convergence of the Twain."

meaning "choke." The enemy chokes the seed, and he himself is choked in the sea. (See Luke 8:33.) Both agreement and difference will be found in many of the twice-repeated words in Scripture, every word of which is pure.

Reference can also be made to F. E. Marsh's valuable work *The Structural Principles of the Bible*, in which he has a profitable chapter called "The Lungs of a Double Action." He said that just as lungs have a double action of inhaling air and exhaling air, most truths in the gospel have a double aspect to them, as well. For Bible students, reading Dr. Marsh's volume is a must.

Another most illuminative work is *The Twofold Life* by A. J. Gordon, in which he expounds on "Christ's work *for* us" and "Christ's work *in* us." He covers lots of twin truths, such as regeneration and renewal, salvation and sealing, ideal and attainment, and so forth. Although this book is out of print, it would be a most worthwhile study if you can lay your hands on a secondhand copy.

ABOUT THE AUTHOR

When Dr. Herbert Lockyer (1886–1984) was first deciding on a career, he considered becoming an actor. Tall and well-spoken, he seemed a natural for the theater. But the Lord had something better in mind. Instead of the stage, God called Herbert to the pulpit, where, as a pastor, a Bible teacher, and the author of more than fifty books, he touched the hearts and lives of millions of people.

Dr. Lockyer held pastorates in Scotland and England for twenty-five years. As pastor of Leeds Road Baptist Church in Bradford, England, he became a leader in the Keswick Higher Life Movement, which emphasized the significance of living in the fullness of the Holy Spirit. This led to an invitation to speak at the Moody Bible Institute's fiftieth anniversary in 1936. His warm reception at that event led to his ministry in the United States. He received honorary degrees from both the Northwestern Evangelical Seminary and the International Academy in London.

In 1955, he returned to England, where he lived for many years. He then returned to the United States, where he spent the final years of his life in Colorado Springs, Colorado, with his son, the Rev. Herbert Lockyer Jr., a Presbyterian minister who eventually became his editor.